YEADON'S REGISTER

of

L N E R

LOCOMOTIVES

Volume Fourteen

CLASS D13, D14, D15 & D16
The Great Eastern 4-4-0s

Copyright Challenger U.K./Booklaw/Railbus
1999
ISBN 1 899624 34 1

YEADON'S REGISTER OF L.N.E.R. LOCOMOTIVES - VOLUME 14

PUBLISHERS NOTE & ACKNOWLEDGEMENTS

Numerous people enquire as to "...and when is the next Register is coming out?". Well, despite an apparently elongated period of time since Volume 13 was published, we can confidently say that Volume 15 will not be too far behind this volume. Hopefully less than three months after the appearance of this volume should see Volume 15 in the shops. Thereafter will come subsequent volumes every four months or so. Despite the seemingly 'fits and starts' of the last couple of years, we have committed ourselves to increasing production to at least four volumes a year until the series is completed.

We apologise to all of you who been constantly disappointed by the none publication of this particular Register; not least the retailers who are always being asked by their customers when a Register is due. Various factors have led to rumours - early advertising, late reviews and misinformation to name but a few. On the other hand it is heartening to know that the series is much awaited and some of the rumours bounding around no doubt have their origins in wishful thinking. However, enough of that - its here now, at last!

The introductory notes concerning this volume are largely the work of Eric Fry whose knowledge of LNER locomotives in general, and the former Great Eastern types in particular, have given the editor and publisher a confidence which would otherwise have been lacking. Our thanks go Eric for his patience, resilience, enthusiasm and sheer dedication to the *Yeadon's Register* series. Even now whilst these notes are being written, EVF is checking proofs for the next volume which is due for publication in the winter of 1999.

The full co-operation of Brian Dyson, the Archivist at Hull University, and his patient staff have enabled us to secure on loan much of the photographic material from the WBY Collection. Usually at short notice, Brian is ever willing to have ready the various albums available for inspection. Like most archivist, Brian Dyson is meticulous in cataloguing, caring for, and storing the archives under his charge; therefore we do not come away from Hull without having give assurances as to the safe keeping of material in our possession during the short time we require it. For those of you who would like to inspect the actual WBY Collection first hand, the University at Hull would be happy to hear from you so that arrangements for a visit can be made. The address, for those willing to visit is at the end of these notes.

Where known the names of the numerous photographers contributing to the illustrative sections of this volume, have been placed alongside the caption, however, there are many unacknowledged pictures. The publisher would like to thank all those cameramen, most of whom are sadly no longer with us. Without your contribution gentlemen the series would have been less than dynamic.

Once again the full backing of Mrs Annie Yeadon and her daughter Jean, along with Simon, have made the publication of this volume possible. They gain much satisfaction from each volume and a certain amount of pride at seeing Willie's 'Register' slowly coming to fruition.

Finally thanks to you the reader who have made the whole thing viable and therefore possible to publish. Please note that due to popular demand the dust jacket is back.

John Hooper, July 1999.

The Yeadon Collection is available for inspection and anyone who wishes to inspect it should contact:-
The Archivist
Brynmor Jones Library
University of Hull
Hull
HU6 7RX
Tel: 01482-465265

First published in the United Kingdom by
CHALLENGER U.K./BOOKLAW/RAILBUS
309 Mapperley Plains, Nottingham, NG3 5RG.
Printed and bound by The Amadeus Press, Huddersfield.

INTRODUCTION

The locomotives covered by Volume 14 of the Register were all of Great Eastern origin except for ten which, though built in 1923, were, for all intents and purposes, GER. Engines with a 4-4-0 wheel arrangement on the GE section of the LNER were encompassed in the D13, D14, D15 and D16 classes, the D14 to D16's being built as 4-4-0s whilst the D13 engines were rebuilt to 4-4-0 from an earlier design of 2-4-0 dating from 1886. All were built at Stratford and most of their maintenance, with some small exception, was carried out there too.

At Stratford, both the 'Old' and 'New Works' were responsible for maintaining and altering the 4-4-0's. However, clerical staff at the 'New Works' were somewhat lax in either recording dates, specific alterations or simply passing on such information to the clerk at the main office in the 'Old Works'.

The Engine Repair Register was kept in the Erecting Shop Foreman's office at the Old Works. Within the register all visits by engines to that Works were recorded i.e. dates 'in', 'out', trial trip and handing over to the Running Dept. Additionally, the register contained notes of alterations carried out in the New Works. However, as already stated many of these notes were either incomplete or did not exist.

Likewise the Engine History Cards for the early years of the LNER and indeed the GER period are lacking much vital information, or have simply disappeared. Consequently certain entries in the tables concerning many of the engines covered by this volume are missing as will become evident to the reader. Hopefully these 'missing' pieces of information should not distract from the vast amount of factual information given and therefore will hopefully not spoil the enjoyment of the record.

D13 Class

In need of new express passenger tender locomotives, the Great Eastern Railway built, in batches of ten, some 110 class T19 2-4-0s, between November 1886 and May 1897 to the design of their newly appointed Locomotive Superintendent James Holden.

Though similar to the earlier G14 2-4-0 tender engines of T.W.Worsdell's design, Holden's T19 class incorporated Stephenson rather than Joy valve gear. Also Holden made his engines somewhat 'steadier' at high speeds by fitting inside and outside frames for the leading axle. During the building period the various batches were further developed and incorporated better boilers, with working pressure reaching 160 lb. in the final batch as opposed to 140 in the initial engines. Oil burning was introduced in 1889 and ten T19's were converted to burn the oil which was a by-product from Stratford's gas plant. Reboilering was carried out to earlier engines from 1895 onwards, many gaining the higher pressure.

However, the increasing weight of passenger trains in the late-1890s led Holden to seek a larger and more powerful design of locomotive more able to cope with the faster schedules then being asked.

The appearance of the new 4-4-0 no.1900 CLAUD HAMILTON in March 1900 was to cast the 2-4-0 wheel arrangement into the history books for express duties, as far as the GER was concerned and the Company set about converting the T19's into 4-4-0's but not until larger boilers had been tried on the existing 2-4-0 frame.

For a two-year period, from July 1902, some twenty-one T19's were rebuilt with 4' 9" diameter Belpaire boilers. These were unsuperheated but pressure was increased to 180 lb. per sq. in. thereby creating a more powerful engine which because of the increase in weight, had more adhesion. Because these larger boilers were pitched a foot higher than the small diameter type, the rebuilt engines took on a somewhat top-heavy and ungainly appearance and became affectionately known as the 'Humpty Dumpty' engines.

In 1905 another phase of rebuilding started which involved the reconstruction of sixty of the original, small diameter boiler, engines from 2-4-0's to 4-4-0's. It is these engines, or to be more precise fifty-eight of them, which are featured in this Register, under the LNER classification D13. The rebuilding took place over a four-year period starting with 10 engines in 1905, 21 in 1906, 19 in 1907 and the final ten in 1908. Meanwhile, as more of the 'Clauds' were coming into traffic a start was made withdrawing those twenty-nine T19's which still had the original, small diameter, boiler. Their demise started in 1908 and the last example, no.768, was scrapped in 1913.

Of the 'Humpty Dumpty' 2-4-0's, none survived to Grouping either and were withdrawn as follows: six in 1913, five in 1914, five in 1915, three in 1919, and the final two, nos.776 and 778 were scrapped in 1920.

The 4-4-0 rebuilds were given second-hand bogies from withdrawn engines of either the E10 class 0-4-4 tank engines or G16 4-4-0 tender engines. Which bogies came from which class was easily discernible because the G16 bogie wheels each had nine spokes, whereas those bogies from the E10's had wheels of 2' 10" inch diameter and had to be replaced by new 3' 1" wheels, the same as the G16 wheels, but had eight spokes only. Because the bogie wheel sets used on the rebuilds were interchangeable with the LNER G4 class, it was possible to see eight and nine spoke combinations on the same bogie and later, a ten-spoke example appeared to add to the variety. To accommodate the bogie, the frames of the T19's were lengthened and the cylinders set at a steeper angle.

Cabs were modified to take into account the larger boiler which at the time of rebuilding was still saturated. Superheating was carried out from December 1913, the first twenty so treated having Schmidt type whilst those engines superheated from June 1915 onwards had the Robinson type superheater. By Grouping some forty-eight engines had superheated boilers. The LNER fitted a further four engines whilst the other six, withdrawn between 1923 and 1930, never had them. Two engines, nos.715 and 747, were condemned on the eve of Grouping in December 1922 and so never became LNER engines. Six of the Schmidt equipped engines changed to Robinson superheater during the mid-1930s, the other fourteen engines with that type being unaltered.

For most of their time on the GER, the rebuilt 4-4-0s ran in the dull grey paint scheme associated with that company, however, the LNER transformed them from 1923 onwards by painting them in lined green with shaded transfer numbers (12") and letters (7½") above them on the tender side sheets. Not all D13's got this treatment though as at least six still had the GER grey when the LNER introduced their own economy colour scheme in 1928 - black with red lining. Numbers had been carried on the tender sides from GE days and renumbering

At Grouping some 48 of the 58 engines comprising class D13 had been superheated. Of the remaining ten (nos. 705, 706, 712, 717, 730, 767, 1018, 1026, 1031, 1033), only four (nos. 706, 712, 767, 1026) received superheated boilers. The other six engines were withdrawn, three of those, including 1031 here, whilst sill carrying GER numbers and livery.

The first twelve engines to be superheated (704, 707, 718, 719, 728, 735, 748, 751, 775, 777, 1016, 1023) were given new frames which had a curved step instead of a sloping upper edge at the front end. No other engines were altered but the twelve kept those frames until withdrawal.

by the LNER added 7000 to the large figures, the letters LNER were carried on a small cast plate attached to the cab sides. At 'shopping' the GER figures were replaced by standard LNER 12" numerals and these remained on the tenders until they were moved to cab sides from March 1929 onwards. However those engines 'shopped' between June 1928 and March 1929 came out black with numbers and letters on the tender similar to the earlier green painted engines. With the cast plate on the cab side only 7½" numbers could be used but eventually the plate was moved to the leading splasher and 12" numerals were used. The small LNER on the tender sides was also eventually changed to 12" letters.

Next in line to the 'Clauds' in the GER express locomotive hierarchy, the rebuilt 4-4-0's could be found on most principal express trains on the GE before the introduction of the Holden 4-6-0s. After that time they were relegated to more secondary duties and were allocated to most of the main depots but could be found in greater numbers in the northern 'flatland' areas of the former GER system by 1923. In GE days they ranged as far north as Doncaster with regular forays to York but rarely went west of Doncaster except on Newmarket horsebox specials to Manchester and Liverpool. These same Newmarket jobs took them to Leicester, Northampton and Birmingham. The GN & GE Joint line provided much traffic for the D13's stationed at March, Lincoln and Doncaster. During the early LNER period they could still be seen at York on local workings from Doncaster where as many as five were allocated during most of 1927. By the mid-1930s however, all the remaining D13's were back in East Anglia. Of the twenty-nine survivors in January 1935, there were seven at King's Lynn, six at Cambridge, five at Norwich, four at Peterborough East, two each at Ipswich, March and Yarmouth Vauxhall, and a solitary example at Colchester.

Over the next four years some twenty-six D13's were withdrawn, replaced mainly by 'Clauds' which had themselves been relegated by newer motive power. The three remaining engines, 8023, 8035 and 8039, literally 'soldiered on' and it was perhaps because of the Second World War that they lasted in service so much longer than the other members of the class. No.8035 got the final calling in May 1943, no.8023 in January 1944 and last to go was no.8039 (the last T19 built incidentally) in March 1944.

The LNER allocated new numbers to the last two engines of D13 class, under the general renumbering scheme but neither got them - 8023 was to be 2057, 8039 as 2058.

D14, D15 and D16 Classes.

The first 'Claud', no.1900 CLAUD HAMILTON was turned out in March 1900 and was, at the time, the largest express passenger engine on the Great Eastern Railway. Although built under the Superintendency of James Holden, No.1900 was actually the design of the Chief Draughtsman Frederick V.Russell and it was the forerunner of a successful locomotive class which was to be subject to numerous changes and improvements during the following twenty-three years which saw 121 examples built at Stratford. The final batch of ten (GER Class H88), built just after Grouping - twelve years after the previous batch, culminated in the large boilered version or 'Super Claud', classified D16 by the LNER. The earlier engines (GER Class S46 and D56) became LNER D14 and D15, the former having a round top firebox and the latter the Belpaire type.

During the LNER period improvements were continued in order to bring the earlier engines into line with later developments. Within the three class groups were a number of sub classes and as engines were rebuilt or altered so they would move up the scale, so to speak, to the higher number class group.

Of the original 41 engines comprising GER Class S46 (LNER D14), no less than twenty-one had been rebuilt by Grouping to Class D15 standard and by 1931 the rest had been rebuilt so rendering the D14 class extinct.

Both saturated and superheated boilers were used within class D15. The distinction between the two types of boiler did not create any separate sub classification until 1927 when saturated and superheated engines with short smokebox became D15/1 and superheated engines with extended smokebox became D15/2.

By 1933 all D15/1 engines had been rebuilt with superheated boilers and Class D15/1 (Sat) also became extinct. Two years later D15/1 class became extinct as the last D15's received the extended smokebox. In 1938 the sub class element was dropped and these engines became simply Class D15.

Further rebuilding to D16 standard was to lessen the ranks of the D15 and of the 80 engines originally classified as such only thirteen were withdrawn as D15, these during the early years of British Railways, and by 1952 Class D15 was extinct.

The ten 'Super Clauds' built in 1923 were supplemented by 30 more rebuilt from class D15 during the years 1923-31. All had the larger diameter boiler with superheater and Belpaire firebox. Extended smokeboxes made their appearance on the class from 1926, these engines being classified D16/2 whilst those still with short smokebox became D16/1. All received extended smokeboxes and Class D16/1 was rendered extinct in 1934.

Meanwhile, from 1933 further rebuilding from Class D15 was with the same size of boiler but to LNER standards with round top firebox. This was the final development of the Claud boiler and introduced D16/3 to the classification scheme. There was a short-lived revival of the D14 classification during 1933-36 in that nine rebuilds to D16/3 standard were classified D14/2. These were from the original D14 series which had shallower frames than the later built D15 engines. However, from May 1936 these nine engines - 8860, 8861, 8863, 8866, 8869, 8870, 8876, 8878, 8900 - were incorporated in Class D16/3, and D14/2 was dropped. Incidentally none of the original D14 engines had been able to be converted to Class D16/1 or D16/2 because of their frame design.

From 1938 to 1949 all but four of the D16/2 engines were further rebuilt to D16/3. Class D16/2 became extinct in January 1952 when no. 62590 (ex 8819) was condemned. By 1949, when rebuilding of the Clauds ceased, 104 had been converted to D16/3, although by then withdrawals had begun. Despite this, new boilers for the class were built as late as 1955. Class D16/3 became extinct in October 1960 with the withdrawal of no. 62613 (ex 8782), built in 1923 under the LNER.

Other than the brief loss of the extended smokebox from Class D15/2 8899, no Claud ever reverted down the ladder of evolution which, essentially, concerned the type of boiler carried. To mention here the various mechanical and technical differences between the classes and sub classes, and the developments leading up to the ultimate version of the Great Eastern 4-4-0, the D16/3, would take up valuable space within this Register so instead the extended and detailed photographic captions along with the tables, and a summary of the evolution,

3

When the Great Eastern Railway built no.1900 CLAUD HAMILTON in April 1900, it was the first of a new, larger type of express tender engine designed to speed up passenger trains to Norfolk and in particular the North Norfolk coast. Initially a 'Watercart' type tender was fitted and the boiler was topped by two Ramsbottom safety valves with a whistle on the same mounting. Beneath the front end of the running plate was a hopper to receive ash ejected from the smokebox. Some ten years later no.1900 had received a new boiler, this time with four Ramsbottom safety valves. The tender was rebuilt in May 1912 to a more conventional form in order to increase water capacity. The original straps on the smokebox door had been replaced by a strengthening ring and the ash ejector had been removed. This view shows the engine in its pre-WW1 condition at Stratford, complete with lamp iron still above the smokebox.

This is no.1900 ex works 27th April 1923 in full LNER livery and looking splendid. A couple of minor changes had taken place over the years since the previous photograph was taken - the cab roof had received rain strips and the lamp iron had been moved to the smokebox door. *L.N.E.R.*

are used to indicate the what, when, where and why these engines had such a long and successful metamorphous.

Renumbering.

The 'Clauds' were subject to numerous renumbering during their somewhat long operational lives. Towards the end of the first year of the LNER the last few (8787, 8788 and 8789) of the 1923 built engines were turned out by Stratford with an 'E' suffix alongside the original Great Eastern designated number. The other engines of that same batch (8780 to 8786) had, by all accounts, also gained the E suffix by year's end. The legend L&NER also adorned the tender sides of those last 'Clauds'.

Into 1924 the suffix was being applied to other 4-4-0's but by February it was decided upon that the former GE Area locomotives would have 7000 added to their numbers. Thus only thirty-one 'Clauds' are known to have actually carried the suffix.

A reliable enthusiast of the period, one S. Lucas, travelled daily into Liverpool St. station and amongst his various notes of sightings at the termini, he also recorded visits to Stratford's sheds and shops. The following are extracts of 'observations' in the London area during the period when certain 4-4-0's were carrying the E suffix and the 7000 was added: *12/23* - 1818*, 1900*; *12/1/24* - 1781*, 1787*, 1789*, 1806, 1864* (full-stops after letters), 1866* (but no suffix); *3/3/24* - 1780*, 1821, 1829; *4/24* - 1867* (full-stops); *26/4/24* - 1782*, 1784*, 1788*, 1796, 1815, 1819, 1833, 1841, 1872, (it was also on this date that the following were seen: 8797, 8893, 8897); *22/5/24* - 1876, 1894; *2/7/24* - 1786*, 1869, 1874; *14/11/24* - 1862, 1785*, 1839*, *12/24* - 1795, 1809*; *1/25* - 1853.
Note: those engines marked * carried L&NER; those without were simply LNER.

In 1942 the Thompson renumbering scheme (7650 to 7770 numbers allotted to 'Clauds') affected only a limited number of 'Clauds' whereas the 1946 scheme was applied to all. Just after Nationalisation the letter E was again used for identification purposes but this time as regional within British Railways and used as a prefix. However, only a small number of engines gained the prefix before 60000 was added to the 1946 number.

Boilers

Until 1914 Stratford Works had not interchanged boilers on locomotives and each boiler carried the same number as the locomotive to which it was fitted. In that year new boilers began to be numbered in a series according to types and in number progression from 2000 upwards (although there was some subsequent use of engine numbers, as with Clauds 1780-9). With the aid of extra spare boilers, a system of rotation of use was inaugurated. The main advantage lay in the reduction of the time locomotives spent in shops during overhaul - boilers usually took longer to repair than the rest of the locomotive.

The series of numbers started in 1914 continued in use throughout the LNER period. Under BR ownership a general renumbering scheme was introduced in August 1950. Boilers of ex-GER locomotives took numbers in the range 23100 to 23999. These new numbers were not alloted in order of the old numbers. It was stipulated that boiler renumbering should be carried out as engines passed through the shops for any class of repair. If a boiler was taken off a frame, it was not to be renumbered until refitted to the same frame or taken for use on another engine. Consequently, boilers taken off and set aside for scrapping were not to be renumbered, nor did spare boilers receive new numbers until taken for use. As a result of this it was May 1956 before renumbering of LNER boilers was completed.

Unfortunately, as far as the Diagram 28A boilers (those used on classes D16/3 and J19/2) are concerned only a small proportion of the old to new numbers are known, hence the large number of "ex-?" entries that appear under the Boiler headings in the individual records in this book.

Types of Boiler

Diagram 28 - 4' 9" diameter, round top firebox, saturated. Used on classes D14 and J16.
Diagram 27 - 4' 9" diameter, Belpaire firebox, saturated or superheated. Used on classes D15 (sat. & sup.), J17 (sat. & sup.), J18 and J19 (sup.).
Diagram 26 - 5' 1⅛" diameter, Belpaire firebox, superheated. Used on classes D16/1 and D16/2.
Diagram 28A - 5' 1⅛" diameter, round top firebox, superheated. Used on classes D16/3 and J19/2.

Boiler Numbers - Built 1914 onwards

Diagram 28	3250 - 3253.	Built 1914.
Diagram 27	3400 - 3542.	Built 1915-1949. Used mostly on J17.
	3550 - 3558.	Built 1914-1918. Saturated. 3551/6/8 converted to superheater 1925-31.
	3559 - 3613.	Built 1914-1922. Superheated.
	3614 - 3618.	Built 1921-1922. Saturated. 3614/6/7 converted to superheater 1928-33.
	3621 - 3685.	Built 1922-1928. Superheated.
	3254 - 3263.	Built 1929-1932. Superheated.
Diagram 26	1780 - 1789.	Built 1923.
	3900 - 3936.	Built 1923-1932.
Diagram 28A	4200 - 4229.	Built 1933-1935. Twin G.E. type snifting valves.
	4230 - 4344*.	Built 1935-1950. Single Gresley snifting valve.
BR	23450 - 23469.	Built 1951-1955. Single Gresley snifting valve.

* Renumbered by BR in the range 23300 - 23449, but not in numerical order of old numbers.

No.1900 was the only one of its class to be named - after the company's Chairman - and the brass nameplate followed very much on the Crewe style even down to the appendage which, in this case, read "Holden's Patent" referring to oil firing. Although oil firing had ceased by 1911 the appendage message was still in place by Grouping, as shown on the previous photograph, but in March 1925 it was removed.

Operation

From their introduction the 'Clauds' reigned supreme for a decade on the important main line express trains on the Great Eastern. Their performance was perhaps nothing less than superb, day in, day out. Even as their trains got heavier they took everything in their stride and worked to very tight timings. One section of the route of the *Norfolk Coast Express* demanded a non-stop run of 130 miles which they handled punctually, even when loaded to over 400 tons. When the 4-6-0's (LNER B12) appeared from 1911 onwards, the Clauds began to give up most of the work on the heavier expresses but still worked many important express trains not least those to and from Cambridge to Liverpool Street, non-stops on the Southend line, main line trains to Colchester, Ipswich and Norwich.

To cut down line occupation on the congested approaches to Liverpool Street station, all the class were fitted with carriage heating connection under the from bufferbeam which enabled them to work ECS into the terminus tender first, as they were often called upon to do, before taking up their rostered working on a later departure.

From 1906 a number of engines were fitted with vacuum brakes and stationed at Doncaster, Lincoln and March to work express goods trains over the GN&GE Joint line. Though not designed as such, they worked well as mixed traffic engines though during GE days they rarely, if ever worked unfitted freight trains.

Due to weight restrictions on the Clacton/Walton route being in place until the 1930s, the 4-6-0's were prohibited and so the Clauds continued to work the morning and evening expresses to and from the Capital. When the trains became too heavy for one engine then doubleheading was resorted to.

Cambridge, Norwich and Stratford sheds usually had the highest numbers of Clauds allocated be they D14, D15 or D16. Ipswich, March and Colchester always had a sizeable stud on which to depend whilst King's Lynn and Yarmouth seem to have had a handful for most of the LNER period.

From the mid 1930s the Clauds began to penetrate the rural branch lines of Norfolk and from 1939 some of the D15/2 engines began work on the Midland & Great Northern Joint line alongside former GC and GN 4-4-0's. By the end of the LNER there were sixteen Clauds (three D15 and thirteen D16) allocated the M&GN Section sheds, six each at Melton Constable and South Lynn, with four at Yarmouth Beach; they continued to be associated with the M&GN until its closure in 1958, though exchanges were made between sheds on the former GE Section.

In the years preceding WW2, the Clauds were doing more and more 'local' work from Cambridge, Colchester, Ipswich and Norwich sheds - the shape of 'things to come.'

During the GER period and through most of the 25 years of the LNER , the Clauds rarely strayed away from their native area except over the Joint line to Lincoln and Doncaster and perhaps on the occasional jaunt to places like Hull and Scarborough. Cambridge used theirs on the King's Cross expresses (Beer Trains) during the 1930s but they were not 'regulars' on those trains even though they handled the loads and timings with ease.

With the ending of hostilities in 1945, newer motive power in the shape of Thompson B1 4-6-0's began a massive influx onto the GE Section. In so doing they released B12 and the B17 4-6-0's to take up the secondary duties then in the hands of the Clauds. Withdrawals were inevitable and the first Claud to succumb was no.8866, one of the 8 inch piston valve D16/3's. Three more were condemned before Nationalisation including no.8900 CLAUD HAMILTON in May 1947.

Between January 1904 and August 1911, Stratford built 66 broadly similar engines to D14 class - nos.1790 to 1792, 1795 to 1797 and 1800 to 1859 - again without superheater. They differed in having Belpaire firebox, and had deeper frames at the front and rear causing the boiler to be pitched 2" higher. This led to a shorter chimney and dome being fitted also the dome cover was less rounded. All these engines were coupled with standard type tender. The cab front windows were shaped to suit the firebox contour. *H.Gordon Tidey.*

The GER called no.1805 into Stratford on 11th October 1922 to be rebuilt with a 5' 1⅛" diameter boiler and when ex works 28th March 1923 it was the first of LNER D16 class. The cab was now 7' 11" instead of 7' 2" wide, and the footplating, at the cab end only, was 7" wider. Note that, although painted grey it still had GER number plate and the cast coat of arms, with no indication of ownership. The larger diameter, higher pitched boiler precluded any use of Ramsbottom safety valves and this and all subsequent rebuilds had Ross 'Pops'.

Having 117 passenger engines, in fairly good condition for their age and useful too, must have been something of a headache for British Railways. Though most of the Clauds were essentially past their 30-year 'scrap-by' date, the various rebuildings had given them a longer lease of life so without further ado BR began to send them to places far and wide totally foreign to the engines.

The first 'new' route tackled by the Clauds was to Oxford on the Cambridge via Bletchley service. From December 1950 until April 1957 any one of a handful of the Cambridge stud of Clauds could be seen on the early morning outward train and the mid-afternoon return. They were replaced by B12's redundant from the Southend line electrification.

In October 1949 no.62535 of Norwich shed was sent to Gorton shed for trials over the Cheshire Lines. During the early LNER period various Clauds had visited Gorton Works for 'shopping' but none had ever taken up residence in Lancashire. No.62535 was transferred to Trafford Park soon after arrival in Manchester and after some six months of 'trials,' on fast and semi-fast trains to Liverpool, it was joined by seven more Clauds - 62532, 62536, 62568, 62587, 62588, 62599, 62609. No.62535 had been welcomed by the former LNER (Great Central) men at Trafford Park hence the eventual allocation. However, an influx of LMS 2-6-4T's onto the CLC routes during the summer of 1951 saw the Clauds being placed into store. In August 1952 the eight engines returned to the Eastern Region after nearly a year of immobility. All, except 62588, went to Peterborough's Spital Bridge shed where they were to find further employment for another three years on former LMS services to Leicester, Northampton and Rugby - more new ground. Though only in a trickle at first, withdrawals were all the time taking their toll on the Clauds during the early years of BR and those at Spital Bridge were not left unscathed. Redundant B12's and B1's took over the Rugby trains and the three remaining Clauds there were transferred away to Lincoln in March 1957, for yet further service with a couple more of the class - 62564 and 62571; this time over the former Midland line to Derby via Nottingham.

The dawn of 1955 saw no less than 90 Clauds still active, or at least in operational condition, all were D16/3; eleven of the survivors having been converted by BR from D16/2. With most engines either approaching or achieving fifty years of age, condemnations began in earnest. The availability of the ever increasing numbers of diesel multiple units for local and cross-country passenger services stole the very traffic that the Clauds needed for existence.

On the former GE lines they could be observed on milk trains, parcels, holiday excursions and even medium distance semi-fast passenger trains. They were a rarity at Liverpool Street by 1955 and by 1959 were virtually non-existent; Stratford had not had any 'on the books' since early BR days.

Only sixteen Clauds were still active in January 1959, all in what could be described as the northern part of East Anglia. Lincoln had given up its last one, 62571, that very month. By the year's end Norwich had just no.62524, Lowestoft no.62604 and Spital Bridge nos.62597 and 62613; all but the latter were withdrawn in the first month of 1960.

No.62613 transferred to March after the closure of the ex-Midland shed at Peterborough in January 1960. March shed kept the engine busy, especially during the spring and summer months but one elderly sole example of a once large class does not stand much of a chance of survival on what was becoming a 'standardised' railway system. When 62613 was withdrawn on 25th October it was not even forty years old, a comparative youngster by 'Claud' standards. Eventually it was sent to Stratford, it's birthplace, for cutting up and so marking the end of a remarkable class of railway locomotive which served three different masters over a sixty year period. The Clauds did the job they were designed for and more; the fact that they had been rebuilt successfully over and over was a tribute to the original design. Perhaps the saddest aspect of their longevity was the fact that none was preserved - surely a classic case of injustice.

After withdrawal in October 1958, no.62588 was used until June 1959 as a temporary steam supply in the works at Stratford. Likewise no.62536, withdrawn in July 1955, found further employment in September when it was made Stationery Boiler no.3339 to supply steam at Stratford works. It was condemned in December 1958 and finally cut up in April 1959. *A.R.Goult.*

Summary Of The Evolution Of Classes D14, D15, D16.

8900 **D14** 3/00; **D15S** 3/25; **D15/2** 1/29; **D14/2** 2/33; **D16/3** 5/36; **W** 5/47.

8890 **D14** 4/00; **D15S** 2/16; **D15/2** 4/29; **W** 6/51.
8891 **D14** 4/00; **D15S** 3/16; **D15/2** 6/32; **W** 2/52.
8892 **D14** 4/00; **D15S** 10/27; **D15/2** 5/32; **W** 2/51.
8893 **D14** 5/00; **D15S** 12/26; **D15/2** 5/31; **W** 6/48.
8894 **D14** 5/00; **D15S** 1/18; **D15/2** 4/32; **W** 11/51.
8895 **D14** 6/00; **D15S** 11/26; **D15/2** 2/30; **W** 4/52.
8896 **D14** 6/00; **D15S** 8/15; **D15/2** 6/33; **W** 4/52.
8897 **D14** 6/00; **D15S** 9/19; **D15/2** 5/29; **W** 10/50.
8898 **D14** 7/00; **D15S** 6/15; **D15/2** 4/33; **W** 9/52.
8899 **D14** 7/00; **D15s** 2/22; **D15S** 6/25; **D15/2** 7/29; **D15S** 4/33; **D15/2** 3/35; **D16/3** 9/43; **W** 10/57.

8880 **D14** 4/01; **D15S** 2/18; **D15/2** 3/28; **D16/3** 9/42; **W** 12/59.
8881 **D14** 5/01; **D15/2** 5/30; **W** 8/50.
8882 **D14** 5/01; **D15S** 12/19; **D15/2** 5/33; **D16/3** 9/42; **W** 11/58.
8883 **D14** 5/01; **D15S** 1/16; **D15/2** 8/28; **D16/3** 5/43; **W** 3/57.
8884 **D14** 5/01; **D15s** 3/22; **D15/2** 12/28; **D16/3** 1/43; **W** 4/58.
8885 **D14** 5/01; **D15S** 5/19; **D15/2** 12/28; **D16/3** 7/37; **W** 8/57.
8886 **D14** 6/01; **D15s** 10/25; **D15/2** 3/29; **D16/3** 4/40; **W** 9/59.
8887 **D14** 6/01; **D15S** 2/18; **D15/2** 4/33; **D16/3** 8/43; **W** 10/58.
8888 **D14** 6/01; **D15S** 11/18; **D15/2** 2/29; **D16/3** 6/39; **W** 1/57.
8889 **D14** 6/01; **D15S** 3/17; **D15/2** 2/30; **W** 8/51.

8870 **D14** 3/02; **D15S** 4/24; **D15/2** 6/28; **D14/2** 5/35; **D16/3** 5/36; **W** 2/58.
8871 **D14** 3/02; **D15S** 4/24; **D15/2** 7/29; **D16/3** 5/38; **W** 8/58.
8872 **D14** 3/02; **D15S** 3/24; **D15/2** 4/28; **D16/3** 5/40; **W** 8/56.
8873 **D14** 3/02; **D15s** 1/30; **D15/2** 3/33; **D16/3** 6/39; **W** 3/60.
8874 **D14** 3/02; **D15S** 5/19; **D15/2** 12/32; **D16/3** 6/38; **W** 9/55.
8875 **D14** 4/02; **D15/2** 3/31; **D16/3** 8/37; **W** 5/57.
8876 **D14** 4/02; **D15/2** 6/29; **D14/2** 3/35; **D16/3** 5/36; **W** 7/52.
8877 **D14** 4/02; **D15/2** 2/28; **W** 6/51.
8878 **D14** 5/02; **D15s** 3/29; **D15/2** 7/31; **D14/2** 5/35; **D16/3** 5/36; **W** 11/59.
8879 **D14** 5/02; **D15/2** 12/27; **D16/3** 4/38; **W** 9/58.

8860 **D14** 5/03; **D15S** 5/19; **D15/2** 6/28; **D14/2** 6/34; **D16/3** 5/36; **W** 3/55.
8861 **D14** 5/03; **D15s** 11/21; **D15/2** 11/29; **D14/2** 4/36; **D16/3** 5/36; **W** 11/56.
8862 **D14** 5/03; **D15S** 12/23; **D15/2** 5/30; **D16/3** 6/40; **W** 9/57.
8863 **D14** 6/03; **D15s** 11/21; **D15S** 6/26; **D15/2** 4/33; **D14/2** 4/35; **D16/3** 5/36; **W** 11/58.
8864 **D14** 6/03; **D15S** 5/23; **D15/2** 3/32; **D16/3** 10/36; **W** 11/57.
8865 **D14** 9/03; **D15/2** 4/30; **D16/3** 7/36; **W** 7/55.
8866 **D14** 9/03; **D15S** 6/23; **D15/2** 6/28; **D14/2** 3/33; **D16/3** 5/36; **W** 9/45.
8867 **D14** 10/03; **D15S** 5/23; **D15/2** 12/33; **W** 4/52.
8868 **D14** 10/03; **D15/2** 9/29; **D16/3** 7/40; **W** 10/57.
8869 **D14** 11/03; **D15s** 1/22; **D15S** 2/24; **D15/2** 7/28; **D14/2** 6/34; **D16/3** 5/36; **W** 8/59.

8850 **D15s** 12/03; **D15S** 12/21; **D15/2** 2/32; **D16/3** 7/39; **W** 10/55.
8851 **D15s** 12/03; **D15S** 11/18; **D16/2** 6/27; **D16/3** 6/38; **W** 10/56.
8852 **D15s** 12/03; **D15S** 7/22; **D16/2** 2/28; **D16/3** 2/49; **W** 10/58.
8853 **D15s** 12/03; **D16/1** 5/26; **D16/2** 11/29; **D16/3** 3/47; **W** 11/59.
8854 **D15s** 1/04; **D15S** 6/16; **D16/3** 3/33; **W** 9/58.
8855 **D15s** 2/04; **D15S** 11/14; **D15/2** 9/28; **D16/3** 1/34; **W** 6/57.
8856 **D15s** 3/04; **D15S** 9/23; **D16/2** 5/27; **W** 2/51.
8857 **D15s** 3/04; **D15S** 11/16; **D15/2** 10/33; **D16/3** 7/39; **W** 10/57.
8858 **D15s** 3/04; **D15S** 5/27; **D15/2** 5/30; **D1o/2** 3/38; **W** 12/55.
8859 **D15s** 4/04; **D15/2** 5/31; **D16/3** 5/34; **W** 11/46.

8840 **D15s** 11/06; **D15S** 8/23; **D15/2** 2/29; **D16/3** 3/35; **W** 7/56.
8841 **D15s** 11/06; **D16/2** 1/29; **D16/3** 2/49; **W** 10/55.
8842 **D15s** 11/06; **D16/2** 9/30; **D16/3** 9/49; **W** 1/57.
8843 **D15s** 11/06; **D16/2** 7/27; **D16/3** 11/38; **W** 11/55.
8844 **D15s** 11/06; **D15S** 10/14; **D15/2** 11/28; **D16/3** 3/39; **W** 3/58.
8845 **D15s** 11/06; **D15S** 10/14; **D16/2** 5/29; **D16/3** 4/46; **W** 1/57.
8846 **D15s** 12/06; **D16/1** 12/24; **D16/2** 3/34; **D16/3** 4/44; **W** 10/55.
8847 **D15s** 12/06; **D15S** 5/21; **D16/1** 7/26; **D16/2** 10/33; **D16/3** 9/48; **W** 5/57.
8848 **D15s** 1/07; **D15S** 9/18; **D15/2** 4/29; **D16/3** 1/33; **W** 12/55.
8849 **D15s** 1/07; **D15S** 5/19; **D15/2** 5/28; **D16/3** 4/33; **W** 9/48.

8830 **D15s** 3/08; **D15S** 1/25; **D15/2** 5/29; **D16/3** 3/40; **W** 2/58.
8831 **D15s** 3/08; **D15S** 4/16; **D16/2** 4/28; **D16/3** 2/46; **W** 10/57.
8832 **D15s** 3/08; **D15S** 7/19; **D15/2** 11/30; **D16/3** 7/36; **W** 8/48.
8833 **D15s** 4/08; **D16/2** 1/30; **D16/3** 1/48; **W** 3/58.
8834 **D15s** 4/08; **D16/2** 3/29; **D16/3** 6/45; **W** 1/57.
8835 **D15s** 5/08; **D15S** 3/25; **D15/2** 5/29; **D16/3** 1/39; **W** 12/58.
8836 **D15s** 5/08; **D15S** 6/28; **D15/2** 2/30; **D16/3** 10/37; **W** 12/56.
8837 **D15s** 6/08; **D15/2** 7/31; **D16/3** 5/33; **W** 4/58.
8838 **D15s** 7/08; **D16/2** 11/29; **D16/3** 5/48; **W** 11/56.
8839 **D15s** 7/08; **D15S** 2/22; **D16/2** 4/28; **D16/3** 9/49; **W** 11/59.

8820 **D15s** 6/09; **D15/2** 5/32; **D16/3** 5/39; **W** 1/59.
8821 **D15s** 6/09; **D15S** 5/20; **D16/3** 5/33; **W** 7/58.
8822 **D15s** 9/09; **D16/2** 6/30; **D16/3** 3/47; **W** 10/55.
8823 **D15s** 11/09; **D15S** 12/21; **D15/2** 12/29; **D16/3** 4/38; **W** 12/55.
8824 **D15s** 11/09; **D15S** 4/18; **D15/2** 1/30; **D16/3** 2/40; **W** 5/57.
8825 **D15s** 11/09; **D15S** 5/22; **D15/2** 6/28; **D16/3** 3/37; **W** 9/57.
8826 **D15s** 12/09; **D15S** 7/22; **D16/2** 4/29; **D16/3** 5/49; **W** 10/56.
8827 **D15s** 12/09; **D16/2** 7/27; **D16/3** 9/44; **W** 10/57.
8828 **D15s** 12/09; **D15/2** 6/28; **D16/3** 3/34; **W** 3/55.
8829 **D15s** 12/09; **D16/2** 2/30; **D16/3** 4/48; **W** 6/58.

8810 **D15s** 3/10; **D15S** 4/22; **D15/2** 3/31; **D16/3** 7/36; **W** 3/53.
8811 **D15s** 3/10; **D15S** 4/22; **D15/2** 3/32; **D16/3** 12/39; **W** 1/59.
8812 **D15s** 3/10; **D15S** 3/22; **D15/2** 4/34; **D16/3** 6/36; **W** 11/48.
8813 **D15s** 4/10; **D15S** 7/14; **D16/2** 4/26; **D16/3** 9/47; **W** 12/57.
8814 **D15s** 4/10; **D15S** 11/21; **D15/2** 12/31; **D16/3** 2/35; **W** 4/55.
8815 **D15s** 5/10; **D15S** 11/22; **D15/2** 5/31; **D16/3** 8/39; **W** 3/58.
8816 **D15s** 6/10; **D15S** 5/20; **D15/2** 12/29; **D16/3** 3/34; **W** 12/56.
8817 **D15s** 6/10; **D15S** 5/24; **D15/2** 5/30; **D16/3** 7/34; **W** 10/58.
8818 **D15s** 6/10; **D16/1** 6/23; **D16/2** 11/33; **D16/3** 3/47; **W** 5/59.
8819 **D15s** 6/10; **D15S** 6/19; **D15/2** 1/26; **D16/2** 1/28; **W** 1/52.

8800 **D15s** 7/10; **D16/2** 7/27; **W** 4/50.
8801 **D15s** 7/10; **D15S** 6/19; **D16/2** 4/29; **D16/3** 6/45. **W** 4/58.
8802 **D15s** 8/10; **D15/2** 5/28; **D16/3** 4/33; **W** 10/57.
8803 **D15s** 8/10; **D15/2** 9/27; **D16/3** 4/37; **W** 3/49.
8804 **D15s** 8/10; **D15/2** 12/28; **D16/3** 3/34; **W** 11/46.
8805 **D15s** 9/10; **D16/1** 3/23; **D16/2** 11/31; **D16/3** 3/47; **W** 10/57.
8806 **D15s** 9/10; **D15/2** 8/29; **D16/3** 1/40; **W** 1/60.
8807 **D15s** 10/10; **D15S** 6/14; **D15/2** 12/29; **D16/3** 1/42; **W** 5/52.
8808 **D15s** 10/10; **D15/2** 7/29; **D16/3** 6/37; **W** 9/58.
8809 **D15s** 11/10; **D15S** 7/29; **D16/3** 6/33; **W** 6/48.

8790 **D15s** 2/11; **D15/2** 8/27; **D16/2** 4/29; **D16/3** 9/44; **W** 1/57.
8791 **D15s** 3/11; **D15S** 4/23; **D15/2** 5/28; **D16/3** 2/37; **W** 9/48.
8792 **D15s** 3/11; **D15/2** 7/14; **D16/2** 3/28; **W** 9/51.
8793 **D15s** 4/11; **D15/2** 5/29; **D16/3** 7/37; **W** 2/60.
8794 **D15S** 5/11; **D16/2** 2/29; **D16/3** 3/40; **W** 6/57.
8795 **D15s** 7/11; **D16/2** 4/31; **D16/3** 3/46; **W** 9/59.
8796 **D15s** 7/11; **D15S** 4/25; **D16/2** 12/28; **D16/3** 12/46; **W** 11/55.
8797 **D15s** 7/11; **D15S** 7/14; **D15/2** 4/28; **D16/3** 7/37; **W** 1/57.
8798 **D15S** 8/11; **D15/2** 4/32; **D16/3** 4/34; **W** 2/57.
8799 **D15S** 8/11; **D15/2** 2/34; **D16/3** 2/40; **W** 1/59.

8780 **D16/1** 6/23; **D16/2** 11/28; **D16/3** 9/44; **W** 1/57.
8781 **D16/1** 6/23; **D16/2** 8/28; **D16/3** 4/49; **W** 11/59.
8782 **D16/1** 6/23; **D16/2** 5/31; **D16/3** 12/48; **W** 10/60.
8783 **D16/1** 7/23; **D16/2** 6/28; **D16/3** 12/39; **W** 8/58.
8784 **D16/1** 7/23; **D16/2** 6/29; **D16/3** 4/47; **W** 10/58.
8785 **D16/1** 7/23; **D16/2** 6/28; **D16/3** 5/44; **W** 2/53.
8786 **D16/1** 8/23; **D16/2** 6/29; **D16/3** 1/45; **W** 5/57.
8787 **D16/1** 8/23; **D16/2** 1/29; **D16/3** 8/44; **W** 11/59.
8788 **D16/1** 9/23; **D16/2** 12/28; **D16/3** 12/38; **W** 10/57.
8789 **D16/1** 9/23; **D16/2** 12/28; **D16/3** 3/48; **W** 10/55.

Key: **S** - superheated; **s** - saturated; **W** - withdrawn.
Note: For nos. 8790-8900 the dates built shown in this table are those officially recorded by the GER and in many cases precede the "to traffic" dates listed individually in the pages that follow.

9

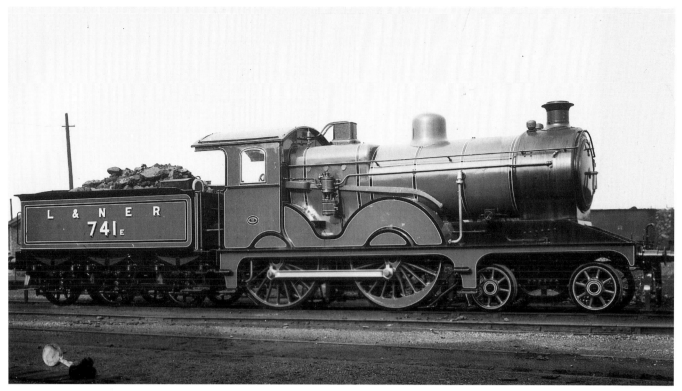

The first twenty to be superheated (nos. 704, 707, 718, 719, 728, 729, 731, 735, 742, 748, 751, 772, 775, 777, 1012, 1016, 1020, 1023, 1025, 1027), between December 1913 and June 1915, received the Schmidt type. At first, element protection consisted of dampers operated by a steam cylinder on the left side of the smokebox. By Grouping all the damper gear had been replaced by anti-vacuum valves fitted each end of the header. Starting with no.756 in June 1915, a change was made to the Robinson pattern of superheater for all further conversions, and these superheaters had the twin anti-vacuum valves from new as seen here on 741E. Except for nos.7707, 7772, 7775, 8016, 8023, 8025, changed to Robinson superheater in 1934-36, the Schmidt pattern was retained on the earlier conversions.

For washing out, there were four plugs on the left side of the firebox and three staggered plugs on the right. Until into the 1930's the plugs had hinged covers.

D13 CLASS

7710

To traffic 11/1886.

REPAIRS:
Str. 26/8/98—3/1/99.**G.**
Str. 9/8/07—14/2/08.**G.**
Rebuilt from 2-4-0.
Str. 7/7—9/11/16.**G.**
Superheated boiler fitted.
Str. ?/?—7/25.**G.**
Str. 11/3—27/7/27.**G.**
Str. ?/?—1/29.**N/C.**
Vacuum brake added.

BOILERS:
710.
710 *(new)* 3/1/99.
710 *(new)* 14/2/08.
3122 *(new)* 9/11/16.
3118 *(ex7718)* 27/7/27.

SHED:
Peterborough East.

RENUMBERED:
7710 1925.

CONDEMNED: 18/12/29.
Cut up at Stratford.

7712

To traffic 5/1887.

REPAIRS:
Str. 1/1—31/5/00.**G.**
Str. 6/2—23/6/06.**G.**
Rebuilt from 2-4-0.
Str. 13/6/19—29/1/20.**G.**
Str. 11/3—13/8/21.**G.**
Str. 10/7—11/11/25.**G.**
Superheated boiler fitted.
Str. ?/?—9/27.**G.**
Str. ?/?—4/29.**N/C.**
Vacuum brake added.
Str. ?/?—2/30.**G.**
Coal guard on tender.

BOILERS:
712.
712 *(new)* 31/5/00.
712 *(new)* 23/6/06.
734 *(ex7734)* 29/1/20.
3137 *(ex8025)* 11/11/25.

SHED:
Cambridge.

RENUMBERED:
7712 1925.

CONDEMNED: 2/11/31.
Cut up at Stratford.

7713

To traffic 5/1887.

REPAIRS:
Str. 26/7/06—29/1/07.**G.**
Rebuilt from 2-4-0.
Str. 21/12/21—18/3/22.**G.**
Superheated boiler fitted.
Str. ?/?—1/26.**G.**
Str. ?/?—1/28.**G.**
Coal guard on tender.
Str. ?/?—11/30.**G.**

BOILERS:
713.
713 *(new)* 29/1/07.
3142 *(new)* 18/3/22.
3128 *(ex8025)* 11/30.

SHED:
Peterborough East

RENUMBERED:
713E *by* 17/1/25.
7713 ?/?/??.

CONDEMNED: 26/5/33.
Cut up at Stratford.

7717

To traffic 6/1887.

REPAIRS:
Str. 17/3—12/11/96.**G.**
Str. 1/5/06—5/2/07.**G.**
Rebuilt from 2-4-0.
Str. 12/4—4/10/18.**G.**
Str. 20/9—21/12/21.**G.**
Str. 25/3—23/9/26.**G.**

BOILERS:
717.
717 *(new)* 12/11/96.
717 *(new)* 5/2/07.
1029 *(ex8029)* 4/10/18.
1032 *(ex8032)* 21/12/21.

SHED:
March

RENUMBERED:
7717 ?/?/??.

CONDEMNED: 27/3/30.
Cut up at Stratford.

7718

To traffic 6/1887.

REPAIRS:
Str. 15/2—5/7/97.**G.**
Str. 11/8/04—14/4/05.**G.**
Rebuilt from 2-4-0.
Str. 18/9/13—27/3/14.**G.**
Str. 12/1—17/6/21.**G.**
Str. 7/4—2/8/23.**G.**
Superheated boiler fitted.
Str. 10/1—23/4/25.**G.**
Str. 25/3—27/7/27.**G.**
Str. ?/?—7/29.**G.**
*Vacuum brake added
and coal guard on tender.*
Str. 16/3—1/5/31.**G.**

BOILERS:
718.
718 *(new)* 5/7/97.
718 *(new)* 14/4/05.
718 *(new)* 27/3/14.
728 *(ex8025)* 17/6/21.
3118 *(ex7708)* 2/8/23.
3132 *(ex7700)* 27/7/27.
3105 *(ex7766)* 1/5/31.

SHEDS:
King's Lynn.
Cambridge 8/3/31.

RENUMBERED:
718E 2/8/23.
7718 23/4/25.

CONDEMNED: 8/5/33.
Cut up at Stratford.

7719

To traffic 6/1887.

REPAIRS:
Str. ?/?—10/95.**G.**
Str. 21/1—8/6/06.**G.**
Rebuilt from 2-4-0.
Str. 8/11/22—8/3/23.**G.**
Superheated boiler fitted.
Str. ?/?—4/27.**G.**
Vacuum brake added.
Str. ?/?—11/29.**G.**
Coal guard on tender.

BOILERS:
719.
719 *(new)* 10/95.
719 *(new)* 8/6/06.
3143 *(new)* 8/3/23.

Note: *According to James
Holden's "Boiler Register",
7719 received a new superheated boiler in March 1914,
probably also numbered 719.
However, WBY did not have
access to this particular
document and has therefore left
out the information. Likewise, a
'shopping' date is also missed
from the list for the same
reason.*

SHEDS:
Peterborough East.
Doncaster 21/4/27.
Peterborough East *by* 8/27.

RENUMBERED:
7719 ?/?/??.

CONDEMNED: 16/3/32.
Cut up at Stratford.

7728

To traffic 4/1888.

REPAIRS:
Str. 27/2—30/8/00.**G.**
Str. 22/1—12/6/06.**G.**
Rebuilt from 2-4-0.
Str. 2/12/13—1/5/14.**G.**
Superheated boiler fitted.
Str. 25/10/17—28/2/18.**G.**
Str. 20/8—25/11/21.**G.**
Str. 27/12/24—28/4/25.**G.**
Str. 6/5—17/9/27.**G.**
Str. ?/?—3/29.**N/C.**
Vacuum brake added.
Str. 12/10—23/11/29.**G.**

BOILERS:
728.

WORKS CODES:- **Bd** - Beardmore. **Ca** - Cambridge shed. **Dn** - Doncaster. **Go** - Gorton. **Ips** - Ipswich shed. **Nr** - Norwich shed. **Str** - Stratford.
REPAIR CODES:- **C/H** - Casual Heavy. **C/L** - Casual Light. **G** - General. **H**- Heavy. **H/I** - Heavy Intermediate. **L** - Light. **L/I** - Light Intermediate. **N/C** - Non-Classified.

11

Chimneys at first had a polished brass cap and at least one is known to have survived to May 1933 on no.8028, although not in a polished state. Soon after Grouping the LNER changed many of the chimneys to a plain and more straight sided cast iron type. Standard safety valves were four-column Ramsbottoms in a rectangular enclosure, painted in the same colour as the engine. The majority of the class kept these until withdrawal.

7728 cont.

728 *(new)* 30/8/00.
728 *(new)* 12/6/06.
728 *(new)* 1/5/14.
3101 *(ex7748)* 28/2/18.
718 *(ex7718)* 25/11/21.
3115 *(ex8032)* 28/4/25.
3141 *(ex7707)* 23/11/29.

SHEDS:
Cambridge.
King's Lynn 5/1/30.

RENUMBERED:
7728 28/4/25.

CONDEMNED: 23/4/31.
Cut up at Stratford.

7729

To traffic 4/1888.

REPAIRS:
Str. 21/2—13/7/98.**G**.
Str. 23/6/04—9/3/05.**G**.
Rebuilt from 2-4-0.
Str. 11/11/14—19/2/15.**G**.
Superheated boiler fitted.
Str. 20/9/21—11/3/22.**G**.
Str. 6/4—27/6/23.**G**.
Str. 29/4—3/9/27.**G**.
Str. ?/?—5/29.**N/C**.
Vacuum brake added.
Str. 23/12/30—5/2/31.**G**.
Str. 22/2—22/3/34.**G**.

BOILERS:
729.
729 *(new)* 13/7/98.
729 *(new)* 9/3/05.
3110 *(new)* 19/2/15.
3119 *(ex7765)* 11/3/22.

3138 *(ex7739)* 27/6/23.
3116 *(ex7765)* 3/9/27.
3142 *(ex7713)* 5/2/31.
3121 *(ex7706)* 22/3/34.

SHEDS:
March.
King's Lynn 24/6/33.

RENUMBERED:
7729 ?/?/??.

CONDEMNED: 11/4/36.
Cut up at Stratford.

G.E. 730

To traffic 5/1888.

REPAIRS:
Str. 17/3—12/11/96.**G**.
Str. 24/10/06—21/2/07.**G**.
Rebuilt from 2-4-0.
Str. 19/12/19—31/3/20.**G**.

BOILERS:
730.
730 *(new)* 12/11/96.
730 *(new)* 21/2/07.
712 *(ex7712)* 31/3/20.

SHED:
Yarmouth.

RENUMBERED:
Allocated 7730 but not applied.

CONDEMNED: 18/8/23.
Cut up at Stratford.

7731

To traffic 5/1888.

REPAIRS:
Str. 6/4—29/9/97.**G**.
Str. 26/10/06—12/3/07.**G**.
Rebuilt from 2-4-0.
Str. 11/11/14—4/2/15.**G**.
Superheated boiler fitted.
Str. 27/1—25/5/22.**G**.
Str. 5/2—22/4/26.**G**.
Str. ?/?—8/28.**G**.
Str. 21/3—9/5/30.**G**.

BOILERS:
731.
731 *(new)* 29/9/97.
731 *(new)* 12/3/07.
3109 *(new)* 4/2/15.
3146 *(new)* 22/4/26.
3138 *(ex8016)* 9/5/30.

SHED:
Ipswich.

RENUMBERED:
7731 3/25.

CONDEMNED: 5/8/31.
Cut up at Stratford.

7732

To traffic 5/1888.

REPAIRS:
Str. 24/3—19/8/98.**G**.
Str. 26/2—21/5/08.**G**.
Rebuilt from 2-4-0.
Str. 20/7/17—2/1/18.**G**.
Str. 24/2—25/5/21.**G**.
Superheated boiler fitted.
Str. ?/?—3/26.**G**.

Coal guard on tender.
Str. 16/12/30—27/1/31.**G**.

BOILERS:
732.
732 *(new)* 19/8/98.
732 *(new)* 21/5/08.
751 *(ex1018)* 2/1/18.
3139 *(new)* 25/5/21.
3131 *(ex7777)* 27/1/31.

SHEDS:
Peterborough East.
Cambridge 3/3/29.
King's Lynn 8/3/31.

RENUMBERED:
7732 ?/?/??.

CONDEMNED: 1/5/33.
Cut up at Stratford.

7733

To traffic 5/1888.

REPAIRS:
Str. 1/12/97—23/5/98.**G**.
Str. 28/4—30/7/08.**G**.
Rebuilt from 2-4-0.
Str. 31/5—13/12/18.**G**.
Str. 11/6/20—11/1/21.**G**.
Superheated boiler fitted.
Str. 26/9/22—23/2/23.**G**.
Str. 24/7—25/11/24.**G**.
Str. 11/2—18/6/26.**G**.
Str. ?/?—11/28.**G**.
Vacuum brake added, & coal guard on tender.

BOILERS:
733.
733 *(new)* 23/5/98.

In 1929 five new boilers, fitted with Ross 'Pop' safety valves, were made for this class. One of these boilers, on no.8025 from June 1932 to February 1934, was unusual in having its two 'Pops' at different heights. *L.Hanson.*

733 (*new*) 30/7/08.
1026 (*ex8026*) 13/12/18.
3111 (*ex8027*) 11/1/21.
3133 (*ex7735*) 25/11/24.
3147 (*new*) 18/6/26.

SHED:
Colchester.

RENUMBERED:
7733 ?/?/??.

CONDEMNED: 11/9/31.
Cut up at Stratford.

7734

To traffic 5/1888.

REPAIRS:
Str. ?/?—12/00.**G**.
Str. 7/3—23/7/07.**G**.
Rebuilt from 2-4-0.
Str. 13/12/18—10/10/19.**G**.
Superheated boiler fitted.
Str. 23/2—18/5/23.**G**.
Str. 14/1—19/5/28.**G**.
Coal guard on tender.
Str. ?/?—3/29.**N/C**.
Vacuum brake added.
Str. ?/?—3/30.**G**.

BOILERS:
734.
734 (*new*) 12/00.
734 (*new*) 23/7/07.
3128 (*new*) 10/10/19.
719 (*ex7719*) 18/5/23.
3152 (*new*) 3/30.

SHED:
Colchester.

RENUMBERED:
7734 ?/?/??.

CONDEMNED: 21/10/31.
Cut up at Stratford.

7735

To traffic 6/1888.

REPAIRS:
Str. 21/12/99—11/9/00.**G**.
Str. 26/4—30/10/07.**G**.
Rebuilt from 2-4-0.
Str. 16/9/13—29/1/14.**G**.
Superheated boiler fitted.
Str. 20/1—23/4/20.**G**.
Str. 17/5/22—5/1/23.**G**.
Str. 18/7—21/11/24.**G**.
Str. 26/11/26—4/2/27.**G**.
Str. ?/?—12/28.**N/C**.
Vacuum brake added.
Str. ?/?—6/29.**G**.
Coal guard on tender.

BOILERS:
735.
735 (*new*) 11/9/00.
735 (*new*) 30/10/07.
735 (*new*) 29/1/14.
3133 (*new*) 23/4/20.
3117 (*ex8015*) 21/11/24.
707 (*ex8035*) 4/2/27.
775 (*ex7767*) 6/29.

SHEDS:
Parkeston.
Colchester 2/11/31.

RENUMBERED:
7735 ?/?/??.

CONDEMNED: 5/4/32.
Cut up at Stratford.

7737

To traffic 6/1888.

REPAIRS:
Str. ?/?—?/99.**G**.
Str. 7/12/06—2/7/07.**G**.
Rebuilt from 2-4-0.
Str. 21/12/15—5/4/16.**G**.
Superheated boiler fitted.
Str. 1/10—23/12/20.**G**.
Str. 21/9/22—24/2/23.**G**.
Str. 1/12/24—5/3/25.**G**.
Str. ?/?—7/27.**G**.
Str. ?/?—6/29.**N/C**.
Vacuum brake added.
Str. ?/?—11/29.**G**.
Coal guard on tender.
Str. 27/4—5/6/31.**G**.

BOILERS:
737.
737 (*new*) ?/99.
737 (*new*) 2/7/07.
3115 (*new*) 5/4/16.
3135 (*new*) 23/12/20.
3126 (*ex8028*) 5/3/25.
3133 (*ex7744*) 5/6/31.

SHEDS:
Ipswich.
Colchester 13/10/31.

RENUMBERED:
7737 ?/?/??.

CONDEMNED: 1/4/33.
Cut up at Stratford.

7738

To traffic 6/1888.

REPAIRS:
Str. ?/?—6/00.**G**.
Str. 27/11/07—28/2/08.**G**.
Rebuilt from 2-4-0.
Str. 12/11/20—23/2/21.**G**.
Superheated boiler fitted.
Str. ?/?—12/26.**G**.
Str. 29/10/27—11/2/28.**G**.
Str. ?/?—2/29.**N/C**.
Vacuum brake added.
Str. 24/10—7/12/29.**G**.
Coal guard on tender.

BOILERS:
738.
738 (*new*) 6/00.

738 (*new*) 28/2/08.
3136 (*new*) 23/2/21.
1023 (*ex8013*) 11/2/28.
3148 (*new*) 7/12/29.

SHED:
Ipswich.

RENUMBERED:
7738 by 25/2/25.

CONDEMNED: 23/7/31.
Cut up at Stratford.

7739

To traffic 6/1888.

REPAIRS:
Str. 23/1—30/5/02.**G**.
Str. 24/6—14/11/07.**G**.
Rebuilt from 2-4-0.
Str. 3/3—14/6/16.**G**.
Superheated boiler fitted.
Str. 7/1—21/4/21.**G**.
Str. 2/3—28/6/23.**G**.
Str. 21/2—12/6/25.**G**.
Str. ?/?—5/27.**G**.
Str. ?/?—5/29.**G**.
Vacuum brake added &
coal guard on tender.

BOILERS:
739.
739 (*new*) 30/5/02.
739 (*new*) 14/11/07.
3116 (*new*) 14/6/16.
3138 (*new*) 21/4/21.
718 (*ex7728*) 12/6/25.
3101 (*ex7772*) 5/29.

SHED:
Colchester.

RENUMBERED:
7739 ?/?/??.

CONDEMNED: 4/9/31.
Cut up at Stratford.

7741

To traffic 4/1889.

REPAIRS:
Str. ?/?—6/00.**G**.
Str. 7/2—9/7/07.**G**.
Rebuilt from 2-4-0.
Str. 27/6/19—25/2/20.**G**.
Superheated boiler fitted.
Str. 22/6—20/10/23.**G**.
Str. ?/?—9/26.**G**.
Str. 17/5—3/10/28.**G**.
Vacuum brake added &
coal guard on tender.
Str. 28/1—13/3/31.**G**.
Str. 27/4—25/5/33.**G**.

BOILERS:
741.
741 *(new)* 6/00.
741 *(new)* 9/7/07.
3131 *(new)* 25/2/20.
3120 *(ex8020)* 20/10/23.
3102 *(ex7751)* 3/10/28.
3116 *(ex7729)* 13/3/31.
3140 *(ex7745)* 25/5/33.

SHEDS:
Ipswich.
King's Lynn 11/10/33.

RENUMBERED:
741ᴇ 20/10/23.
7741 ?/?/??.

CONDEMNED: 12/12/35.
Cut up at Stratford.

7742

To traffic 4/1889.

REPAIRS:
Str. ?/?—?/96.**G**.
Str. 26/10/06—7/3/07.**G**.
Rebuilt from 2-4-0.
Str. 17/9—17/12/14.**G**.
Superheated boiler fitted.
Str. 1/3—24/6/22.**G**.
Str. 30/1—8/6/26.**G**.
Str. 20/10—18/12/26.**H**.
New cylinders.
Str. 20/7—12/10/28.**G**.
Vacuum brake added &
coal guard on tender.
Str. 24/4—19/5/33.**G**.

BOILERS:
742.

742 *(new)* ?/96.
742 *(new)* 7/3/07.
3107 *(new)* 17/12/14.
3106 *(ex8023)* 24/6/22.
3113 *(ex8023)* 12/10/28.

SHEDS:
Cambridge.
King's Lynn 26/4/31.

RENUMBERED:
7742 ?/?/??.

CONDEMNED: 25/11/35.
Cut up at Stratford.

7744

To traffic 5/1889.

REPAIRS:
Str. 15/4—5/9/02.**G**.
Str. 24/6—31/10/07.**G**.
Rebuilt from 2-4-0.
Str. 27/3—31/8/15.**G**.
Superheated boiler fitted.
Str. 5/1—25/5/22.**G**.
Str. ?/?—11/26.**G**.
Str. ?/?—1/29.**G**.
Vacuum brake added &
coal guard on tender.
Str. 23/1—6/3/31.**G**.
Str. 5/7—1/8/33.**G**.

BOILERS:
744.
744 *(new)* 5/9/02.
744 *(new)* 31/10/07.
3114 *(new)* 31/8/15.
3133 *(ex7779)* 1/29.
3127 *(ex8035)* 6/3/31.
3131 *(ex7732)* 1/8/33.

SHEDS:
Colchester.
Ipswich 18/10/29.

RENUMBERED:
7744 ?/?/??.

CONDEMNED: 2/4/35.
Cut up at Stratford.

7745

To traffic 5/1889.

REPAIRS:
Str. 11/2—9/7/02.**G**.
Str. 9/12/05—29/6/06.**G**.

Rebuilt from 2-4-0.
Str. 30/11/17—20/3/18.**G**.
Superheated boiler fitted.
Str. 28/3—29/7/22.**G**.
Str. 24/4—26/7/24.**G**.
Str. ?/?—3/27.**G**.
Str. ?/?—7/29.**G**.
Vacuum brake added &
coal guard on tender.
Str. 26/6—7/8/31.**G**.

BOILERS:
745.
745 *(new)* 9/7/02.
745 *(new)* 29/6/06.
3124 *(new)* 20/3/18.
3125 *(ex8036)* 26/7/24.
3140 *(ex7700)* 7/8/31.

SHED:
Colchester.

RENUMBERED:
7745 26/7/24.

CONDEMNED: 27/1/33.
Cut up at Stratford.

7748

To traffic 5/1889.

REPAIRS:
Str. 29/10/95—27/4/96.**G**.
Str. 26/7/04—23/2/05.**G**.
Rebuilt from 2-4-0.
Str. 27/1—9/6/14.**G**.
Superheated boiler fitted.
Str. 12/10/17—8/2/18.**G**.
Str. 11/11/21—13/4/22.**G**.
Str. ?/?—2/24.**G**.
Str. 19/2—12/5/27.**G**.
Str. ?/?—8/29.**G**.
Vacuum brake added &
coal guard on tender.

BOILERS:
748.
748 *(new)* 27/4/96.
748 *(new)* 23/2/05.
3101 *(new)* 9/6/14.
3108 *(ex8020)* 8/2/18.
3110 *(ex7729)* 13/4/22.
3123 *(ex8030)* 2/24.

SHED:
Colchester.

RENUMBERED:
7748 by 25/2/25.

CONDEMNED: 11/9/31.
Cut up at Stratford.

7751

To traffic 6/1889.

REPAIRS:
Str. 14/3—2/8/99.**G**.
Str. 27/11/06—29/6/07.**G**.
Rebuilt from 2-4-0.
Str. 9/2—12/6/14.**G**.
Superheated boiler fitted.
Str. 6/4—29/7/22.**G**.
Str. 22/1—21/5/26.**G**.
Str. 10/4—7/7/28.**G**.
Vacuum brake added &
coal guard on tender.
Str. 1/9—6/10/30.**G**.

BOILERS:
751.
751 *(new)* 2/8/99.
751 *(new)* 29/6/07.
3103 *(new)* 12/6/14.
3102 *(ex7777)* 29/7/22.
3103 *(ex7777)* 7/7/28.
3130 *(ex8021)* 6/10/30.

SHED:
March.

RENUMBERED:
7751 ?/?/??.

CONDEMNED: 24/1/33.
Cut up at Stratford.

7756

To traffic 9/1889.

REPAIRS:
Str. 14/6/00—26/2/01.**G**.
Str. 10/4—10/7/08.**G**.
Rebuilt from 2-4-0.
Str. 18/2—25/6/15.**G**.
Superheated boiler fitted.
Str. 28/10/21—16/2/22.**G**.
Str. 13/3—27/9/23.**G**.
Str. 19/2—30/6/25.**G**.
Str. 25/3—27/7/27.**G**.
Str. ?/?—10/29.**G**.
Vacuum brake added &
coal guard on tender.
Str. 27/6—11/8/32.**G**.
Str. 30/5—13/7/34.**G**.
Str. ?/?—29/1/37.**G**.

WORKS CODES:- Bd - Beardmore. Ca - Cambridge shed. Dn - Doncaster. Go - Gorton. Ips - Ipswich shed. Nr - Norwich shed. Str - Stratford.
REPAIR CODES:- **C/H** - Casual Heavy. **C/L** - Casual Light. **G** - General. **H**- Heavy. **H/I** - Heavy Intermediate. **L** - Light. **L/I** - Light Intermediate. **N/C** - Non-Classified.

Until superheaters were put in, the smokebox door had two hinge straps across it, and was fastened by two handles. Superheating required a new, and longer, smokebox and the door was then changed to the type with a strengthening ring instead of the two straps. Although the upper lamp iron was originally on top of the smokebox, all the replacement doors at superheating had the iron fixed on them. By 1923 the unsuperheated engines also had the lamp iron fixed to this more accessible position.

When these engines were rebuilt in 1905-08 from 2-4-0 to 4-4-0 type, the bogies from withdrawn engines were used. Most of these came from Bromley 0-4-4 tank engines but needed new 3' 1" diameter wheels in place of the 2' 10" originals; the new wheels all had eight spokes. Some bogies came from withdrawn Worsdell 4-4-0s which although having 3' 1" wheels, they had nine spokes. Consequently it was possible to see bogies with both types of wheel - 7738 for instance had a Wordsell bogie with nine-spoke wheels on the rear axle whilst the front axle had eight-spoke wheels. There were even cases where the difference was more marked, because in its LNER years no.1031 ran with eight spokes on the front wheels and ten on the rear wheels. There were other variations too - no.8028 ran for at least its last five years with 9-spoke front bogie wheels and 8-spoke on the rear.

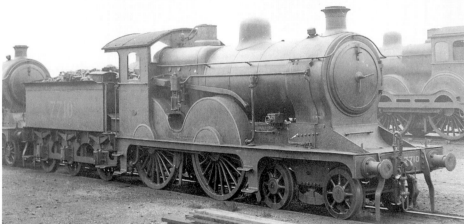

(above) **Front buffers were originally taper shank type with solid spindle but when replacements were required, the parallel shank type with hollow spindle was usually fitted. No D13 was ever recorded with Group Standard buffers.**

(left) **The D13 cab roof was of traditional GER style with wood planking clad in canvas. Cab roof rain strips were put on most of the class during the early years of the LNER but none ever acquired a steel roof as introduced on other classes after 1930. In this March 1927 view, no.7710 was still not fitted with rain strips at the eaves but probably got them in July.** *H.C.Casserley.*

In 1901, nos.1020 to 1029 exchanged tenders with those of the 4-2-2 engines, nos.10 to 19. With one exception they retained those unusual type of tenders until withdrawal. The exception was no.8021 which, at some time after 1929, exchanged tenders with no.8032. Nos.1022 and 1024 never survived to become D13, being scrapped in 1913 and 1908 respectively. On the other hand no.8023 survived to January 1944 and its tender went to E4 class where it was in use until May 1955. *W.L.Good.*

7756 cont.
BOILERS:
 756.
 756 *(new)* 26/2/01.
 756 *(new)* 10/7/08.
 3113 *(new)* 25/6/15.
 3101 *(ex7728)* 16/2/22.
 728 *(ex7718)* 27/9/23.
 3146 *(ex7772)* 11/8/32.
 3147 *(ex8020)* 13/7/34.
 3149 *(ex7772)* 29/1/37.

SHEDS:
Colchester.
Norwich 15/11/35.

RENUMBERED:
7756 30/6/25.

CONDEMNED: 5/12/38.
Cut up at Stratford.

7765

To traffic 6/1890.

REPAIRS:
Str. 26/10/04—23/3/05.**G.**
Rebuilt from 2-4-0.
Str. 25/8/16—23/3/17.**G.**
Superheated boiler fitted.
Str. 1/7—28/10/21.**G.**
Str. 23/1—30/5/25.**G.**
Str. 4/3—23/6/27.**G.**
Str. ?/?—1/29.**N/C.**
Vacuum brake added.

BOILERS:
 765.
 765 *(new)* 23/3/05.
 3119 *(new)* 23/3/17.
 3116 *(ex7739)* 28/10/21.
 3110 *(ex????)* 23/6/27.

SHED:
Ipswich.

RENUMBERED:
7765 30/5/25.

CONDEMNED: 21/1/30.
Cut up at Stratford.

7766

To traffic 6/1890.

REPAIRS:
Str. ?/?—6/02.**G.**
Str. 1/11/07—28/2/08.**G.**
Rebuilt from 2-4-0.
Str. 15/11/18—2/9/19.**G.**
Superheated boiler fitted.
Str. 29/2—28/5/24.**G.**

Str. ?/?—2/26.**G.**
Str. 17/3—30/4/27.**H.**
Boiler work only.
Str. 30/9—1/11/27.**H.**
New cylinders.
Str. 19/5—24/8/28.**G.**
Vacuum brake added &
coal guard on tender.
Str. 24/2--5/4/30.**G.**
Str. 31/3—29/4/32.**G.**

BOILERS:
 766.
 766 *(new)* 6/02.
 766 *(new)* 28/2/08.
 3105 *(ex7772)* 2/9/19.
 3104 *(ex8036)* 24/8/28.
 3118 *(ex7710)* 5/4/30.
 3150 *(ex8029)* 29/4/32.

SHEDS:
Norwich.
Yarmouth 23/9/28.
Norwich 20/7/30.
Yarmouth 11/1/31.
Norwich 15/5/32.
Yarmouth 26/2/33.
Norwich 9/10/34.

RENUMBERED:
7766 28/5/24.

CONDEMNED: 21/1/35.
Cut up at Stratford.

7767

To traffic 6/1890.

REPAIRS:
Str. 5/11/01—30/4/02.**G.**
Str. 30/7/07—6/2/08.**G.**
Rebuilt from 2-4-0.
Str. ?/?—1/16.**G.**
Str. 21/9/22—9/2/23.**G.**
Superheated boiler fitted.
Str. ?/?—12/26.**G.**
Str. ?/?—4/29.**G.**
Vacuum brake added &
coal guard on tender.
Str. 1/1—14/2/31.**G.**
Str. 20/1—23/2/33.**G.**

BOILERS:
 767.
 767 *(new)* 30/4/02.
 767 *(new)* 6/2/08.
 744 *(ex7744)* 1/16.
 775 *(ex7775)* 9/2/23.
 3114 *(ex7744)* 4/29.
 3113 *(ex7742)* 14/2/31.
 3145 *(ex8026)* 23/2/33.

SHEDS:
Norwich.

RENUMBERED:
7767 ?/?/??.

CONDEMNED: 19/12/34.
Cut up at Stratford.

7700

To traffic 5/1892.

REPAIRS:
Str. 12/1—14/4/05.**G.**
Rebuilt from 2-4-0.
Str. 20/6/19—30/3/20.**G.**
Superheated boiler fitted.
Str. 17/9/20—22/1/21.**H.**
Str. ?/?—9/24.**G.**
Str. 12/2—14/5/27.**G.**
Coal guard on tender.
Str. ?/?—?/29.**N/C.**
Vacuum brake added.
Str. 25/3—15/5/31.**G.**

BOILERS:
 700.
 700 *(new)* 14/4/05.
 3132 *(new)* 30/3/20.
 3140 *(ex7706)* 14/5/27.
 3139 *(ex7732)* 15/5/31.

SHEDS:
Doncaster.
Norwich 23/5/25.
Ipswich 17/8/31.
King's Lynn 28/10/33.

RENUMBERED:
7700 9/24.

CONDEMNED: 17/10/35.
Cut up at Stratford.

7704

To traffic 5/1892.

REPAIRS:
Str. 29/3/05—16/3/06.**G.**
Rebuilt from 2-4-0.
Str. 15/4—1/7/14.**G.**
Superheated boiler fitted.
Str. 20/9/23—1/2/24.**G.**
Str. 22/9—10/12/27.**G.**
Coal guard on tender.
Str. ?/?—2/29.**N/C.**
Vacuum brake added.

BOILERS:
 704.
 704 *(new)* 16/3/06.
 3104 *(new)* 1/7/14.

3131 *(ex7741)* 1/2/24.
3122 *(ex7710)* 10/12/27.

SHEDS:
Peterborough East.
Norwich 25/5/32.

RENUMBERED:
 704ᴇ as at 13/4/25*.
7704 ?/?/??.

* *The E suffix gave way to the*
addition of 7000 from 2/24 to
4/25 so the sighting of 704 with
the suffix on the given date
would appear to be the end of
the period when 704 actually
carried the suffix.

CONDEMNED: 22/12/32.
Cut up at Stratford.

7705

To traffic 6/1892.

REPAIRS:
Str. 7/7/99—22/2/00.**G.**
Str. 24/7—26/11/07.**G.**
Rebuilt from 2-4-0.
Str. 7/3—29/8/19.**G.**
Str. 26/5—5/9/23.**G.**

BOILERS:
 705.
 705 *(new)* 22/2/00.
 705 *(new)* 26/11/07.
 747 *(ex??)* 29/8/19.

SHED:
Peterborough East.

RENUMBERED:
7705 by 13/3/25.

CONDEMNED: 20/12/26.
Cut up at Stratford.

7706

To traffic 6/1892.

REPAIRS:
Str. 25/11/04—4/4/05.**G.**
Rebuilt from 2-4-0.
Str. 13/9/18—3/6/19.**G.**
Str. 9/2—30/6/25.**G.**
Superheated boiler fitted.
Str. 21/1—22/4/27.**G.**
Coal guard on tender.
Str. 15/10—19/11/27.**L.**
Str. ?/?—3/29.**G.**
Vacuum brake added.
Str. 22/9—28/10/31.**G.**

Str. 4/9—3/10/33.**G.**
Str. 9/10—1/11/35.**G.**

BOILERS:
 706.
 706 *(new)* 4/4/05.
3140 *(ex8039)* 30/6/25.
3117 *(ex7735)* 22/4/27.
3121 *(ex8037)* 28/10/31.
3128 *(ex7713)* 3/10/33.
3150 *(ex7766)* 1/11/35.

SHEDS:
March.
King's Lynn 29/2/36.
March 2/10/36.
King's Lynn 8/4/37.

RENUMBERED:
7706 30/6/25.

CONDEMNED: 8/6/38.
Cut up at Stratford.

7707

To traffic 6/1892.

REPAIRS:
Str. 28/6/04—17/2/05.**G.**
Rebuilt from 2-4-0.
Str. 4/3—31/12/13.**G.**
Superheated boiler fitted.
Str. 8/3—10/9/18.**G.**
Str. 10/11/21—28/2/22.**G.**
Str. 29/1—28/4/25.**G.**
Str. 19/5—1/10/27.**G.**
Coal guard on tender.
Str. ?/?—?/?.**N/C.**
Vacuum brake added.
Str. 16/3—1/5/31.**G.**
Str. 10/5—8/6/33.**G.**
Str. 24/6—23/7/35.**G.**

BOILERS:
 707.
 707 *(new)* 17/2/05.
 707 *(new)* 31/12/13.
1023 *(ex8023)* 10/9/18.
3141 *(new)* 28/2/22.
3102 *(ex7741)* 1/5/31.
3129 *(ex????)* 8/6/33.
3144 *(ex8015)* 23/7/35.

SHEDS:
Norwich.
Yarmouth 4/10/31.
Norwich 26/2/33.
Yarmouth 5/8/33.
Norwich 24/5/35.

RENUMBERED:
7707 28/4/25.

CONDEMNED: 25/5/37.
Cut up at Stratford.

7708

To traffic 6/1892.

REPAIRS:
Str. 6/9/05—1/5/06.**G.**
Rebuilt from 2-4-0.
Str. 30/8—23/11/17.**G.**
Superheated boiler fitted.
Str. 5/2—3/5/23.**G.**
Str. 4/3—9/7/27.**G.**
Str. ?/?—8/29.**G.**
*Vacuum brake added &
coal guard on tender.*
Str. 1/6—3/7/31.**G.**
Str. 26/6—25/7/33.**G.**

BOILERS:
 708.
 708 *(new)* 1/5/06.
3118 *(new)* 23/11/17.
3100 *(ex8016)* 3/5/23.
 707 *(ex7735)* 8/29.
3141 *(ex7728)* 3/7/31.
3102 *(ex7707)* 25/7/33.

SHEDS:
Cambridge.
King's Lynn 4/8/29.

RENUMBERED:
7708 *by* 2/25.

CONDEMNED: 15/11/35.
Cut up at Stratford.

7772

To traffic 6/1892.

REPAIRS:
Str. 14/4/05—16/3/06.**G.**
Rebuilt from 2-4-0.
Str. 20/8/14—5/1/15.**G.**
Superheated boiler fitted.
Str. 25/10/18—3/4/19.**G.**
Str. 20/5—4/9/23.**G.**
Str. ?/?—10/26.**G.**
Str. ?/?—11/28.**G.**
Coal guard on tender.
Str. 17/11—31/12/30.**G.**
Str. 23/5—30/6/32.**G.**
Str. 19/3—20/4/34.**G.**
Str. ?/?—12/12/36.**G.**

BOILERS:
 783.
 772 *(new)* 16/3/06.
3105 *(new)* 5/1/15.
 707 *(ex7707)* 3/4/19.
3101 *(ex7756)* 4/9/23.
3106 *(ex7742)* 11/28.
3146 *(ex7731)* 31/12/30.
3119 *(ex8021)* 30/6/32.
3149 *(ex8025)* 20/4/34.
3147 *(ex7756)* 12/12/36.

SHEDS:
Peterborough East.
Immingham ?/26.
Norwich 30/10/27.
Yarmouth 20/7/30.
Norwich 11/1/31.
Yarmouth 19/5/34.
Norwich 19/1/35.
Yarmouth 7/2/35.
Norwich 1/3/36.

RENUMBERED:
7772 ?/?/??.

CONDEMNED: 1/9/38.
Cut up at Stratford.

7775

To traffic 6/1892.

REPAIRS:
Str. 16/9/04—3/3/05.**G.**
Rebuilt from 2-4-0.
Str. 4/3—18/12/13.**G.**
Superheated boiler fitted.
Str. 3/1—28/6/22.**G.**
Str. ?/?—?/24.**G.**
Str. 5/3—11/9/26.**G.**
Str. ?/?—6/29.**G.**
*Vacuum brake added &
coal guard on tender.*
Str. 26/11/31—15/1/32.**G.**
Str. 1/5—9/6/34.**G.**

BOILERS:
 786.
 775 *(new)* 3/3/05.
 775 *(new)* 18/12/13.
3108 *(ex7748)* 28/6/22.
 718 *(ex7739)* 6/29.
3123 *(ex7748)* 15/1/32.
3119 *(ex7772)* 9/6/34.

SHEDS:
Peterborough East.
King's Lynn 17/4/35.

RENUMBERED:
7775 31/5/24.

CONDEMNED: 5/5/36.
Cut up at Stratford.

7777

To traffic 6/1892.

REPAIRS:
Str. 11/5/05—21/4/06.**G.**
Rebuilt from 2-4-0.
Str. 29/1—5/6/14.**G.**
Superheated boiler fitted.
Str. 9/3—25/8/22.**G.**
Str. 6/2—12/6/26.**G.**
Str. 9/2—19/5/28.**G.**
*Vacuum brake added &
coal guard on tender.*
Str. 19/11/30—7/1/31.**G.**

BOILERS:
 788.
 777 *(new)* 21/4/06.
3102 *(new)* 5/6/14.
3103 *(ex7751)* 25/8/22.
3131 *(ex7704)* 19/5/28.
3103 *(ex7751)* 7/1/31.

SHEDS:
March.
King's Lynn 19/6/33.

RENUMBERED:
7777 *by* 8/24.

CONDEMNED: 9/6/34.
Cut up at Stratford.

7779

To traffic 7/1892.

REPAIRS:
Str. 19/1—25/5/06.**G.**
Rebuilt from 2-4-0.
Str. 18/1—22/5/18.**G.**
Superheated boiler fitted.
Str. 17/5—1/11/22.**G.**
Str. 8/5—5/7/24.**G.**
Str. 12/4—17/9/26.**G.**
Str. 27/7—31/10/28.**G.**
*Vacuum brake added &
coal guard on tender.*
Str. 20/1—2/3/33.**G.**

BOILERS:
 790.
 779 *(new)* 25/5/06.

WORKS CODES:- Bd - Beardmore. Ca - Cambridge shed. Dn - Doncaster. Go - Gorton. Ips - Ipswich shed. Nr - Norwich shed. Str - Stratford.
REPAIR CODES:- **C/H** - Casual Heavy. **C/L** - Casual Light. **G** - General. **H** - Heavy. **H/I** - Heavy Intermediate. **L** - Light. **L/I** - Light Intermediate. **N/C** - Non-Classified.

18

These tenders were known as 'Bohemian' or 'Watercart' tenders and had been built to carry oil fuel tanks, but these were stripped out at the time the exchange was made. The frames and wheels were the same as those of the other tenders coupled with nos.8012 to 8016 and 1018, also 8030 to 8039 but the tank body had rounded top edges as did the four corners.

During 1927-30 all eight of these tenders had coal guard fitted to help stop spillage. When running with D13 class the tenders were equipped with water pick-up apparatus, although in LNER days the D13's were on duties where the use of the apparatus was most unlikely to be needed. Normal equipment included two large boxes, one on each side at the front, each with rounded hinged lid, for tools, food, and clothing. No.8029 had a third box but this appears to be an isolated case.

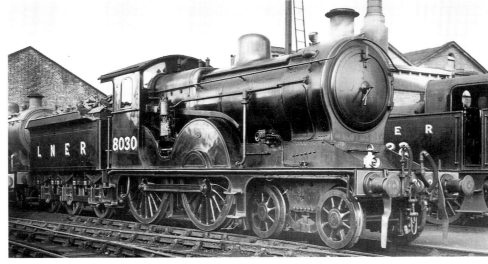

8030, at Peterborough East shed 16th June 1935, had the conventional tender design as used by the rest of the class.

Engines built prior to 1890 had square ended balance weights in their coupled wheels, and some of these wheels survived into the 1930's.

Sanding was applied by compressed air ahead of the leading coupled wheels. For running in reverse gravity sanding, from boxes in the cab, was provided. 7772 is at Norwich shed 30th June 1936. *H.C.Casserley.*

7779 cont.
3127 *(new)* 22/5/18.
3133 *(ex7733)* 17/9/26.
3120 *(ex7741)* 31/10/28.
3122 *(ex7704)* 2/3/33.

SHED:
Cambridge.

RENUMBERED:
7779 5/7/24.

CONDEMNED: 2/4/35.
Cut up at Stratford.

8012

To traffic 6/1893.

REPAIRS:
Str. 5/1—30/5/06.**G.**
Rebuilt from 2-4-0.
Str. 2/2—14/5/15.**G.**
Superheated boiler fitted.
Str. 22/5—30/11/22.**G.**
Str. 20/10/24—3/2/25.**G.**
Str. ?/?—7/27.**G.**
Str. ?/?—3/29.**N/C.**
Vacuum brake added.
Str. 11/11—14/12/29.**G.**
Coal guard on tender.
Str. 23/10—27/11/31.**G.**

BOILERS:
1012.

1012 *(new)* 30/5/06.
3112 *(new)* 14/5/15.
3111 *(ex7733)* 3/2/25.
3109 *(ex8030)* 14/12/29.
3138 *(ex7731)* 27/11/31.

SHED:
Cambridge.

RENUMBERED:
8012 ?/?/??.

CONDEMNED: 18/12/35.
Cut up at Stratford.

8013

To traffic 6/1893.

REPAIRS:
Str. 27/11/05—11/5/06.**G.**
Rebuilt from 2-4-0.
Str. 27/1—17/6/22.**G.**
Superheated boiler fitted.
Str. ?/?—2/28.**G.**
Coal guard on tender.
Str. ?/?—5/29.**N/C.**
Vacuum brake added.
Str. 8/2—9/3/32.**G.**
Str. 15/1—15/2/34.**G.**

BOILERS:
1013.
1013 *(new)* 11/5/06.
1023 *(ex7707)* 17/6/22.

3134 *(ex8020)* 9/3/32.
3125 *(ex8028)* 15/2/34.

SHEDS:
Yarmouth.
Norwich 11/1/31.

RENUMBERED:
8013 ?/?/??.

CONDEMNED: 17/10/35.
Cut up at Stratford.

8015

To traffic 6/1893.

REPAIRS:
Str. 5/2—13/6/06.**G.**
Rebuilt from 2-4-0.
Str. 31/3—23/8/22.**G.**
Superheated boiler fitted.
Str. 5/2—20/5/24.**G.**
Str. 11/3—6/8/26.**G.**
Str. 3/28—6/28.**G.**
*Vacuum brake added &
coal guard on tender.*
Str. 3/4—21/5/30.**G.**
Str. 30/5—7/7/32.**G.**

BOILERS:
1015.
1015 *(new)* 13/6/06.
3117 *(new)* ?/11/16.
???? *(new)* 23/8/22.

3121 *(ex8035)* 20/5/24.
735 *(ex8027)* 6/8/26.
3144 *(ex8029)* 21/5/30.
3143 *(ex7719)* 7/7/32.

Note: *According to Holden's
"Boiler Register" 1015 received
a superheated boiler in November 1916. See previous note
affecting 7719.*

SHED:
Cambridge.

RENUMBERED:
8015 ?/?/??.

CONDEMNED: 17/10/34.
Cut up at Stratford.

8016

To traffic 7/1893.

REPAIRS:
Str. 8/5/05—30/3/06.**G.**
Rebuilt from 2-4-0.
Str. 29/12/13—14/5/14.**G.**
Superheated boiler fitted.
Str. 21/9/22—1/2/23.**G.**
Str. 17/1—29/4/25.**G.**
Str. 19/5—22/9/27.**G.**
Str. ?/?—3/29.**N/C.**
Vacuum brake added.
Str. 31/12/29—7/2/30.**G.**

Braking was Westinghouse both on engine and for train. Before Grouping, nos.713, 772, 1030, 1031, 1032, 1033, 1035, 1036, 1037, 1038 and 1039 had been fitted with vacuum ejector for alternative train braking. On saturated engines the ejector pipe passed through the boiler.

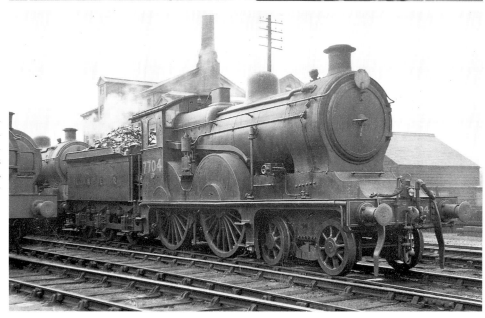

Beginning with no.7719 in April 1927, vacuum brake was added to all the surviving engines except no.7717. On these, the exhaust pipe was external on the right hand side. 7704 is at Peterborogh East shed, 12th July 1931. *A.B.Crompton.*

Until well after Grouping the tenders were not fitted with any coping. Those with engines numbered 700 to 779 had hemispherical slots in the frames. During the period 1927-30, sheet metal copings, or coal guards, were added. Tenders with engines numbered between 8012 and 8039 had different frame slots - sausage instead of D-shaped.

No.765 in GER Royal blue livery pre-1917 when it was superheated. Note lamp iron on top of smokebox. and pipe from smokebox ash ejector to receiving box between the bogie wheels. By 1923 all had upper lamp iron moved to the door whilst the ash ejection gear had been removed. *H.Gordon Tidey.*

During the 1914-18 War the blue livery was discarded and grey, without lining was then used. By 1920 yellow painted 19" figures appeared on the tender sides and the only evidence as to ownership was the company name in 1" letters cast on the brass number plate.

By October 1923 Stratford was painting some D13s in fully lined green livery, but still including the ampersand. Note that the 'E' suffix was not applied to the number on the buffer beam. On this engine the brass beading to the splashers had been painted over in black.

8016 cont.
Coal guard on tender.
Str. 29/2—7/4/32.**G.**
Str. 24/4—25/5/34.**G.**
Str. 23/3—1/5/36.**G.**

BOILERS:
1016.
1016 *(new)* 30/3/06.
3100 *(new)* 14/5/14.
3107 *(ex7742)* 1/2/23.
3138 *(ex7729)* 22/9/27.
3126 *(ex7737)* 7/2/30.
3152 *(ex7734)* 7/4/32.
3101 *(ex8023)* 25/5/34.
3140 *(ex7741)* 1/5/36.

SHED:
Cambridge.

RENUMBERED:
8016 ?/?/??.

CONDEMNED: 17/5/38.
Cut up at Stratford.

G.E. 1018

To traffic 7/1893.

REPAIRS:
Str. 26/9/00—27/3/01.**G.**
Str. 6/2—24/7/07.**G.**
Rebuilt from 2-4-0.
Str. 9/2—28/5/14.**G.**
Str. 7/12/16—13/6/17.**G.**
Str. 18/6—24/9/20.**G.**

BOILERS:
1018.
1018 *(new)* 27/3/01.
1018 *(new)* 24/7/07.
 751 *(ex7751)* 28/5/14.
1028 *(ex8028)* 13/6/17.
 730 *(ex7730)* 24/9/20.

SHED:
King's Lynn.

CONDEMNED: 11/6/25.
Cut up at Stratford.

8020

To traffic 6/1895.

REPAIRS:
Str. 26/10/06—4/4/07.**G.**
Rebuilt from 2-4-0.
Str. 17/9/14—13/1/15.**G.**
Superheated boiler fitted.
Str. 1/6—29/11/17.**G.**
Str. ?/?—5/5/20.**G.**
Str. 2/3—23/8/23.**G.**

Str. 11/3—14/8/26.**G.**
Str. ?/?—2/29.**N/C.**
Vacuum brake added.
Str. 29/1—8/3/30.**G.**
Coal guard on tender.
Str. 23/12/31—5/2/32.**G.**

BOILERS:
1020.
1020 *(new)* 4/4/07.
3108 *(new)* 13/1/15.
3120 *(new)* 29/11/17.
3119 *(ex7729)* 23/8/23.
3134 *(ex8023)* 8/3/30.
3147 *(ex7733)* 5/2/32.

SHEDS:
Doncaster.
Cambridge 13/6/25.
March *by* 5/30.
King's Lynn 2/3/36.

RENUMBERED:
8020 ?/?/??.

CONDEMNED: 7/4/36.
Cut up at Stratford.

8021

To traffic 6/1895.

REPAIRS:
Str. 27/7/05—28/4/06.**G.**
Rebuilt from 2-4-0.
Str. 29/11/18—14/11/19.**G.**
Superheated boiler fitted.
Str. 31/1—26/4/21.**G.**
Str. 20/2—7/7/25.**G.**
Str. ?/?—12/27.**G.**
Coal guard on tender.
Str. ?/?—12/28.**N/C.**
Vacuum brake added.
Str. 17/4—10/6/30.**G.**
Str. 13/4—17/5/32.**G.**
Str. 13/9—8/10/34.**G.**

BOILERS:
1021.
1021 *(new)* 28/4/06.
3130 *(new)* 14/11/19.
3119 *(ex8020)* 10/6/30.
3126 *(ex8016)* 17/5/32.
3118 *(ex8030)* 8/10/34.

SHED:
Cambridge.

RENUMBERED:
8021 ?/?/??.

CONDEMNED: 27/8/36.
Cut up at Stratford.

8023

To traffic 7/1895.

REPAIRS:
Str. 30/12/05—29/5/06.**G.**
Rebuilt from 2-4-0.
Str. 17/10/13—5/5/14.**G.**
Superheated boiler fitted.
Str. 11/1—21/6/18.**G.**
Str. 11/10/21—26/4/22.**G.**
Str. 10/7—16/12/25.**G.**
Str. 20/10/27—26/1/28.**G.**
Coal guard on tender.
Str. ?/?—12/28.**N/C.**
Vacuum brake added.
Str. 19/12/29—8/2/30.**G.**
Str. 14/1—26/2/32.**G.**
Str. 20/11—22/12/33.**G.**
Str. 15—26/1/35.**G.**
Str. 17/12/35—23/1/36.**G.**
Str. ?/?—18/3/38.**G.**
Str. ?/?—27/7/40.**G.**

BOILERS:
1023.
1023 *(new)* 29/5/06.
1023 *(new)* 5/5/14.
3106 *(ex8025)* 21/6/18.
3113 *(ex7756)* 26/4/22.
3134 *(ex8037)* 26/1/28.
3111 *(ex8012)* 8/2/30.
3101 *(ex7739)* 26/2/32.
3124 *(ex8032)* 22/12/33.
3128 *(ex7706)* 23/1/36.
3145 *(ex8025)* 18/3/38.
3152 *(ex8030)* 27/7/40.

SHEDS:
Cambridge.
King's Lynn ?/38.
Cambridge 22/8/38.

RENUMBERED:
8023 ?/?/??.
2057 *allocated but not applied.*

CONDEMNED: 22/1/44.
Cut up at Stratford.

8025

To traffic 7/1895.

REPAIRS:
Str. 29/8/05—28/4/06.**G.**
Rebuilt from 2-4-0.
Str. 20/8—5/11/14.**G.**
Superheated boiler fitted.
Str. 2/11/17—12/4/18.**G.**
Str. 3/11/20—29/1/21.**G.**
Str. 7/4—27/8/25.**G.**
Str. ?/?—6/28.**G.**
Vacuum brake added &

coal guard on tender.
Str. 12/5—1/7/30.**G.**
Str. 2/5—9/6/32.**G.**
Str. 7/2—9/3/34.**G.**
Str. 8/8—6/9/35.**G.**

BOILERS:
1025.
1025 *(new)* 28/4/06.
3106 *(new)* 5/11/14.
 728 *(ex7728)* 12/4/18.
3137 *(new)* 29/1/21.
3128 *(ex????)* 27/8/25.
3151 *(new)* 1/7/30.
3149 *(ex8030)* 9/6/32.
3127 *(ex7744)* 9/3/34.
3145 *(ex7767)* 6/9/35.

SHEDS:
Lincoln.
Stratford 6/6/25.
Ipswich 12/10/27.
Colchester 12/9/35.
Ipswich 17/12/36.

RENUMBERED:
8025 ?/?/??.

CONDEMNED: 25/10/37.
Cut up at Stratford.

8026

To traffic 8/1895.

REPAIRS:
Str. 11/10/05—2/5/06.**G.**
Rebuilt from 2-4-0.
Str. 27/3—1/11/18.**G.**
Str. ?/?—7/22.**G.**
Str. 8/11/23—4/3/24.**G.**
Str. 5/2—29/5/26.**G.**
Superheated boiler fitted.
Str. ?/?—6/28.**G.**
Vacuum brake added &
coal guard on tender.
Str. 25/5—1/7/32.**G.**
Str. 26/11—28/12/34.**G.**

BOILERS:
1026.
1026 *(new)* 2/5/06.
 748 *(ex7748)* 1/11/18.
 712 *(ex7730)* 4/3/24.
3145 *(new)* 29/5/26.
3151 *(ex8025)* 1/7/32.
3143 *(ex8015)* 28/12/34.

SHEDS:
Stratford.
Norwich 6/10/27.
Yarmouth 5/8/33.
Norwich 9/9/33.

RENUMBERED:
8026 ?/?/??.

CONDEMNED: 19/2/37.
Cut up at Stratford.

8027

To traffic 8/1895.

REPAIRS:
Str. 8/2—23/6/06.**G**.
Rebuilt from 2-4-0.
Str. 22/1—21/4/15.**G**.
Superheated boiler fitted.
Str. 24/2—19/6/20.**G**.
Str. ?/?—7/23.**G**.
Str. 18/12/35—20/3/26.**G**.
Str. ?/?—8/28.**G**.
Vacuum brake added &
coal guard on tender.
Str. 9/5—26/6/30.**G**.
Str. 30/1—27/3/33.**G**.

BOILERS:
1027.
1027 *(new)* 23/6/06.
3111 *(new)* 21/4/15.
 735 *(ex7735)* 19/6/20.
3129 *(ex8029)* 20/3/26.
3136 *(ex8036)* 26/6/30.
3130 *(ex7751)* 27/3/33.

SHEDS:
Stratford.
Norwich 1/10/27.

RENUMBERED:
8027 ?/?/??.

CONDEMNED: 28/1/36.
Cut up at Doncaster.

8028

To traffic 8/1895.

REPAIRS:
Str. 28/11/06—17/4/07.**G**.
Rebuilt from 2-4-0.
Str. 4/1—16/5/18.**G**.
Superheated boiler fitted.
Str. 5/1—19/5/22.**G**.
Str. 8/9/24—2/1/25.**G**.
Str. 29/4—27/8/27.**G**.
Str. ?/?—3/29.**G**.
Vacuum brake added.
Str. 16/7—21/8/31.**G**.
Str. ?/?—9/33.**G**.
Str. 15/11—19/12/35.**G**.

BOILERS:
1028.
1028 *(new)* 17/4/07.
3126 *(new)* 16/5/18.
3124 *(ex7745)* 2/1/25.
3125 *(ex7745)* 21/8/31.
3133 *(ex7737)* 9/33.
3132 *(ex????)* 19/12/35.

SHEDS:
Lincoln.
Cambridge 6/7/25.
King's Lynn 22/2/31.
Cambridge 5/3/31.
King's Lynn 7/3/37.

RENUMBERED:
8028 ?/?/??.

CONDEMNED: 22/1/38.
Cut up at Doncaster.

8029

To traffic 8/1895.

REPAIRS:
Str. 26/10/06—12/4/07.**G**.
Rebuilt from 2-4-0.
Str. 31/1—31/10/19.**G**.
Superheated boiler fitted.
Str. 29/8—22/12/25.**G**.
Str. ?/?—3/28.**G**.
Coal guard on tender.
Str. ?/?—1/29.**N/C**.
Vacuum brake added.
Str. 12—28/2/30.**G**.
Str. 14/3—22/4/32.**G**.
Str. 3/10—22/11/34.**G**.
Str. 18/6—24/7/36.**G**.

BOILERS:
1029.
1029 *(new)* 12/4/07.
3129 *(new)* 31/10/19.
3144 *(new)* 22/12/25.
3150 *(new)* 28/2/30.
3135 *(ex8036)* 22/4/32.

SHEDS:
March.
King's Lynn 19/6/33.

RENUMBERED:
8029 ?/?/??.

CONDEMNED: 1/3/38.
Cut up at Stratford.

8030

To traffic 3/1897.

REPAIRS:
Str. 1/12/05—15/5/06.**G**.
Rebuilt from 2-4-0.
Str. 26/5—15/9/16.**G**.
Superheated boiler fitted.
Str. 14/10/26—27/1/27.**G**.
Str. 9/10—19/11/29.**G**.
Coal guard on tender.
Str. 18/4—20/5/32.**G**.
Str. ?/?—12/2/37.**G**.

BOILERS:
1030.
1030 *(new)* 15/5/06.
3123 *(new)* 15/9/16.
3109 *(ex7731)* 27/1/27.
3149 *(new)* 19/11/29.
3118 *(ex7766)* 20/5/32.
3152 *(ex8016)* 12/2/37.

SHEDS:
Peterborough East.
Norwich 23/11/35

RENUMBERED:
8030 ?/?/??.

CONDEMNED: 18/11/38.
Cut up at Stratford.

8031

To traffic 3/1897.

REPAIRS:
Str. 31/12/07—29/4/08.**G**.
Rebuilt from 2-4-0.
Str. 6/4—28/7/22.**G**.

BOILERS:
1031.
1031 *(new)* 29/4/08.
 739 *(ex8033)* 28/7/22.

SHEDS:
Cambridge.
Doncaster 8/6/25.

RENUMBERED:
8031 ?/?/??.

CONDEMNED: 20/12/26.
Cut up at Stratford.

8032

To traffic 3/1897.

REPAIRS:
Str. 20/1—1/6/06.**G**.
Rebuilt from 2-4-0.
Str. 10/12/20—16/3/21.**G**.
Superheated boiler fitted.
Str. 24/5—2/11/22.**G**.
Str. 22/11/24—27/2/25.**G**.
Str. 13/7—3/11/27.**G**.
Str. 12/10—13/11/31.**G**.
Str. 27/10—23/11/33.**G**.

BOILERS:
1032.
1032 *(new)* 1/6/06.
3115 *(ex7737)* 16/3/21.
???? *(ex????)* 27/2/25
3107 *(ex8016)* 3/11/27.
3124 *(ex8028)* 13/11/31.
3138 *(ex8012)* 23/11/33.

SHEDS:
Doncaster.
Norwich 30/10/27.
Yarmouth 11/1/31.
Norwich 22/11/31.
Yarmouth 15/5/32.
Norwich 5/8/33.

RENUMBERED:
8032 ?/?/??.

CONDEMNED: 16/9/36.
Cut up at Stratford.

8033

To traffic 4/1897.

REPAIRS:
Str. 25/10/04—29/3/05.**G**.
Rebuilt from 2-4-0.
Str. 27/9—19/12/16.**G**.
Str. 24/1—18/9/19.**G**.
Str. 2/4—25/8/25.**G**.

BOILERS:
1033.
1033 *(new)* 29/3/05.
 739 *(ex7739)* 19/12/16.
1037 *(ex8037)* 18/9/19.
 730 *(ex1018)* 25/8/25.

SHEDS:
Stratford.
Lincoln 6/6/25.

WORKS CODES:- Bd - Beardmore. Ca - Cambridge shed. Dn - Doncaster. Go - Gorton. Ips - Ipswich shed. Nr - Norwich shed. Str - Stratford.
REPAIR CODES:- **C/H** - Casual Heavy. **C/L** - Casual Light. **G** - General. **H**- Heavy. **H/I** - Heavy Intermediate. **L** - Light. **L/I** - Light Intermediate. **N/C** - Non-Classified.

Similarly green painted, and with both ampersand and suffix, no.1030 retained polished brass beading on main and coupling rod splashers, also brass cap to chimney. Until the 1928 economies, standard livery for the class was green with black and white lining though not all the class were so treated - no.1031 was still in grey when withdrawn whilst some (no.7772 for instance) retained grey until 1928 when black was applied. Early in 1924 both the ampersand and the suffix were discarded.

Ex works on 2nd August 1923, in green as L&NER 718, this engine was noted 17th January 1925 as having had the 'E' added at its shed. It was then at Stratford awaiting 'general' repair. When ex works 23rd April 1925 it had not been repainted, but the number on the tender had been patched to 7718. It would thus still have ampersand to 25th March 1927 when it next went to works.

(left) When Stratford moved the number from tender to cab side, they made difficulties for themselves by leaving the small numberplate where it was on the side sheet and also assuming the continuation of the rear splasher profile. This led them to use 9" numbers high on the cab side which looked completely adrift from the 7½" letters which they kept on the tender. No.7719 was put in this style in November 1929 and kept it to withdrawal in 1932.

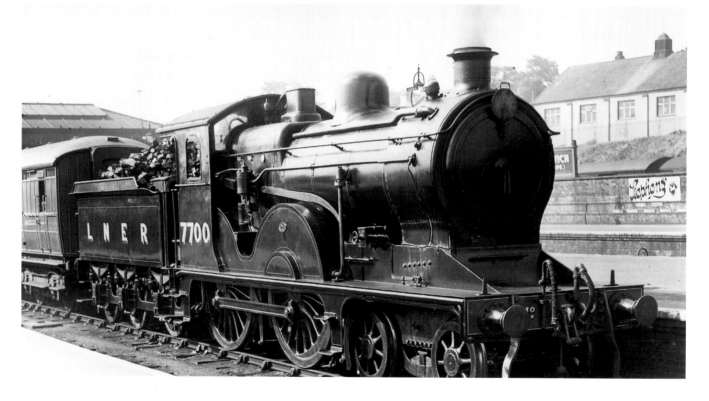

When no.8028 was withdrawn on 22nd January 1938, the white instruction shows it consigned to Mechanical Engineer, Plant Works, Doncaster, where it was duly cut up. Note that the cab window was of the carriage type and adjustable by means of a leather strap.

8033 cont.
RENUMBERED:
8033 ?/?/??.

CONDEMNED: 30/6/27.
Cut up at Stratford.

8035

To traffic 4/1897.

REPAIRS:
Str. 2/5/04—18/2/05.**G.**
Rebuilt from 2-4-0.
Str. 30/11/17—5/4/18.**G.**
Superheated boiler fitted.
Str. 20/10/23—29/1/24.**G.**
Str. 21/8—30/10/26.**G.**
Str. 31/8—15/11/28.**G.**
Coal guard on tender.
Str. 6/2—27/3/31.**G.**
Str. 10/3—4/5/34.**G.**
Str. 8/4—25/6/36.**G.**
Str. 24/4—1/6/38.**G.**
Str. 6/11—30/12/40.**G.**
Str. 19/4/43. *Not repaired.*

BOILERS:
1035.
1035 *(new)* 18/2/05.
3121 *(new)* 5/4/18.
 707 *(ex7772)* 29/1/24.
3127 *(ex7779)* 30/10/26.
3114 *(ex7767)* 27/3/31.
3148 *(ex8036)* 25/6/36.
3151 *(ex8039)* 30/12/40.

SHEDS:
Cambridge.
Lincoln 6/7/25.
Peterborough East 3/1/28.
King's Lynn 26/11/35.
Norwich 13/6/39.
King's Lynn 11/10/39.
Cambridge 6/10/40.

RENUMBERED:
1035ᴇ 29/1/24.
8035 ?/?/??.

(opposite, centre) **Some improvement was made in February 1930 when no.7712 was given 12" numerals on the cab but still above the plate, and well above the tender lettering. Before the end of the year the final style was adopted and no.7713 was ex works in November with 12" numbers and letters on the same level. This was achieved by moving the plate to the leading splasher. All subsequent painting was in this style as worn by 7700 here at Norwich, and included the single red lining.** *T.G.Hepburn.*

CONDEMNED: 29/5/43.
Cut up at Stratford.

8036

To traffic 5/1897.

REPAIRS:
Str. 24/10/06—25/2/07.**G.**
Rebuilt from 2-4-0.
Str. 11/1—12/4/18.**G.**
Superheated boiler fitted.
Str. 29/11/23—8/3/24.**G.**
Str. 17/4—9/10/26.**G.**
Str. 1/3—30/6/28.**G.**
Coal guard on tender.
Str. 7/2—14/3/30.**G.**
Str. 4/10—26/11/31.**G.**
Str. 20/1—14/2/36.**G.**

BOILERS:
1036.
1036 *(new)* 25/2/07.
3125 *(new)* 12/4/18.
3104 *(ex7704)* 8/3/24.
3136 *(ex7738)* 30/6/28.
3135 *(ex8039)* 14/3/30.
3148 *(ex7738)* 26/11/31.
3124 *(ex8023)* 14/2/36.

SHEDS:
Cambridge.
Doncaster 13/6/25.
Lincoln ?/?
Cambridge 10/1/28.
King's Lynn 8/7/29.
Cambridge 22/2/31.
King's Lynn 5/3/31.

RENUMBERED:
8036 ?/?/??.

CONDEMNED: 25/2/37.
Cut up at Stratford.

8037

To traffic 5/1897.

REPAIRS:
Str. 23/3—30/6/08.**G.**
Rebuilt from 2-4-0.
Str. 18/10/18—2/4/19.**G.**
Str. 21/6—17/12/20.**G.**
Superheated boiler fitted.
Str. 30/6—2/12/22.**G.**
Str. 11/4—23/7/27.**G.**
Str. ?/?—8/29.**G.**
Coal guard on tender.
Str. 30/4—18/6/31.**G.**
Str. 5/4—11/5/33.**G.**

BOILERS:
1037.
1037 *(new)* 30/6/08.
1039 *(ex8039)* 2/4/19.
3134 *(new)* 17/12/20.
3121 *(ex8015)* 23/7/27.
3132 *(ex7718)* 18/6/31.
3136 *(ex8027)* 11/5/33.

SHEDS:
Norwich.
Doncaster 27/5/25.
Norwich 23/7/27.
Stratford 1/10/27.
Ipswich 27/7/29.
King's Lynn 12/10/33.

RENUMBERED:
8037 *by* 25/2/25.

CONDEMNED: 19/12/34.
Cut up at Stratford.

8039

To traffic 5/1897.

REPAIRS:
Str. 24/6—14/11/07.**G.**
Rebuilt from 2-4-0.
Str. 12/4—26/11/18.**G.**
Str. 29/8—15/12/21.**G.**
Superheated boiler fitted.
Ca. 13/11/22—20/3/23.**H.**
Str. 7/2—12/6/25.**G.**
Str. 14/7—6/8/25.**L.**
Str. 31/12/27—5/4/28.**G.**
Coal guard on tender.
Str. 2/11/29—7/1/30.**G.**
Str. 5/12/32—27/1/33.**G.**
Str. 16/3—23/5/35.**G.**
Str. 24/2—4/5/38.**G.**
Str. 29/9—23/11/40.**G.**
Str. 6/2/44. *Not repaired.*

BOILERS:
1039.
1039 *(new)* 14/11/07.
 717 *(ex7717)* 26/11/18.
3140 *(new)* 15/12/21.
3135 *(ex7737)* 12/6/25.
3115 *(ex7728)* 7/1/30.
3151 *(ex8026)* 23/5/35.
3147 *(ex7772)* 23/11/40.

SHEDS:
Lincoln.
Doncaster 12/7/24.
Norwich 15/9/27.
Stratford 5/10/27.
Peterborough East 7/1/30.
King's Lynn 26/11/35.
March 3/10/36.
King's Lynn 5/6/37.
Cambridge 13/6/39.

RENUMBERED:
8039 ?/?/??.
2058 allocated but not applied.

CONDEMNED: 1/3/44.
Cut up at Stratford.

Between May and July 1900, ten more 'Clauds' (nos.1890 to 1899) were built to the same specifications as no.1900. In February 1908 no.1893 got a new boiler with four instead of the usual two safety valves. By 1921 the engine had taken on additional changes such as buffers with stepped parallel shanks, whistle to cab roof and perhaps most important was the fitting of vacuum brake for train working. A further ten engines (nos.1880 to 1889) were built between May and July of 1901. These ten had wider cabs, 7' 2" against 6' 3" with a higher arch roof. The circular front windows were however unchanged. Also of note in this photograph is the change in the position of the sandboxes from the splasher to underneath the running plate; the footsteps also were moved further back. These changes caused modification to the piping to the clack box. At building 1880-1889 were turned out with 'Watercart' tenders but these were quickly changed (July 1901 to March 1902) in favour of new conventional tenders with greater water capacity.

A total of 41 were built as D14 but when the LNER took over this had been reduced to 21, the others having been rebuilt to D15 class. The 21 were: 1862, 1864, 1865, 1866, 1867, 1868, 1870, 1871, 1872, 1873, 1875, 1876, 1877, 1878, 1879, 1881, 1886, 1892, 1893, 1895, 1900. Of these only 1892, 1893 and 1895 had 'Watercart' tenders. This shows no.8892 as it became in September 1924.

28

D14, D15 & D16 CLASS

8900

To traffic 4/1900.

REPAIRS:
Str. 13/10/09—28/1/10.**G.**
Str. 8/2—13/3/18.**G.**
Str. 28/2—20/8/19.**G.**
Str. 5/10/22—27/4/23.**G.**
Str. 11/12/24—27/3/25.**G.**
Rebuilt to D15.
Superheated boiler fitted.
Str. 5—7/8/26.**N/C.**
Liquid fuel fitted.
Str. ?/4—?/6/27.**G.**
Liquid fuel removed.
Vacuum brake added.
Str. ?/?/28—?/1/29.**G.**
Altered to D15/2.
Str. ?/?—?/4/30.**G.**
Str. 23/11/32—3/2/33.**G.**
Rebuilt to D14/2.
Str. 21—22/9/33.**N/C.**
Pyrometer fitted.
Str. ?/?—?/1/34.**N/C.**
Indicator gear fitted.
Str. 5/11—14/12/34.**G.**
Str. 9/3—9/4/36.**G.**
Str. ?/?—14/1/38.**G.**
Str. ?/?—25/1/40.**G.**
Str. ?/?—1/10/40.**L.**
Str. ?/?—5/12/41.**L.**
Str. ?/?—25/8/42.**G.**
Str. ?/?—24/12/42.**L.**
Str. ?/?—9/3/45.**G.**
Str. ?/?—27/4/46.**L.**
Str. ?/?—14/3/47.**L.**

BOILERS:
1900.
1900 (new) 28/1/10.
3252 (ex8877) 13/3/18.
1869 (ex8869) 20/8/19.
1874 (ex8868) 27/4/23.
3662 (new) 27/3/25.
3257 (new) ?/4/30.
4200 (new) 3/2/33.
4204 (ex8849) 14/12/34.
4243 (new) 9/4/36.
4242 (ex8837) 14/1/38.
4302 (new) 25/1/40.
4316 (new) 25/8/42.
4309 (ex8883) 9/3/45.

SHEDS:
Stratford.
Southend 13/9/30.

Stratford 20/9/30.
Colchester 10/3/40.
Stratford 8/9/40.

RENUMBERED:
1900ᴇ 12/23.
8900 27/3/25
7770 21/12/42.
2500 16/4/46.

CONDEMNED: 27/5/47.
Cut up at Stratford.

8890

To traffic 5/1900.

REPAIRS:
Str. 4/2—18/6/09.**G.**
Str. 17/9—30/12/14.**G.**
Str. 4/10/15—3/3/16.**G.**
Rebuilt to D15.
Superheated boiler fitted.
Str. 16/1—7/6/23.**G.**
Str. 4/5—18/9/25.**G.**
Str. 29/4—20/8/27.**G.**
Str. 13/2—19/4/29.**G.**
Altered to D15/2.
Coal guard on tender.
Str. 20/10/30—15/1/31.**G.**
Str. 30/4—30/6/32.**G.**
Str. 18/7—19/8/32.**L.**
Str. 15/1—2/3/34.**G.**
Str. 15/10—20/12/35.**G.**
Str. 8—11/6/36.**L.**
Str. 5/10—12/11/37.**G.**
Str. 23/2—3/5/40.**G.**
Str. 29/12/42—18/3/43.**G.**
Str. 15/12/44—30/1/45.**G.**
Str. 7/5—14/6/46.**L.**
Str. 2/4—17/6/47.**G.**
Str. 12/7—27/8/49.**G.**
Str. 27/9—3/10/50.**N/C.**
Str. 14/6/51 *Not repaired.*

BOILERS:
1890.
1890 (new) 18/6/09.
3250 (new) 30/12/14.
3577 (new) 3/3/16.
3586 (ex8880) 7/6/23.
3577 (ex8862) 20/8/27.
3254 (new) 19/4/29.
3578 (ex8891) 30/6/32.
3634 (ex8884) 2/3/34.
3465 (ex8836) 20/12/35.
3631 (ex8880) 3/5/40.

3443 (ex8894) 18/3/43.
3467 (ex8889) 17/6/47.
3257 (ex8892) 27/8/49.

SHEDS:
Cambridge.
Norwich 3/10/24.
Cambridge 23/12/24.
King's Lynn 16/1/39.

RENUMBERED:
8890 5/25??
2501 8/12/46.
62501 27/8/49.

CONDEMNED: 25/6/51.
Cut up at Stratford.

8891

To traffic 5/1900.

REPAIRS:
Str. 9/11/10—1/3/11.**G.**
Str. 25/11/15—23/3/16.**G.**
Rebuilt to D15.
Superheated boiler fitted.
Str. 31/7/22—6/1/23.**G.**
Str. 16/2—24/5/24.**G.**
Str. 26/2—20/7/26.**G.**
Oil fuel equipment fitted.
Str. ?/?—24/3/27.**N/C.**
Oil fuel equipment taken off.
Str. 14/3—11/7/28.**G.**
Coal guard on tender.
Str. 11/1—5/4/30.**G.**
Str. 26/3—15/6/32.**G.**
Altered to D15/2.
Str. 22/4—23/6/34.**G.**
Str. 23/11/35—15/1/36.**H.**
Str. 2/4—22/5/36.**G.**
Str. 27/4—3/6/38.**G.**
Str. 11/6—26/7/39.**G.**
Str. 6/4—28/5/41.**G.**
Str. 5/2—25/3/42.**L.**
Str. 4/10—19/11/43.**G.**
Str. 3/6—13/7/45.**G.**
Str. 14/7—2/9/47.**G.**
Str. 4/1—8/3/50.**G.**
Str. 31/3—3/4/50.**N/C.**
Str. 24/1/52 *Not repaired.*

BOILERS:
1891.
1891 (new) 1/3/11.
3578 (new) 23/3/16.
3587 (ex8887) 6/1/23.

3675 (new) 20/7/26.
3578 (ex8894) 5/4/30.
3635 (ex8883) 15/6/32.
3681 (ex8869) 23/6/34.
3624 (ex8879) 22/5/36.
3661 (ex8887) 3/6/38.
3681 (ex8888) 26/7/39.
3683 (ex8889) 28/5/41.
3467 (ex8896) 19/11/43.
3464 (exJ17 8178) 13/7/45.
3453 (ex8894) 2/9/47.

SHEDS:
Cambridge.
Stratford 8/8/26.
Southend *by* 24/8/29.
Stratford 11/1/30.
Southend 31/5/30.
Stratford 11/10/30.
Cambridge 29/9/44.
Bury St Edmunds 30/3/45.
King's Lynn 19/8/45.

RENUMBERED:
8891 24/5/24.
2502 6/10/46.
62502 8/3/50.

CONDEMNED: 4/2/52.
Cut up at Stratford.

8892

To traffic 5/1900.

REPAIRS:
Str. 19/12/12—1/5/13.**G.**
Str. 8/3—30/8/18.**G.**
Str. 21/7—9/10/20.**G.**
Str. 30/3—29/6/22.**G.**
Str. 2/5—3/9/24.**G.**
Str. 26/5—7/10/27.**G.**
Rebuilt to D15.
Superheated boiler fitted.
Coal guard on tender.
Str. 11/12/29—24/2/30.**G.**
Str. 21/2—11/5/32.**G.**
Altered to D15/2.
Str. 3/3—9/5/34.**H.**
Str. 7/3—3/5/35.**G.**
Str. 23/4—3/6/36.**G.**
Str. 11/3—16/4/37.**G.**
Str. 5/1—18/3/39.**G.**
Str. 9/7—2/10/40.**G.**
Str. 18/3—31/7/42.**G.**
Str. 26/5—25/6/43.**L.**
Str. 30/1—26/5/44.**G.**

WORKS CODES:- Bd - Beardmore. Ca - Cambridge shed. Dn - Doncaster. Go - Gorton. Ips - Ipswich shed. Nr - Norwich shed. Str - Stratford.
REPAIR CODES:- **C/H** - Casual Heavy. **C/L** - Casual Light. **G** - General. **H** - Heavy. **H/I** - Heavy Intermediate. **L** - Light. **L/I** - Light Intermediate. **N/C** - Non-Classified.

29

Str. 26/4—26/8/46.**G.**
Str. 5/10—2/12/48.**G.**
Str. 5/9—13/10/49.**C/L.**

BOILERS:
1892.
1892 *(new)* 1/5/13.
3251 *(ex8879)* 30/8/18.
1862 *(ex8862)* 9/10/20.
1891 *(ex8866)* 29/6/22.
3678 *(new)* 7/10/27.
3682 *(ex8872)* 11/5/32.
3681 *(ex8891)* 3/6/36.
3256 *(ex8867)* 16/4/37.
3258 *(ex8898)* 18/3/39.
3624 *(ex8868)* 2/10/40.
3256 *(ex8893)* 31/7/42.
3681 *(ex8893)* 26/5/44.
3257 *(ex8877)* 26/8/46.
3681 *(ex8897)* 2/12/48.

SHEDS:
Cambridge.
Norwich 3/10/24.
Cambridge 7/10/24.
Ipswich 22/2/30.
Peterborough East 14/7/34.
Ipswich 15/11/34.
Bury St Edmunds 5/6/38.

RENUMBERED:
8892 3/9/24.
2503 10/11/46.
62503 27/11/48.

CONDEMNED: 12/2/51.
Cut up at Stratford.

8893

To traffic 5/1900.

REPAIRS:
Str. 10/9/07—12/2/08.**G.**
Str. 20/8/20—8/1/21.**G.**
Str. 1/4—30/6/22.**G.**
Str. 11/1—17/4/24.**G.**
Str. 13/8—23/12/26.**G.**
Rebuilt to D15.
Superheated boiler fitted.
Str. ?/?—?/5/31.**G.**
Altered to D15/2.
Str. 3/5—14/6/33.**G.**
Str. 28/2—5/4/35.**G.**
Str. ?/?—?/3/37.**G.**
Str. ?/?—21/4/39.**G.**
Str. ?/?—?/4/42.**G.**
Str. ?/?—14/4/44.**G.**
Str. 2/2—15/3/46.**G.**
Str. 14/4/48 *Not repaired.*

BOILERS:
1893.
1893 *(new)* 12/2/08.

1897 *(ex spare)* 8/1/21.
1886 *(ex8872)* 17/4/24.
3584 *(ex8889)* 23/12/26.
3676 *(ex8898)* ?/5/31.
3663 *(ex8863)* 14/6/33.
3614 *(ex8863)* 5/4/35.
3660 *(ex8864)* ?/3/37.
3256 *(ex8892)* 21/4/39.
3681 *(ex8891)* ?/4/42.
3256 *(ex8892)* 14/4/44.

SHEDS:
Cambridge.
King's Lynn 25/8/29.

RENUMBERED:
8893 17/4/24.
2504 8/9/46.

CONDEMNED: 12/6/48.
Cut up at Stratford.

8894

To traffic 6/1900.

REPAIRS:
Str. 22/1—27/5/09.**G.**
Str. 13/9/17—15/1/18.**G.**
Rebuilt to D15.
Superheated boiler fitted.
Str. 29/8—2/2/22.**G.**
Str. 21/11/23—15/3/24.**G.**
Str. 26/10/25—22/1/26.**G.**
Str. 12/9—10/12/27.**G.**
Coal guard on tender.
Str. 22/10—24/12/29.**G.**
Str. 8/2—7/4/32.**G.**
Altered to D15/2.
Str. 2/5—22/6/34.**G.**
Str. 19—28/9/34.**L.**
Str. 23/5—7/6/35.**L.**
Str. 27/4—11/6/36.**G.**
Str. 22/4—10/6/38.**G.**
Str. 8—27/10/39.**L.**
Str. 17/7—18/9/40.**G.**
Str. 17/10/42—6/1/43.**G.**
Str. 8—18/5/43.**L.**
Str. 6—26/4/44.**L.**
Str. 15/10—1/12/44.**G.**
Str. 5/1—29/3/45.**H.**
After being hit by an aircraft.
Str. 25/5—22/8/47.**G.**
Str. 19/2—7/3/49.**C/L.**
Str. 25/8—15/10/49.**G.**

BOILERS:
1894.
1894 *(new)* 27/5/09.
3585 *(new)* 15/1/18.
3663 *(new)* 15/3/24.
3578 *(ex8887)* 10/12/27.
3637 *(ex8889)* 24/12/29.
3610 *(ex-spare)* 7/4/32.

1269 *(ex8879)* 22/6/34.
3635 *(ex8887)* 11/6/36.
3254 *(ex8882)* 10/6/38.
3443 *(ex8883)* 18/9/40.
3627 *(ex8882)* 6/1/43.
3421 *(exJ17 8229)* 1/12/44.
3453 *(exJ17 8220)* 29/3/45.
3443 *(ex8890)* 22/8/47.
3531 *(new)* 15/10/49.

SHEDS:
Cambridge.
Stratford 22/1/26.
Cambridge 13/3/26.
March 25/6/28.
Peterborough East 25/10/30.
March 8/6/31.
King's Lynn 28/2/40.
March 18/3/40.
Cambridge 31/5/42.
King's Lynn 27/5/45.

RENUMBERED:
1894E 15/3/24.
8894 ?/?/??.
7764 6/1/43.
2505 24/3/46.
62505 15/10/49.

CONDEMNED: 19/11/51.
Cut up at Stratford.

8895

To traffic 6/1900.

REPAIRS:
Str. 12/8—26/11/09.**G.**
Str. 9/1—31/3/22.**G.**
Str. 4/2—16/5/24.**G.**
Str. 12/1—7/3/25.**L.**
Str. 9/7—16/11/26.**G.**
Rebuilt to D15.
Superheated boiler fitted.
Coal guard on tender.
Str. 25/6—23/7/28.**G.**
Str. 30/12/29—26/2/30.**G.**
Altered to D15/2.
Str. 17/3—11/5/33.**G.**
Str. 18/1—9/2/34.**L.**
Str. 20/1—25/4/35.**G.**
Str. 8—11/6/36.**L.**
Str. 3/12/36—28/1/37.**G.**
Str. 9/4—9/6/39.**G.**
Str. 30/3—19/5/41.**G.**
Str. 20/11/43—8/1/44.**G.**
Str. 11/11—21/12/45.**G.**
Str. 3/11—22/12/47.**G.**
Str. 1/1—18/2/50.**G.**
Str. 1—22/12/50.**C/L.**
Str. 30/3/52 *Not repaired.*

BOILERS:
1895.

1895 *(new)* 26/11/09.
3677 *(new)* 16/11/26.
3261 *(ex8899)* 11/5/33.
3258 *(ex8896)* 25/4/35.
3606 *(ex8899)* 28/1/37.
3255 *(ex8873)* 9/6/39.
3254 *(ex8894)* 19/5/41.
3678 *(ex8898)* 8/1/44.
3464 *(ex8891)* 22/12/47.

SHEDS:
March.
Norwich 8/1/40.
King's Lynn 18/1/40.

RENUMBERED:
8895 16/5/24.
2506 8/9/46.
62506 18/2/50.

CONDEMNED: 21/4/52.
Cut up at Stratford.

8896

To traffic 7/1900.

REPAIRS:
Str. 13/1—8/9/15.**G.**
Rebuilt to D15.
Superheated boiler fitted.
Str. 25/10/22—18/4/23.**G.**
Str. 25/10—23/12/24.**G.**
Gr. 6/12/26—18/3/27.**G.**
Str. 7/9—21/12/28.**G.**
Coal guard on tender.
Str. 25/2—4/6/31.**G.**
Str. 20/4—2/6/33.**G.**
Altered to D15/2.
Str. 15/11—8/12/33.**L.**
Str. 27/11/34—15/2/35.**G.**
After Wormley accident.
Str. 25—31/7/35.**L.**
Str. 2/5—25/6/36.**G.**
Str. 28/8—8/10/37.**G.**
Str. 28/5—23/8/40.**G.**
Str. 14—23/9/41.**L.**
Str. 28/3—1/7/43.**G.**
Str. 11/3—19/4/45.**G.**
Str. 17/3—10/5/47.**G.**
Str. 25/6—16/8/47.**L.**
Str. 4/8—14/10/49.**G.**
Str. 30/3/52 *Not repaired.*

BOILERS:
1896.
3575 *(new)* 8/9/15.
3256 *(ex8868)* 4/6/31.
3258 *(ex8898)* 2/6/33.
3262 *(ex8868)* 15/2/35.
3637 *(ex8881)* 8/10/37.
3467 *(ex8881)* 23/8/40.
3665 *(ex8884)* 1/7/43.
3255 *(ex8867)* 10/5/47.

(above) **The class had been completed by building a further ten in 1902 (nos.1870 to 1879) and ten more in the following year (1860 to 1869). These twenty had the wider cab and high roof but the circular windows on the front plate of the cab were changed to shaped ones. Nos.1876-9 and 1860-9 were fitted with four-column Ramsbottom safety valves from new. This is no.1876, one of the eighteen D14 fitted with a conventional tender at Grouping. No.1876 was ex works 20th February 1924 in green livery with the 'E' suffix.**

(right) **Ex works 9th September 1924, no.8873 had unlined grey paint but with black boiler bands. Later, whilst still D14, it did receive lined green livery.**

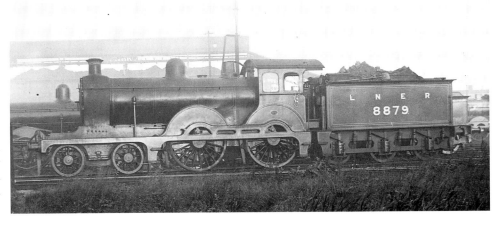

(right) **Although rebuilding from D14 was continued every year after Grouping, several had further general repairs whilst remaining D14. No.8879 had them in July 1924 and February 1926 and, like most of them, got green livery. Note that there is no coal guard on the tender - this was only added 31st December 1927 when 8879 changed to D15.**

No.8868 was the last D14 to get green painting, ex works 28th April 1928 when it also acquired a coal guard on the tender. No.8875 was the only D14 to get black livery - 3rd January 1929. At that same 'shopping' it came out with number on tender but this was moved to the cab side in May 1930. When 8875 went for re-boilering in January 1931, D14 became extinct.

Between January 1933 and April 1936 nine engines from the number range 8860 to 8900 were rebuilt with 5' 1⅛" diameter boilers and round top firebox and the classification D14 was revived for them, though as Part 2 (D14/2). The nine engines concerned were: 8860, 8861, 8863, 8866, 8869, 8870, 8876, 8878, 8900, all having been previously rebuilt to class D15. During the same period other engines from the later series, which had been rebuilt as D15, were being similarly rebuilt and these were classified D16/3. The difference lay in the frame design, nos.8860 to 8900 having shallower frames than those that followed. In May 1936 it was decided to merge D14/2 into class D16/3 and the classification D14 then lapsed. Strangely when the original D14 engines with small boiler were rebuilt to class D15, it had not been thought necessary to differentiate them.

By Grouping this class had been augmented in 1921 (+2) and 1922 (+3) by the reboiling with Belpaire firebox of D14. Of those five engine, 1861, 1863, 1869, 1884 and 1899, only the latter retained its 'Watercart' tender.

8896 cont.
3530 *(new)* 14/10/49.

SHEDS:
King's Lynn
Cambridge 25/8/29.
King's Lynn 21/3/38.
South Lynn 5/11/50.
King's Lynn 1/7/51.

RENUMBERED:
8896 23/12/24.
2507 23/11/46.
62507 14/10/49.

CONDEMNED: 21/4/52.
Cut up at Stratford.

8897

To traffic 7/1900.

REPAIRS:
Str. 23/9/09—28/1/10.**G.**
Str. 13/6—7/10/19.**G.**
Rebuilt to D15.
Superheated boiler fitted.
Str. 26/5—8/11/22.**G.**
Str. 30/11/23—29/2/24.**G.**
Str. 17—30/4/26. *Not repaired.*
Gr. 1/5—11/12/26.**G.**
Str. 24/12/28—6/5/29.**G.**
Altered to D15/2.
Coal guard on tender.
Str. 11/10—25/11/32.**G.**
Str. 3/7—31/8/34.**G.**
Str. 5/3—3/4/36.**G.**
Str. 25—28/5/36.**L.**
Str. 24/11/37—6/1/38.**G.**
Str. 19/12/38—12/1/39.**L.**
Str. 7/5—3/6/39.**H.**
Str. 18/1—16/3/40.**G.**
Str. 10/4—1/5/40.**L.**
Str. 8/3—19/5/42.**G.**
Str. 27/5—17/6/42.**L.**
Str. 24/9—28/10/44.**G.**
Str. 5/10—26/11/46.**G.**
Str. 5/10—19/11/48.**G.**
Str. 15—26/11/49.**C/L.**
Str. 9/10/50 *Not repaired.*

BOILERS:
1897.
1897 *(new)* 28/1/10.
3592 *(new)* 7/10/19.
3662 *(ex8886)* 25/11/32.
3610 *(ex8894)* 31/8/34.
3633 *(exJ17 8160)* 3/4/36.
3638 *(ex8886)* 6/1/38.
3262 *(ex8886)* 16/3/40.
3445 *(exJ17 8177)* 19/5/42.
3681 *(ex8892)* 26/11/46.
3423 *(ex8877)* 19/11/48.

SHEDS:
Colchester.
Ipswich 22/6/37.
Bury St Edmunds 5/6/38.

RENUMBERED:
8897 29/2/24.
2508 18/11/46.
62508 13/11/48.

CONDEMNED: 30/10/50.
Cut up at Stratford.

8898

To traffic 7/1900.

REPAIRS:
Str. 11/12/14—6/7/15.**G.**
Rebuilt to D15.
Superheated boiler fitted.
Str. 10/3—8/7/20.**G.**
Str. 6/1—7/7/22.**G.**
Str. 24/12/23—2/5/24.**G.**
Vacuum brake added.
Str. 22/5—14/6/24.**L.**
Str. 18/3—9/7/26.**G.**
Coal guard on tender.
Str. 16/3—3/7/28.**G.**
Str. 1/1—29/3/29.**L.**
Str. 9/11/30—18/2/31.**G.**
Str. 9/3—21/4/33.**G.**
Altered to D15/2.
Str. 11/12/34—11/2/35.**G.**
Str. 2—5/6/36.**L.**
Str. 22/2—1/4/37.**G.**
Str. 30/11/38—17/1/39.**G.**
Str. 12—15/8/40.**L.**
Str. 20/10—8/11/40.**L.**
Str. 16/5—11/7/41.**G.**
Str. 2/9—31/12/43.**G.**
Str. 12/8—5/10/45.**G.**
Str. 24/2—8/4/48.**G.**
Str. 16/2—21/4/50.**G.**
Str. 22—28/2/51.**C/L.**
Str. 21/5—13/6/52.**N/C.**

BOILERS:
1898.
3574 *(new)* 6/7/15.
3676 *(new)* 9/7/26.
3258 *(ex8888)* 18/2/31.
3593 *(ex8868)* 21/4/33.
3255 *(ex8865)* 11/2/35.
3258 *(ex8895)* 1/4/37.
3676 *(ex8867)* 17/1/39.
3678 *(ex8899)* 11/7/41.
3457 *(exJ17 8232)* 31/12/43.
3678 *(ex8895)* 8/4/48.
3255 *(ex8896)* 21/4/50.
3255 re-no.23266 13/6/52.

SHEDS:
Parkeston.

Colchester 28/4/33.
Cambridge 27/7/34.
Ipswich 7/8/34.
Peterborough East 17/8/34.
Norwich 30/6/36.
Yarmouth 13/12/36.
Norwich 31/1/37.
Yarmouth 3/6/37.
Ipswich 29/1/38.
Colchester 27/3/38.
Stratford 25/9/39.
Melton Constable 7/1/49.
Norwich 27/1/52.

RENUMBERED:
8898 2/5/24.
2509 15/11/46.
62509 3/4/48.

CONDEMNED: 22/9/52.
Cut up at Stratford.

8899

To traffic 7/1900.

REPAIRS:
Str. 13/12/11—5/3/12.**G.**
Str. 8/11/21—18/2/22.**G.**
Rebuilt to D15 Saturated.
Str. 21/7—23/11/23.**G.**
Str. 20/2—25/6/25.**G.**
Superheated boiler fitted.
Go. 6/11/26—4/3/27.**G.**
Str. 13/3—5/7/29.**G.**
Altered to D15/2.
Coal guard on tender.
Str. 27/12/30—31/3/31.**G.**
Str. 18/1—13/4/33.**G.**
Altered to D15 Superheated.
Str. 1/1—28/3/35.**G.**
Reverted to D15/2.
Str. 29/6—4/7/36.**L.**
Str. 26/10—4/12/36.**G.**
Str. 7/2—3/3/37.**L.**
Str. 3/10—16/12/38.**G.**
Str. 30/7—9/11/40.**G.**
Str. 25/4—10/9/43.**G.**
Rebuilt to D16/3.
Str. 10/6—20/7/45.**G.**
Str. 9/3—13/5/46.**G.**
Str. 11/12/48—4/2/49.**G.**
Str. 7/1—16/2/51.**G.**
Str. 17/5—26/6/53.**G.**
Str. 21/8—24/9/55.**G.**

BOILERS:
1899.
1899 *(new)* 5/3/12.
3617 *(new)* 18/2/22.
3589 *(ex8885)* 25/6/25.
3261 *(new)* 31/3/31.
3257 *(ex8900)* 13/4/33.
3606 *(ex8810)* 28/3/35.

3636 *(ex8868)* 4/12/36.
3678 *(ex8879)* 16/12/38.
3637 *(ex8896)* 9/11/40.
4281 *(ex8876)* 10/9/43.
4287 *(ex8798)* 20/7/45.
4297 *(exJ19 8265)* 13/5/46.
4302 *(ex8794)* 4/2/49.
23330 *(ex ?)* 16/2/51.
23319 *(ex8837)* 26/6/53.
23315 *(ex8884)* 24/9/55.

SHEDS:
Doncaster.
March 13/6/25.
Cambridge 26/5/29.
King's Lynn 25/8/29.
Cambridge 11/10/30.
King's Lynn 13/6/39.
Melton Constable 18/1/40.
Yarmouth Beach 21/1/40.
Norwich 13/12/40.
Yarmouth Beach 3/1/41.
Melton Constable 1/4/41.
Stratford 7/8/45.
Colchester 17/8/46.
Norwich 3/3/47.
Melton Constable 24/7/55.
Norwich 14/8/55.
Cambridge 17/6/56.
King's Lynn 6/1/57.

RENUMBERED:
1899E 23/11/23.
8899 ?/?/??.
2510 24/11/46.
62510 29/1/49.

CONDEMNED: 7/10/57.
Cut up at Stratford.

8880

To traffic 5/1901.

REPAIRS:
Str. 30/12/07—5/5/08.**G.**
Str. 28/9/17—22/2/18.**G.**
Rebuilt to D15.
Superheated boiler fitted.
Str. 20/12/22—4/5/23.**G.**
Str. 19/7—16/10/24.**G.**
Str. 12/5—2/7/25.**L.**
Str. 11/3—13/10/26.**G.**
Str. 28/12/27—31/3/28.**G.**
Altered to D15/2.
Coal guard on tender.
Str. 24/7—17/8/28.**L.**
Vacuum brake added.
Str. 5/3—9/5/30.**G.**
Str. 15/11/31—16/1/32.**G.**
Str. 1/2—27/4/34.**G.**
Str. 27/1—12/3/36.**G.**
Str. 27/4—1/5/36.**L.**
Str. 14/2—25/3/38.**G.**

After Grouping three more D14 were reboilered to non-superheated D15; 8886 in October 1925; 8878 in March 1929; 8873 in January 1930. Note that no.8886 retained its 2" taller chimney as the Belpaire boiler pitch was not altered on engines with shallow frames, but these engines did have a shorter dome. However, a chimney change was just a matter of circumstance and it was possible to see short chimneys on shallow framed engines - no.8861 was ex works 23rd May 1925 with a short chimney. Note alteration to cab front windows on 8886. *H.C.Casserley.*

Str. 26/2—19/4/40.**G.**
Str. 27/7—29/9/42.**G.**
Rebuilt to D16/3.
Str. 20/6—5/8/44.**G.**
Str. 25/1—16/3/46.**G.**
Str. 29/5—27/8/47.**G.**
Str. 1—28/5/49.**H/I.**
Str. 2—13/6/49.**N/C.**
Str. 2/10—10/11/51.**G.**
Str. 17/1—27/2/54.**G.**
Str. 2/1—3/3/56.**G.**

BOILERS:
1880.
1880 *(new)* 5/5/08.
3586 *(new)* 22/2/18.
3636 *(new)* 4/5/23.
3680 *(new)* 31/3/28.
3617 *(ex8861)* 16/1/32.
3605 *(exJ17 8221)* 27/4/34.
3631 *(ex8877)* 25/3/38.
3638 *(ex8897)* 19/4/40.
4318 *(new)* 29/9/42.
4326 *(new)* 5/8/44.
4315 *(exJ19 8249)* 16/3/46.
4288 *(ex8883)* 27/8/47.
23373 *(ex ?)* 10/11/51.
23397 *(ex8823)* 27/2/54.
23332 *(ex8823)* 3/3/56.

SHEDS:
Yarmouth.
Norwich 14/2/32.
Yarmouth 10/7/32.
Norwich 12/5/34.
Yarmouth 22/6/35.
Norwich 26/1/36.
Yarmouth 17/5/36.
Norwich 5/3/38.
Yarmouth 19/2/39.
Norwich 3/9/39.
Yarmouth 22/10/39.
Norwich 19/5/40.

Yarmouth 24/11/40.
Norwich 2/6/57.

RENUMBERED:
8880 16/4/24.
2511 24/11/46.
62511 28/5/49.

CONDEMNED: 17/12/59.
Cut up at Stratford.

8881

To traffic 5/1901.

REPAIRS:
Str. 27/4—28/7/09.**G.**
Str. 7/7—12/8/16.**G.**
Str. 11/10/20—6/1/21.**G.**
Str. 18/5—30/11/23.**G.**
Str. 26/2—26/4/24.**H.**
Boiler repairs only.
Nr. 8—15/8/24.**L.**
Str. 21/2--3/7/25.**G.**
Str. 27/5—8/10/27.**G.**
Coal guard on tender.
Str. 31/12/28—15/1/29.**N/C.**
Vacuum brake added.
Str. 20/2—1/5/30.**G.**
Rebuilt to D15/2.
Str. 25/2—26/4/32.**G.**
Str. 25/1—8/3/34.**G.**
Str. 30/9—22/11/35.**G.**
Str. 24/6—1/7/36.**L.**
Str. 31/7—17/9/37.**G.**
Str. 10/3—31/5/40.**G.**
Str. 6/10—15/11/41.**G.**
Str. 12/12/43—10/3/44.**G.**
Str. 23/12/45—15/2/46.**G.**
Str. 7/3—25/5/48.**G.**
Str. 26/7/50 *Not repaired.*

BOILERS:
1881.
1881 *(new)* 28/7/09.
1190 *(exJ16 1190)* 12/8/16.
3250 *(ex-spare)* 6/1/21.
3587 *(ex-spare)* 1/5/30.
3637 *(ex8894)* 26/4/32.
3574 *(ex8883)* 8/3/34.
3637 *(ex8875)* 22/11/35.
3467 *(ex8883)* 17/9/37.
3465 *(ex8890)* 31/5/40.
3255 *(ex8895)* 15/11/41.
3683 *(ex8891)* 10/3/44.

SHEDS:
Lowestoft.
Yarmouth 9/10/28.
Norwich 14/10/28.
Lowestoft 28/4/29.
Norwich 20/7/30.
Yarmouth 8/6/32.
Norwich 5/8/33.
Yarmouth 17/3/34.
Norwich 23/2/35.
Yarmouth 22/4/35.
Norwich 28/9/35.
Lowestoft 1/1/36.
Yarmouth 12/1/36.
Norwich 1/8/37.
King's Lynn 16/5/39.
March 6/10/40.
King's Lynn 15/12/40.

RENUMBERED:
8881 26/4/24.
2512 13/10/46.
62512 22/5/48.

CONDEMNED: 15/8/50.
Cut up at Stratford.

8882

To traffic 5/1901.

REPAIRS:
Str. 21/1—9/6/10.**G.**
Str. 25/7—10/12/19.**G.**
Rebuilt to D15.
Superheated boiler fitted.
Str. 19/7—30/12/22.**G.**
Str. 5/6—24/10/24.**G.**
Str. 2/10/26—14/1/27.**G.**
Str. 17/9—26/11/28.**G.**
Vacuum brake added &
coal guard on tender.
Str. 26/10/30—16/1/31.**G.**
Str. 16/3—5/5/33.**G.**
Altered to D15/2.
Str. 23/5—1/6/34.**L.**
Str. 18—20/6/34.**L.**
Str. 6/11—21/12/34.**G.**
Str. 11/4—28/5/36.**G.**
Str. 19/2—18/3/37.**L.**
Str. 11/9—8/10/37.**L.**
Str. 27/3—13/5/38.**G.**
Str. 10/3—17/5/40.**G.**
Str. 16/7—11/9/42.**G.**
Rebuilt to D16/3.
Str. 1/10—4/11/44.**G.**
Str. 26/6—21/7/45.**L.**
Str. 22/6—19/9/47.**G.**
Str. 21/8—15/10/49.**G.**
Str. 9/3—7/4/51.**C/L.**
Str. 23/11—22/12/51.**G.**
W.P.U. gear removed.
Str. 30/5—8/8/53.**G.**
Str. 9/8—11/9/54.**G.**
Str. 6/4—5/5/55.**C/L.**
Str. 20/4—16/6/56.**G.**

In March 1915 no.1791 received a Weir feed water heater and pump, in place of the left hand injector. The pump could operate very slowly and work constantly whilst the engine was in motion. It was still in use when the engine became superheated in April 1923 but was removed in June 1924. Note the tender axleboxes are Iracier type with shield shape covers.

BOILERS:
1882.
1882 *(new)* 9/6/10.
3593 *(new)* 10/12/19.
3591 *(ex8874)* 24/10/24.
3634 *(ex8867)* 14/1/27.
3638 *(ex8869)* 26/11/28.
3589 *(ex8878)* 5/5/33.
3659 *(ex8874)* 21/12/34.
3254 *(ex8874)* 28/5/36.
3627 *(ex8806)* 13/5/38.
4317 *(new)* 11/9/42.
4259 *(exJ19 8142)* 4/11/44.
4244 *(exJ19 8244)* 19/9/47.
4326 *(exJ19 8267)* 15/10/49.
4326 renum 23343 7/4/51.
23377 *(ex ?)* 22/12/51.
23407 *(ex8811)* 11/9/54.
23346 *(ex8870)* 16/6/56.

SHEDS:
Ipswich.
Cambridge 17/1/31.
Peterborough East 28/2/31
Cambridge 2/4/31
King's Lynn 31/10/37.
Cambridge 21/3/38.
King's Lynn 28/5/39.

March 6/10/40.
King's Lynn 15/12/40.
Cambridge 13/5/47.
King's Lynn 26/10/47.
Bury St Edmunds 15/4/51.
Cambridge 24/3/57.
March 16/6/57.
Cambridge 17/8/58.

RENUMBERED:
8882 24/10/24.
2513 23/6/46.
62513 15/10/49.

CONDEMNED: 3/11/58.
Cut up at Stratford.

8883

To traffic 6/1901.

REPAIRS:
Str. 22/12/07—6/5/08.**G.**
Str. 23/9/15—4/2/16.**G.**
Rebuilt to D15.
Superheated boiler fitted.
Str. 31/3—13/9/22.**G.**
Str. 19/2—13/5/24.**G.**

Str. 23/9—13/11/24.**H.**
Str. 12/11/25—10/3/26.**G.**
Str. 9/7—21/10/26.**G.**
Str. 13/4—10/8/28.**G.**
Altered to D15/2.
Vacuum brake added &
coal guard on tender.
Str. 3/2—15/4/30.**G.**
Str. 1/2—16/3/32.**G.**
Str. 4/12/33—25/1/34.**G.**
Str. 7/10/35—16/1/36.**G.**
Str. 2—4/6/36.**L.**
Str. 2/7—20/8/37.**G.**
Str. 8/5—22/6/40.**G.**
Str. 21/2—14/5/43.**G.**
Rebuilt to D16/3.
Str. 31/12/44—27/1/45.**G.**
Str. 13/9—5/11/46.**G.**
Str. 14/11/48—4/1/49.**G.**
Str. 18/1—12/2/49.**L.**
Str. 16/2—19/3/49.**N/C.**
Str. 6/5—23/6/51.**G.**
Str. 12/5—13/6/53.**G.**
Str. 7/3—9/4/55.**G.**

BOILERS:
1883.
1883 *(new)* 6/5/08.

3576 *(new)* 4/2/16.
3585 *(ex8888)* 21/10/26.
3635 *(ex8864)* 10/8/28.
3574 *(ex8889)* 16/3/32.
3638 *(ex8882)* 25/1/34.
3467 *(ex8824)* 16/1/36.
3443 *(ex8885)* 20/8/37.
3633 *(ex8862)* 22/6/40.
4309 *(ex8872)* 14/5/43.
4288 *(ex-spare)* 27/1/45.
4282 *(ex8810)* 5/11/46.
4311 *(ex8835)* 4/1/49.
23353 *(ex ?)* 23/6/51.
23425 *(ex ?)* 13/6/53.
23372 *(exJ19 8243)* 9/4/55.

SHEDS:
Norwich.
Ipswich 13/3/26.
Norwich 11/3/27.
Yarmouth ?/?/??
Norwich 28/4/29.
Yarmouth 7/4/34.
Norwich 22/6/35.
Yarmouth 14/3/37.
Norwich 2/7/37.
Cambridge 1/4/38.
King's Lynn 15/4/38.

8883 cont.
Cambridge 30/4/39
King's Lynn 21/5/39.
Cambridge 6/10/40.
King's Lynn 15/10/40.

RENUMBERED:
8883 13/5/24.
2514 23/6/46.
62514 1/1/49.

CONDEMNED: 11/3/57.
Cut up at Stratford.

8884

To traffic 6/1901.

REPAIRS:
Str. 14/12/08—13/5/09.**G**.
Str. 1/12/15—24/3/16.**G**.
Str. 26/4—3/7/20.**G**.
Str. 2/12/21—18/3/22.**G**.
Rebuilt to D15.
Nr. 10/4—16/6/23.**H**.
Str. 30/10/24—4/4/25.**G**.
Str. 25/9/26—14/1/27.**G**.
Coal guard on tender.
Str. 27/9—27/12/28.**G**.
Altered to D15/2.
Superheated boiler fitted.
Vacuum brake added.
Str. 24/4—5/7/30.**G**.
Str. 3/12/30—29/1/31.**L**.
Str. 19/5—14/7/32.**G**.
Str. 16/9—10/11/33.**G**.
Str. 11/11/35—3/1/36.**G**.
Str. 4—7/5/36.**L**.
Str. 21/1—25/2/38.**G**.
Cab side screens fitted.
Str. 28/2—1/6/40.**G**.
Str. 9/11/42—28/1/43.**G**.
Rebuilt to D16/3.
Str. 29/10—1/12/44.**G**.
Str. 16/6—26/8/46.**G**.
Str. 5/8—29/9/48.**G**.
Str. 6/8—8/9/50.**G**.
Str. 9—30/12/50.**C/L**.
Str. 15/1—21/2/53.**G**.
Str. 21/5—1/7/55.**G**.

BOILERS:
1884.
1884 *(new)* 13/5/09.
1885 *(ex8885)* 24/3/16.
3252 *(ex8900)* 3/7/20.
3618 *(new)* 18/3/22.
3590 *(ex8874)* 27/12/28.
3634 *(ex8879)* 14/7/32.
3683 *(ex8887)* 10/11/33.
3665 *(exJ17 8221)* 25/2/38.
4319 *(new)* 28/1/43.
4317 *(ex8882)* 1/12/44.
4264 *(exJ19 8146)* 26/8/46.

4241 *(exJ19 8249)* 29/9/48.
23300 *(ex ?)* 8/9/50.
23315 *(ex8786)* 21/2/53.
23414 *(ex8794)* 1/7/55.

SHEDS:
Norwich.
Yarmouth 28/4/29.
Norwich 20/7/30.
Yarmouth 27/7/30.
Norwich 13/5/33.
Yarmouth 5/8/33.
Norwich 7/11/35.
Yarmouth 31/5/36.
Norwich 1/8/37.
Melton Constable 28/9/39.
Norwich 2/12/45.
Melton Constable 12/12/45.

RENUMBERED:
8884 ??/??
2515 22/8/46.
62515 25/9/48.

CONDEMNED: 1/4/58.
Cut up at Stratford.

8885

To traffic 6/1901.

REPAIRS:
Str. 20/10/08—20/4/09.**G**.
Str. 13/10/15—22/2/16.**G**.
Str. 21/12/18—16/5/19.**G**.
Rebuilt to D15.
Superheated boiler fitted.
Str. 1/6—1/9/23.**G**.
Nr. 17—25/6/24.**L**.
Str. 24/1—23/6/25.**G**.
Ash ejector fitted.
Str. 11/2—8/6/27.**G**.
Str. 1/9—29/12/28.**G**.
Altered to D15/2.
Vacuum brake added &
coal guard on tender.
Str. 29/4—14/6/29.**L**.
Str. 7/12/30—7/5/31.**G**.
Ash ejector removed.
Str. 31/1—10/3/33.**G**.
Str. 11/3—17/5/35.**G**.
Str. 22—24/6/36.**L**.
Str. 24/5—23/7/37.**G**.
Rebuilt to D16/3.
Str. 28/8—13/10/39.**G**.
Str. 31/8—4/10/41.**G**.
Str. 1/1—31/3/43.**G**.
Str. 21/1—16/2/45.**G**.
Str. 7—30/3/45.**L**.
Str. 18/11—26/12/46.**G**.
Str. 2/1—21/2/49.**G**.
Str. 12—26/3/49.**C/L**.
Str. 17/4—6/5/49.**C/L**.
Str. 15—22/12/49.**C/L**.

Str. 26/5—21/6/50.**C/L**.
Str. 18/10—9/12/50.**G**.
Str. 28/9—25/10/52.**G**.
Str. 6/8—22/10/54.**C/L**.
Str. 29/4—4/6/55.**G**.

BOILERS:
1885.
1885 *(new)* 20/4/09.
3250 *(ex8890)* 22/2/16.
3589 *(new)* 16/5/19.
3593 *(ex8882)* 23/6/25.
3586 *(ex8887)* 7/5/31.
3260 *(ex8875)* 10/3/33.
3443 *(ex-spare)* 17/5/35.
4212 *(ex8798)* 23/7/37.
4210 *(ex8817)* 13/10/39.
4218 *(ex8871)* 4/10/41.
4200 *(ex8870)* 31/3/43.
4209 *(ex8868)* 16/2/45.
4203 *(ex8843)* 26/12/46.
4207 *(ex8858)* 21/2/49.
23317 *(ex8844)* 9/12/50.
23324 *(ex8820)* 25/10/52.
23409 *(exJ19 8145)* 4/6/55.

SHEDS:
Norwich.
Ipswich 27/5/31.
Norwich 16/7/34.
Yarmouth 15/1/35.
Norwich 9/3/35.
Lowestoft 5/10/35.
Norwich 23/5/37.
Peterborough East 25/4/38.
March 30/4/39.
Cambridge 27/10/40.
King's Lynn 14/9/47.
Cambridge 21/9/47.
King's Lynn 21/3/48.
Cambridge 13/5/48.
King's Lynn 15/11/51.

RENUMBERED:
8885 ??/??.
2516 2/6/46.
62516 19/2/49.

CONDEMNED: 19/8/57.
Cut up at Stratford.

8886

To traffic 6/1901.

REPAIRS:
Str. 10/4—20/7/11.**G**.
Str. 1/4—17/12/21.**G**.
Str. 20/4—13/7/23.**G**.
Str. 30/4—6/10/25.**G**.
Rebuilt to D15.
Str. 25/2—9/7/27.**G**.
Vacuum brake added.
Str. 29/11/28—22/3/29.**G**.

Altered to D15/2.
Superheated boiler fitted.
Coal guard on tender.
Str. 23/9—19/12/30.**G**.
Str. 9/6—10/8/32.**G**.
Str. 26/2—11/5/34.**G**.
Str. 11/1—26/2/36.**G**.
Str. 11—15/5/36.**L**.
Str. 9/11—17/12/37.**G**.
Str. 3—18/2/38.**L**.
Str. 6/12/39—5/4/40.**G**.
Rebuilt to D16/3.
Str. 20/6—13/8/42.**G**.
Str. 29/10—24/11/44.**G**.
Str. 9/6—29/8/46.**G**.
Str. 28/11/48—26/1/49.**G**.
Str. 1/4—5/5/51.**G**.
Str. 1/11—12/12/53.**G**.
Str. 6/6—11/8/56.**G**.
Str. 16/9/59. *Not repaired.*

BOILERS:
1886.
1886 *(new)* 20/7/11.
1860 *(ex8860)* 17/12/21.
3617 *(ex8899)* 6/10/25.
3576 *(ex8867)* 22/3/29.
3662 *(ex8900)* 19/12/30.
3678 *(ex8892)* 10/8/32.
3617 *(ex8880)* 11/5/34.
3638 *(ex8883)* 26/2/36.
3262 *(ex8896)* 17/12/37.
4306 *(new)* 5/4/40.
4303 *(ex8824)* 13/8/42.
4265 *(ex8855)* 24/11/44.
4317 *(ex8884)* 29/8/46.
4243 *(ex8785)* 26/1/49.
23347 *(ex ?)* 5/5/51.
23358 *(ex8848)* 12/12/53.
23362 *(ex8817)* 11/8/56.

SHEDS:
Stratford.
Norwich 9/7/27.
Yarmouth 28/4/29.
Norwich 20/7/30.
Yarmouth 8/2/31.
Norwich 25/4/33.
Yarmouth 2/6/34.
Norwich 27/3/35.
Yarmouth 5/4/35.
Norwich 12/1/36.
Yarmouth 11/3/36.
Norwich 12/4/36.
Yarmouth 31/5/36.
Norwich 29/12/37.
Yarmouth 14/4/40.
Norwich 19/5/40.
Yarmouth 24/11/40.
Norwich 23/11/41.
Yarmouth 7/12/41.
Norwich 3/5/46.
Yarmouth 9/5/46.
Lowestoft 17/1/54.

Normally there was just the Westinghouse brake for engine and for train working. A number had vacuum ejector added - nos.1858 and 1859 were the first in June 1904 so that they could work the Great Northern Royal Train on journeys to and from Wolferton. Note that the exhaust pipe was through the boiler. No.1829E, ex works 29th December 1923, was one of the first to get LNER. *H.Gordon Tidey.*

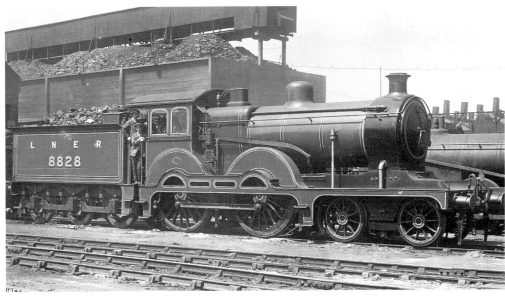

No.8828 got the fully lined green livery when ex works in May 1924. It had carried dual brakes from new but now had the ejector exhaust pipe along the outside of the boiler. Note the stepped parallel shanks of the buffers.

No.8833 had vacuum brake added when ex works 9th March 1926 and the coal guard was put on at its next repair in 1928 when it retained green paint which lasted its career as a non-superheated engine. Note buffers have taper shanks, and that the cab side windows drop vertically.

No.8873 was the last to become D15 non-superheated, in January 1930, when it was painted black and had number put high on cab side, and got 12" LNER on tender. When it next went to works in January 1933, Class D15NS was then extinct. From December 1927 it had been included with the superheated engines in Class D15/1.

(left) Part 1, although not officially introduced as such until December 1927, was normally regarded as comprising Belpaire firebox, superheater and short smokebox. In 1911, four of the last batch of ten with 4' 9" diameter boilers (nos.1793, 1794, 1798, 1799) came out new fitted with superheater and in April 1914 no.1793 was the first to have an anti-vacuum valve at each end of the header. The general addition of superheater began with no.1807, in July 1914, which got a Robinson 18-element type, and a slightly longer smokebox, with two anti-vacuum valves. Between then and 5th July 1929, some 41 had superheater added - 31 by the GER and 10 by the LNER. This class was also augmented by superheating and rebuilding with Belpaire firebox twenty-nine which had been built as class D14, fifteen before Grouping and ten by the LNER. No.1793 traverses Ipswich water troughs. *H.Gordon Tidey.*

Two of the first batch of superheated boilers were fitted with top feed through the dome, but no more were so equipped. Originally on nos.1845 and 1855, by Grouping nos.1810 and 1794 had them, and that from no.1810 also served on no.8826. 1810 stands in the yard at Nottingham Low Level station. *T.G.Hepburn.*

Yarmouth 28/3/54.
Yarmouth Beach 26/8/56.
Norwich 25/1/59.
March 21/6/59.

RENUMBERED:
8886 6/10/25.
2517 23/8/46.
62517 15/1/49.

CONDEMNED: 28/9/59.
Cut up at Stratford.

8887

To traffic 6/1901.

REPAIRS:
Str. 13/12/09—22/4/10.**G.**
Str. 5/10/17—15/2/18.**G.**
Rebuilt to D15.
Superheated boiler fitted.
Str. 15/6—12/12/22.**G.**
Str. 8/2—27/5/24.**G.**
Str. 28/4—14/10/25.**G.**
Str. 15/12/25—10/2/26.**H.**
New cylinders fitted.
Str. 17/5—30/9/27.**G.**
Coal guard on tender.
Str. 23/2—17/5/29.**G.**
Vacuum brake added.
Str. 20/11/30—16/1/31.**G.**
Str. 28/2—13/4/33.**G.**
Altered to D15/2.
Str. 19/8—21/9/34.**G.**
Str. 2/4—15/5/36.**G.**
Str. 26/1—18/2/37.**L.**
Str. 18—26/8/37.**L.**
Str. 5/3—19/5/38.**G.**
Str. 4/12/40—1/2/41.**G.**
Str. 17—20/12/42.**N/C.**
Str. 29/4—20/8/43.**G.**
Rebuilt to D16/3.
Str. 15/2—17/3/45.**G.**
Str. 5/1—1/3/47.**G.**
Str. 30/10—27/12/48.**H.**
Str. 19/10—19/11/49.**G.**
Str. 1/1—9/2/52.**G.**
Str. 24/1—12/3/54.**G.**
Str. 16/7—7/9/56.**G.**

BOILERS:
  1887.
  1887 *(new)* 22/4/10.
  3587 *(new)* 15/2/18.
  3578 *(ex8891)* 12/12/22.
  3586 *(ex8890)* 30/9/27.
  3683 *(ex8866)* 16/1/31.
  3675 *(ex8888)* 13/4/33.
  3635 *(ex8891)* 21/9/34.
  3661 *(ex8889)* 15/5/36.
  3677 *(ex spare)* 19/5/38.
  3258 *(ex8892)* 1/2/41.
  4280 *(ex8798)* 20/8/43.

4256 *(ex8799)* 17/3/45.
4308 *(ex8786)* 1/3/47.
4286 *(ex8797)* 19/11/49.
23387 *(ex ?)* 9/2/52.
23337 *(exJ19 8240)* 12/3/54.
23398 *(exJ19 8269)* 7/9/56.

SHEDS:
Norwich.
Stratford 20/10/34.
Cambridge 7/2/39.
King's Lynn 14/6/39.
South Lynn 22/2/40.
Cambridge 9/2/41.
March 8/10/44.
Cambridge 31/12/44
King's Lynn 29/7/45.
Cambridge 15/11/51.
King's Lynn 2/3/52.

RENUMBERED:
8887 27/5/24.
2518 23/6/46.
62518 24/12/48.

CONDEMNED: 13/10/58.
Cut up at Stratford.

8888

To traffic 7/1901.

REPAIRS:
Str. 29/3—21/7/10.**G.**
Str. 9/5—41/11/18.**G.**
Rebuilt to D15.
Superheated boiler fitted.
Str. 26/5—16/11/22.**G.**
Str. 8/2—5/6/24.**G.**
Vacuum brake added.
Str. 21/5—1/10/26.**G.**
Str. 8/11/28—4/2/29.**G.**
Altered to D15/2.
Coal guard on tender.
Str. 16/10/30—2/1/31.**G.**
Str. 25/8—7/10/32.**G.**
Str. 3—20/4/34.**G.**
Str. 21/12/34—1/3/35.**G.**
Str. 10/3—3/4/36.**L.**
Str. 14—18/7/36.**L.**
Str. 8/4—3/6/37.**G.**
Str. 15/3—2/6/39.**G.**
Rebuilt to D16/3.
Str. 20/8—16/9/40.**H.**
Str. 23/12/41—3/2/42.**G.**
Str. 17—26/2/42.**L.**
Str. 4/7—25/9/43.**G.**
Str. 18/10—18/11/44.**L.**
Str. 2/7—18/8/45.**G.**
Str. 27/2—26/4/47.**G.**
Str. 7—9/1/48.**N/C.**
Tablet apparatus fitted.
Str. 31/12/48—23/3/49.**G.**
Str. 13/5—10/6/50.**C/L.**

Str. 28/5—21/7/51.**G.**
Str. 15/11—5/12/52.**C/L.**
Str. 31/10—28/11/53.**G.**
Str. 5—28/4/56.**C/L.**

BOILERS:
  1888.
  1888 *(new)* 21/7/10.
  3588 *(new)* 14/11/18.
  3585 *(ex8894)* 5/6/24.
  3574 *(ex8898)* 1/10/26.
  3258 *(new)* 4/2/29.
  3675 *(ex8891)* 2/1/31.
  3590 *(ex8884)* 7/10/32.
  3593 *(ex8898)* 1/3/35.
  3681 *(ex8892)* 3/6/37.
  4288 *(new)* 2/6/39.
  4312 *(new)* 3/2/42.
  4248 *(exJ19 8242)* 18/8/45.
  4281 *(ex8804)* 26/4/47.
  4327 *(exJ19 8251)* 23/3/49.
23356 *(ex ?)* 21/7/51.
23345 *(ex8781)* 28/11/53.

SHEDS:
Ipswich.
Colchester 24/7/34.
Cambridge 9/8/34.
Bury St Edmunds 22/1/39.
Stratford 21/11/42.
Colchester 2/1/43.
Stratford 18/11/44.
Colchester 25/11/44.
Melton Constable 16/1/48.

RENUMBERED:
8888 5/6/24.
2519 2/6/46.
62519 19/3/49.

CONDEMNED: 1/1/57.
Cut up at Stratford.

8889

To traffic 7/1901.

REPAIRS:
Str. ?/?—?/12/08.**G.**
Str. 18/8/16—22/3/17.**G.**
Rebuilt to D15.
Superheated boiler fitted.
Str. 5/1—1/7/22.**G.**
Str. 25/3—27/6/24.**G.**
Str. 23/10/25—6/1/26.**L.**
Str. 15/4—29/7/26.**G.**
Str. 24/5/27.**N/C.**
Vacuum brake added.
Str. 14/10/27—28/1/28.**G.**
Coal guard on tender.
Str. 24—31/7/29.**H.**
Str. 9/11/29—3/2/30.**G.**
Altered to D15/2.
Str. 31/10/31—1/1/32.**G.**

Str. 8/4—15/6/34.**G.**
Str. 23/3—20/5/36.**G.**
Str. 14/3—20/5/38.**G.**
Str. 24/2—12/4/41.**G.**
Str. 25/6—19/7/41.**L.**
Str. 29/8—27/11/43.**G.**
Str. 24/6—17/8/45.**G.**
Str. 23/3—22/5/47.**G.**
Str. 3—23/10/47.**L.**
Str. 21/11—22/12/48.**L.**
Str. 7/10—11/11/49.**G.**
Str. 21/12/50—26/1/51.**C/L.**
Str. 12/8/51. *Not repaired.*

BOILERS:
1889.
1889 *(new)* 12/08.
3584 *(new)* 22/3/17.
3637 *(ex8866)* 29/7/26.
3574 *(ex8888)* 31/7/29.
3263 *(new)* 1/1/32.
3661 *(ex8875)* 15/6/34.
3674 *(ex8861)* 20/5/36.
3683 *(ex8884)* 20/5/38.
3677 *(ex8887)* 12/4/41.
3258 *(ex8887)* 27/11/43.
3467 *(ex8891)* 17/8/45.
3665 *(ex8896)* 22/5/47.
3475 *(exJ17 8213)* 11/11/49.
3475 renum 23219 26/1/51.

SHEDS:
Cambridge.
Stratford 31/10/24.
Southend 15/2/30.
Stratford 14/6/30.
Southend 21/6/30.
Stratford 12/7/30.
Norwich 20/10/34.
Yarmouth 26/1/35.
Norwich 27/2/35.
Yarmouth 1/6/35.
Norwich 22/3/36.
Yarmouth Beach 12/7/39.
Melton Constable 22/10/39.

RENUMBERED:
8889 27/6/24.
2520 29/9/46.
62520 18/12/48.

CONDEMNED: 27/8/51.
Cut up at Stratford.

Until after Grouping, all boilers were fitted with four-column Ramsbottom safety valves whilst the final eleven new boilers, built May 1926 to May 1928, had two Ross 'Pop' safety valves. The first of this batch of new boilers went to no.8891 in July 1926 whilst the second went to no.8898 in the same month. *L.N.E.R.*

(*below*) For washout purposes there were four plugs on the right hand side of the firebox, supplemented on the left side by three plugs pitched opposite the spaces on the other side. Until about 1929 all the plugs had cover plates but the last five boilers built in 1928 did not have covers fitted. *L.N.E.R.*

8870

To traffic 4/1902.

REPAIRS:
Str. 3/2—8/6/09.**G**.
Str. 5/1—15/6/17.**G**.
Str. 25/3—29/6/20.**G**.
Str. ?/?—3/22.**G**.
Str. 25/10/23—14/4/24.**G**.
Rebuilt to D15.
Superheated boiler fitted.
Vacuum brake added.
Str. 9/3—23/7/26.**G**.
Str. 15/3—22/6/28.**G**.
Altered to D15/2.
Coal guard on tender.
Str. 9/1—1/4/31.**G**.
Str. 14/4—4/6/32.**H**.
Str. 2/1—10/2/33.**G**.
Str. 11/2—10/5/35.**G**.
Reb. to D16/3 (D14/2 to 5/36).
Str. 21/12/36—5/2/37.**G**.
Str. 3/3—6/5/39.**G**.
Str. 2/10—9/12/42.**G**.
Str. 24/9—21/10/44.**G**.
Str. 1—13/4/45.**L**.
Str. 25/11/45—5/1/46.**G**.
Str. 11/8—5/10/47.**G**.
Str. 20/6—20/8/49.**G**.
Str. 12/9—17/10/51.**G**.
Str. 7/3—8/4/54.**G**.
Str. 17—28/6/55.**C/L**.
Str. 9/4—26/5/56.**G**.

BOILERS:
1870.
1870 *(new)* 8/6/09.
1861 *(ex8861)* 15/6/17.
1878 *(ex-spare)* 29/6/20.
3660 *(new)* 14/4/24.
3262 *(new)* 1/4/31.
3679 *(ex8871)* 10/2/33.
4222 *(new)* 10/5/35.
4208 *(ex8814)* 5/2/37.
4200 *(exJ19 8146)* 6/5/39.
4206 *(ex8854)* 9/12/42.
4228 *(exJ19 8140)* 21/10/44.
4223 *(ex8821)* 5/1/46.
4202 *(ex8843)* 5/10/47.
4222 *(ex8821)* 20/8/49.
23366 *(ex ?)* 17/10/51.
23346 *(ex8841)* 8/4/54.
23454 *(ex8808)* 26/5/56.

SHEDS:
Ipswich.
Norwich 17/2/25.
Ipswich 13/3/25.
Colchester *by* 6/31.
Norwich 18/7/34.
Yarmouth 19/1/35.
Norwich 7/2/35.
Melton Constable 19/8/45.

Norwich 30/9/45.
Melton Constable 4/11/45.
Norwich 20/11/45.
Yarmouth 7/7/46.
Norwich 4/5/47.
Yarmouth 22/6/47.
Cambridge 5/4/53.
King's Lynn 6/1/57.
Cambridge 7/4/57.
King's Lynn 16/6/57.

RENUMBERED:
8870 4/24.
7740 9/12/42.
2521 17/3/46.
62521 20/8/49.

CONDEMNED: 10/2/58.
Cut up at Stratford.

8871

To traffic 4/1902.

REPAIRS:
Str. ?/?—6/09.**G**.
Str. 9/5—12/12/18.**G**.
Str. 9/4—22/7/20.**G**.
Str. 31/3—1/7/22.**G**.
Str. 16/11/23—29/4/24.**G**.
Rebuilt to D15.
Superheated boiler fitted.
Vacuum brake added.
Str. 17/11/25—17/2/26.**G**.
Str. 12/8—29/10/27.**G**.
Coal guard on tender.
Str. 19/4—25/7/29.**G**.
Altered to D15/2.
Str. 5/11—30/12/32.**G**.
Str. 22/6—1/8/34.**G**.
Str. 23/4—19/6/36.**G**.
Str. 5/3—13/5/38.**G**.
Rebuilt to D16/3.
Str. 7/12/40—30/1/41.**G**.
Str. 6—16/4/43.**L**.
Str. 23/10—8/12/43.**G**.
Str. 11/6—27/7/45.**G**.
Str. 4/3—6/5/47.**G**.
Str. 6/2—2/4/49.**G**.
Str. 15/4—26/5/51.**G**.
Str. 8/3—23/5/53.**C/H**.
Str. 21/9—14/11/53.**H/I**.
Str. 31/12/54—20/1/55.**N/C**.
Str. 24/4—9/6/56.**G**.

BOILERS:
1871.
1871 *(new)* 6/09.
1888 *(ex8888)* 12/12/18.
1864 *(ex8864)* 22/7/20.
3661 *(new)* 29/4/24.
3679 *(new)* 29/10/27.
3259 *(ex8877)* 30/12/32.
3263 *(ex8889)* 1/8/34.

4218 *(ex8821)* 13/5/38.
4221 *(exJ19 8261)* 30/1/41.
4204 *(exJ19 8261)* 8/12/43.
4222 *(ex8836)* 27/7/45.
4206 *(ex8874)* 6/5/47.
4334 *(ex8818)* 2/4/49.
23450 *(new)* 26/5/51.
23303 *(ex8781)* 9/6/56.

SHEDS:
Colchester.
Stratford 25/9/39.
Colchester 13/11/39.
Stratford 2/1/43.
Colchester 18/11/44.
Norwich 18/8/45.
Yarmouth Beach 19/7/46.
Norwich 27/10/46.
King's Lynn 8/1/56.
Cambridge 8/6/58.

RENUMBERED:
8871 4/24.
2522 23/6/46.
62522 2/4/49.

CONDEMNED: 4/8/58.
Cut up at Stratford.

8872

To traffic 4/1902.

REPAIRS:
Str. 21/9—29/11/10.**G**.
Str. 1/5—29/11/18.**G**.
Str. 30/3—4/7/22.**G**.
Str. 29/10/23—28/3/24.**G**.
Rebuilt to D15.
Superheated boiler fitted.
Vacuum brake added.
Str. 13/11/25—23/3/26.**G**.
Str. 13/1—28/4/28.**G**.
Altered to D15/2.
Coal guard on tender.
Str. 28/9—7/12/29.**G**.
Str. 5/12/31—13/2/32.**G**.
Str. 2/11/33—4/1/34.**G**.
Str. 19/9—6/11/35.**G**.
Str. 10/9—5/11/37.**G**.
Str. 13/1—3/5/40.**G**.
Rebuilt to D16/3.
Str. 30/11/42—22/2/43.**G**.
Str. 8/4—4/5/45.**G**.
Str. 1—6/1/48.**N/C**.
Tablet apparatus fitted.
Str. 4/4—12/5/48.**G**.
Str. 8—9/6/48.**N/C**.
Str. 25/10—17/12/49.**G**.
Str. 20/1—23/2/52.**G**.
W.P.U. gear removed.
Str. 20/6—7/8/54.**G**.
Str. 14/8/56. *Not repaired.*

BOILERS:
1872.
1872 *(new)* 29/11/10.
1887 *(ex8887)* 29/11/18.
1886 *(ex8886)* 4/7/22.
3659 *(new)* 28/3/24.
3682 *(new)* 28/4/28.
3674 *(ex8865)* 13/2/32.
3676 *(ex8893)* 4/1/34.
3257 *(ex8899)* 6/11/35.
4309 *(new)* 3/5/40.
4298 *(ex8837)* 22/2/43.
4319 *(ex8884)* 4/5/45.
4277 *(ex8787)* 12/5/48.
4252 *(ex8817)* 17/12/49.
23314 *(exJ19 8147)* 23/2/52.
23352 *(ex8839)* 7/8/54.

SHEDS:
Stratford.
Southend 4/1/30.
Stratford 8/2/30.
Southend 22/2/30.
Stratford 22/3/30.
Southend 26/7/30.
Stratford 9/8/30.
Parkeston 16/1/43.
Colchester 7/6/47.
Melton Constable 7/1/48.
Norwich 9/3/52.

RENUMBERED:
1872E 28/3/24.
8872 ?/25.
2523 15/6/46.
62523 8/5/48.

CONDEMNED: 27/8/56.
Cut up at Stratford.

8873

To traffic 4/1902.

REPAIRS:
Str. ?/?—?/6/10.**G**.
Str. 6/12/18—2/7/19.**G**.
Str. 3/12/20—22/2/21.**G**.
Str. 31/8/22—24/1/23.**G**.
Str. 16/5—9/9/24.**G**.
Str. 18/3—21/7/26.**G**.
Str. 17/2—12/5/28.**G**.
Coal guard on tender.
Str. 22/2—12/3/29.**N/C**.
Vacuum brake added.
Str. 2/11/29—18/1/30.**G**.
Rebuilt to D15 Saturated.
Str. 26/1—9/3/33.**G**.
Altered to D15/2.
Superheated boiler fitted.
Str. 4/3—2/5/35.**G**.
Str. 15—18/6/36.**L**.
Str. 5/4—14/5/37.**G**.
Str. 28/3—22/6/39.**G**.

Rebuilt to D16/3.
Str. 16/6—25/7/42.**G.**
Str. 25/6—17/8/44.**G.**
Str. 28/9—17/10/44.**L.**
Str. 2/12/45—5/1/46.**G.**
Str. 20/2—17/3/47.**L.**
Str. 18/1—17/3/48.**G.**
Str. 22/11—30/12/50.**G.**
Str. 22/7—22/8/53.**G.**
Str. 28/10—20/11/54.**C/L.**
Str. 14/12/55—25/2/56.**G.**
Str. 14/8—14/9/56.**C/L.**

BOILERS:
 1873.
 1873 *(new)* ?/6/10.
 1865 *(ex8865)* 2/7/19.
 3251 *(ex8892)* 22/2/21.
 3252 *(ex8884)* 24/1/23.
 1863 *(ex8865)* 21/7/26.
 1892 *(ex8877)* 12/5/28.
 3614 *(ex8861)* 18/1/30.
 3616 *(ex8866)* 9/3/33.
 3663 *(ex8893)* 2/5/35.
 3255 *(ex8898)* 14/5/37.
 4291 *(new)* 22/6/39.
 4257 *(exJ19 8244)* 25/7/42.
 4333 *(new)* 17/8/44.
 4324 *(exJ19 8246)* 5/1/46.
 4294 *(ex8788)* 17/3/48.
 23323 *(ex8885)* 30/12/50.
 23348 *(ex8824)* 22/8/53.
 23418 *(exJ19 8267)* 25/2/56.

SHEDS:
 Ipswich.
 Norwich 24/5/27.
 Yarmouth ?/?
 Lowestoft 20/7/30.
 Norwich 17/8/30.
 Lowestoft 13/5/33.
 Norwich 27/1/34.
 Yarmouth 5/5/34.
 Norwich 9/6/34.
 Yarmouth 22/3/36.
 Norwich 12/2/39.
 Yarmouth 8/2/42.
 Norwich 23/3/42.
 Yarmouth 1/4/42.
 Norwich 7/6/42.
 Yarmouth 11/11/45.
 Yarmouth Beach 22/6/58.
 Norwich 25/1/59.

RENUMBERED:
 8873 9/24.
 2524 23/6/46.
 E2524 17/3/48
 62524 30/12/50.

CONDEMNED: 10/3/60.
Cut up at Stratford.

8874

To traffic 4/1902.

REPAIRS:
Str. ?/?—?/12/08.**G.**
Str. 1/11/18—6/6/19.**G.**
Rebuilt to D15.
Superheated boiler fitted.
Str. 9/9/21—10/3/22.**G.**
Str. 22/5—22/10/24.**G.**
Str. 14/10—11/11/25.**L.**
Str. 24—30/4/26. *Not repaired.*
Go. 1/5—30/9/26.**G.**
Str. 14/3—18/7/28.**G.**
Vacuum brake added.
Coal guard on tender.
Str. 5/3—14/5/30.**G.**
Str. 19/1—24/4/31.**G.**
Str. 7/10—8/12/32.**G.**
Altered to D15/2.
Str. 18/9—25/10/34.**G.**
B17 tender axleboxes fitted.
Str. 31/3—16/5/36.**G.**
Str. 22/2—2/6/38.**G.**
Rebuilt to D16/3.
Str. 25/1—9/3/40.**G.**
Str. 13/8—9/10/42.**G.**
Str. 27/9—5/11/43.**G.**
Str. 8/4—5/5/45.**G.**
Str. 12/2—22/3/46.**L.**
Str. 23/8—6/10/46.**L.**
Str. 25/2—2/8/47.**G.**
Str. 26/3—14/5/49.**G.**
Str. 6/2—9/3/51.**G.**
Str. 21/6—21/7/51.**C/L.**
Str. 30/7—22/8/51.**C/L.**
Str. 10/12/52—3/1/53.**C/L.**
Str. 25/10—5/12/53.**G.**
Str. 12/9/55. *Not repaired.*

BOILERS:
 1874.
 1874 *(new)* 12/08.
 3591 *(new)* 6/6/19.
 3590 *(ex8860)* 22/10/24.
 3616 *(exJ17 8188)* 18/7/28.
 3661 *(ex8879)* 14/5/30.
 3659 *(ex8869)* 8/12/32.
 3254 *(ex8877)* 25/10/34.
 3610 *(ex8897)* 16/5/36.
 4207 *(ex8802)* 2/6/38.
 4209 *(ex8866)* 9/3/40.
 4207 *(ex8862)* 9/10/42.
 4216 *(ex8868)* 5/11/43.
 4206 *(ex8870)* 5/5/45.
 4210 *(ex8868)* 2/8/47.
 4251 *(ex8805)* 14/5/49.
 23334 *(ex ?)* 9/3/51.
 23393 *(exJ19 8142)* 5/12/53.

SHEDS:
 Ipswich.
 Stratford 25/10/24.

Cambridge 20/11/26.
Lincoln 20/7/30.
Peterborough East 17/10/32.
Cambridge 4/2/37.
South Lynn 31/10/48.
King's Lynn 9/11/48.
Cambridge 16/1/49.
King's Lynn 13/4/52.
Cambridge 26/10/52.

RENUMBERED:
 1874E ?/?/?
 8874 10/24.
 2525 16/3/46.
 62525 14/5/49.

CONDEMNED: 19/9/55.
Cut up at Stratford.

8875

To traffic 5/1902.

REPAIRS:
Str. ?/?—?/12/09.**G.**
Str. 4/3—7/5/21.**G.**
Str. 6/3—25/6/24.**G.**
Vacuum brake added.
Str. 6/11/25—28/5/26.**G.**
Str. 22/11/27—27/1/28.**L.**
Str. 22/9/28—3/1/29.**G.**
Coal guard on tender.
Str. 23/2—29/5/30.**G.**
Str. 26/1—27/3/31.**G.**
Rebuilt to D15/2.
Superheated boiler fitted.
Str. 2/1—15/2/33.**G.**
Str. 7/1—19/4/34.**G.**
Str. 28/7—16/9/35.**G.**
Str. 4—7/5/36.**L.**
Str. 18—28/7/36.**G.**
Str. 24/5—19/8/37.**G.**
Rebuilt to D16/3.
Str. 4/12/39—10/2/40.**G.**
Str. 7/2—26/3/43.**G.**
Str. 13/5—7/6/44.**L.**
Str. 21/7—1/9/45.**G.**
Str. 24/7—12/9/46.**L.**
Str. 4/1—28/2/48.**G.**
Str. 10/6—9/7/48.**L.**
Str. 31/5—20/7/50.**G.**
Str. 27/4—28/5/52.**G.**
Str. 3/8—11/9/54.**G.**
Str. 22/6—27/7/56.**G.**

BOILERS:
 1875.
 1875 *(new)* ?/12/09.
 1865 *(ex8873)* 7/5/21.
 1897 *(ex8893)* 25/6/24.
 3251 *(ex8868)* 28/5/26.
 1863 *(ex8873)* 3/1/29.
 3253 *(ex8865)* 9/5/30.
 3260 *(new)* 27/3/31.

3661 *(ex8874)* 15/2/33.
3637 *(ex8881)* 19/4/34.
3261 *(ex8895)* 16/9/35.
1269 *(ex8894)* 28/7/36.
4223 *(exJ19 8245)* 19/8/37.
4220 *(ex8854)* 10/2/40.
4320 *(new)* 26/3/43.
4271 *(ex8803)* 1/9/45.
4258 *(ex8795)* 28/2/48.
4344 *(new)* 20/7/50.
23350 *(ex8783)* 28/5/52.
23413 *(ex8835)* 11/9/54.

SHEDS:
Stratford.
Southend 15/2/30.
Stratford 22/2/30.
Southend 14/6/30.
Stratford 21/6/30.
Ipswich 27/3/31.
March 7/6/53.

RENUMBERED:
 8875 25/6/24.
 2526 29/8/46.
 E2526 28/2/48
 62526 9/7/48.

CONDEMNED: 21/5/57.
Cut up at Stratford.

8876

To traffic 5/1902.

REPAIRS:
Str. 11/4—27/7/10.**G.**
Str. 17/8/18—4/4/19.**G.**
Str. 23/3—17/6/22.**G.**
Str. 27/10/23—20/2/24.**G.**
Str. 20/12/24—10/6/25.**G.**
Str. 29/4—27/8/27.**G.**
Vacuum brake added.
Str. ?/?—14/9/27.**N/C.**
Str. 5/4—14/6/29.**G.**
Rebuilt to D15/2.
Superheated boiler fitted.
Coal guard on tender.
Str. 12/2—14/4/31.**G.**
Str. 30/3—26/5/33.**G.**
Str. 10/1—22/3/35.**G.**
Rebuilt to D16/3 (14/2 to 5/36).
Str. 27/1—14/2/36.**L.**
Str. 4/10—6/11/36.**G.**
Str. 20/11/38—9/1/39.**G.**
Str. 17/10—7/12/40.**G.**
Str. 20/8—16/10/42.**G.**
Str. 9/1—16/2/44.**L.**
Str. 1/10—2/11/44.**G.**
Str. 5/5—27/6/46.**G.**
Str. 28/9—20/10/46.**L.**
Str. 21/5—7/8/48.**G.**
Dn. 5/3—12/4/49.**C/L.**
Str. 23/3—21/4/50.**C/L.**

Although the smokebox door with strengthening ring had been introduced in 1901, and only the eleven built in 1900 seem to have had hinge straps, one such door was still in use on no.8866 to at least March 1926. Even this door had the top lamp iron moved onto it. All others in this class were noted as having door with strengthening ring which was usually kept well burnished until black paint took over. *H.Gordon Tidey.*

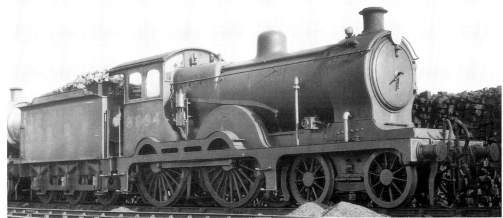

The original chimney had a brass cap to it and this was often well polished, as were the splasher beadings. Where a replacement chimney was needed after Grouping a plain straight sided type was fitted. 8854 is at Yarmouth South Town, October 1932. *Photomatic.*

Until 1924 the majority just had Westinghouse brake both for engine and for train working. At the front end there was usually a connection for carriage heating fitted below the buffer beam. By Grouping seventeen in this class were dual fitted having had vacuum ejector added for train braking. More were fitted in 1924 and again during 1926-27. Under the 1928 Unification of Brakes programme all the others became dual braked. The last to be fitted, on 29th March 1930, was no.8820 whilst still saturated.

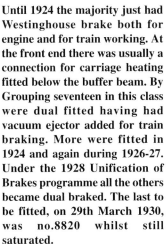

All, except nos.8891 to 8896 and 8898, which had the 'Watercart' type, had the standard tender (8898's 'Watercart' had been rebuilt to conventional type in 1926) but it was not until 1926 that coal guards began to be fitted, all had these by March 1930. Note this is one of the few on which Iracier axleboxes were tried, shown by the shield shaped covers. There was some swapping with the 'Watercart' type - between November 1923 and February 1925, no.8897 exchanged its tender rebuilt in 1919 for 1899ᴇ's 'Watercart'.

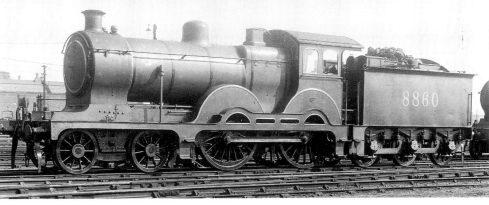

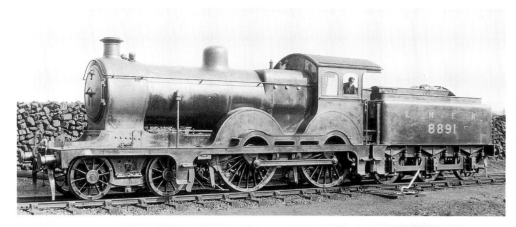

8891 with its 'Watercart' type tender. Southend shed, 24th August 1929.

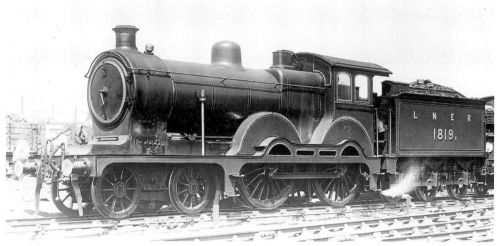

Four of the class got the Area suffix 'E' but with LNER (1862ᴇ 7th December 1923; 1819ᴇ 18th January 1924; 1869ᴇ 5th February 1924; 1872ᴇ 28th March 1924) whilst others, such as 1839ᴇ, ex works 3rd November 1923, had the L&NER with ampersand. The inclusion of the ampersand lasted much longer at Stratford than at other works hence the reason why 1839 got it so late. *W.J.Reynolds.*

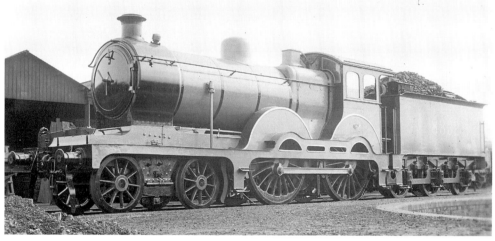

The green livery was not at first applied to all this class, nos.8832, 8855 and 8860 continuing in unlined grey at least into 1926.

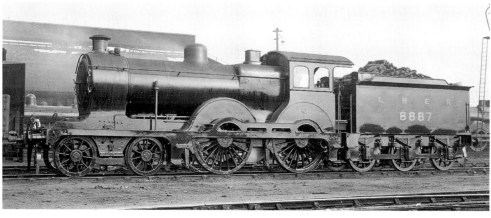

Lined green livery became the normal standard until June 1928 when the painting economies decreed black with single red lining for this class. The number was still carried on the tender and this was to be so for at least another year.

8876 cont.
Str. 4/9—7/10/50.**G.**
Str. 24/6/52. *Not repaired.*

BOILERS:
1876.
1876 *(new)* 27/7/10.
1892 *(ex8892)* 4/4/19.
3253 *(ex8869)* 17/6/22.
1862 *(ex8878)* 10/6/25.
3255 *(new)* 14/6/29.
3586 *(ex8885)* 26/5/33.
4229 *(new)* 22/3/35.
4224 *(ex8804)* 6/11/36.
4249 *(exJ19 8253)* 9/1/39.
4281 *(ex8788)* 7/12/40.
4255 *(ex8869)* 16/10/42.
4318 *(ex8880)* 2/11/44.
4332 *(ex8827)* 27/6/46.
4314 *(ex8827)* 7/8/48.
23307 *(ex ?)* 7/10/50.

SHEDS:
Cambridge.
Ipswich 13/3/26.
Cambridge 10/4/26.

RENUMBERED:
1876ᴇ 20/2/24.
8876 10/6/25.
2527 19/6/46.
62527 7/8/48.

CONDEMNED: 7/7/52.
Cut up at Stratford.

8877

To traffic 5/1902.

REPAIRS:
Str. 18/1—18/6/09.**G.**
Str. 19/2—20/5/14.**G.**
Str. 17/8/17—28/3/18.**G.**
Str. 29/9/22—23/4/23.**G.**
Str. 3/11/24—25/3/25.**G.**
Str. 9/3—2/7/26.**G.**
Str. 11/11/27—2/2/28.**G.**
Rebuilt to D15/2.
Superheated boiler fitted.
Coal guard on tender.
Str. 22/6—3/10/29.**G.**
Vacuum brake added.
Str. 8/12/30—17/2/31.**G.**
Str. 22/5—22/7/32.**G.**
Str. 15/5—29/6/34.**G.**
Str. 20/2—27/3/36.**G.**
Str. 17—20/5/36.**L.**
Str. 31/1—3/3/38.**G.**
Str. 22/1—7/6/40.**G.**
Str. 25/6—11/9/42.**G.**
Str. 1/1—20/2/43.**L.**
Str. 15/10—2/12/44.**G.**
Str. 29/12/44—19/1/45.**L.**

Str. 12—25/5/45.**L.**
Str. 3/4—20/6/46.**G.**
Str. 18/9—25/10/48.**G.**
Str. 6/6/51. *Not repaired.*

BOILERS:
1877.
1877 *(new)* 18/6/09.
3252 *(new)* 20/5/14.
1894 *(ex8894)* 28/3/18.
1892 *(ex8876)* 23/4/23.
3663 *(ex8894)* 2/2/28.
3259 *(new)* 17/2/31.
3254 *(ex8890)* 22/7/32.
3678 *(ex8886)* 29/6/34.
3631 *(exJ17 8184)* 27/3/36.
3261 *(ex8862)* 3/3/38.
3257 *(ex8872)* 7/6/40.
3423 *(exJ17 8226)* 20/6/46.
3519 *(new)* 25/10/48.

SHEDS:
Norwich.
Peterborough East 18/11/29.
Norwich 1/7/36.
Melton Constable 29/1/39.
Yarmouth Beach 1/4/41.
Norwich 13/1/42.
Yarmouth 23/2/46.
Norwich 6/3/46.
Yarmouth 4/10/46.
Norwich 19/10/46.
Melton Constable 18/12/46.
Yarmouth Beach 20/4/47.
Melton Constable 13/5/47.

RENUMBERED:
8877 ?/?/24.
2528 7/6/46.
62528 23/10/48.

CONDEMNED: 25/6/51.
Cut up at Stratford.

8878

To traffic 5/1902.

REPAIRS:
Str. ?/?—?/6/09.**G.**
Str. 2/2—11/6/15.**G.**
Str. 11/2—4/5/21.**G.**
Str. 13/10/22—15/2/23.**G.**
Str. 28/2—19/6/24.**G.**
Str. 12/10/25—28/1/26.**G.**
Str. 27/4—23/7/27.**G.**
Str. ?/?—20/3/29.**G.**
Rebuilt to D15 saturated.
Coal guard on tender.
Str. 7/5—11/7/31.**G.**
Altered to D15/2.
Superheated boiler fitted.
Str. 20/2—31/3/33.**G.**
Str. 21/1—3/5/35.**G.**

Rebuilt to D16/3 (14/2 to 5/36).
Str. 1/2—12/3/37.**G.**
Str. 21/3—18/5/39.**G.**
Str. 31/8—14/10/41.**G.**
Str. 12/12/43—28/1/44.**G.**
Str. 27/1—10/2/45.**L.**
Str. 4/11—1/12/45.**G.**
Str. 4—21/6/46.**L.**
Str. 10/1—3/3/48.**G.**
Str. 26/10—26/11/49.**C/L.**
Str. 3/3—22/4/50.**G.**
Str. 20/11/51—11/1/52.**G.**
W.P.U. gear removed.
Str. 6/3—10/4/54.**G.**
Str. 29/8—19/10/56.**G.**
Str. 17—20/12/57.**N/C.**
Tender change only.

BOILERS:
1878.
1878 *(new)* ?/6/09.
1867 *(ex8867)* 11/6/15.
1890 *(ex8868)* 4/5/21.
1862 *(ex8892)* 15/2/23.
1864 *(ex8871)* 19/6/24.
3252 *(ex8873)* 23/7/27.
3618 *(ex8884)* 20/3/29.
3589 *(ex8899)* 11/7/31.
3660 *(ex8870)* 31/3/33.
4220 *(new)* 3/5/35.
4213 *(ex8855)* 12/3/37.
4205 *(ex8855)* 18/5/39.
4217 *(exJ19 8245)* 14/10/41.
4207 *(ex8874)* 28/1/44.
4216 *(ex8874)* 1/12/45.
4212 *(ex8802)* 3/3/48.
4223 *(ex8802)* 22/4/50.
4223 reno.23379 11/1/52.
23460 *(new)* 10/4/54.
23452 *(exJ19 8268)* 19/10/56.

SHEDS:
Norwich.
Yarmouth 9/10/28.
Lowestoft 30/10/28.
Norwich 28/4/29.
Yarmouth 13/7/30.
Norwich 19/7/31.
Yarmouth 20/10/34.
Norwich 22/12/34.
Yarmouth 29/1/38.
Norwich 11/3/38.
Yarmouth 3/4/38.
Norwich 12/3/39.
Yarmouth 13/8/39
Norwich 19/5/40.
Yarmouth 12/11/44.
Norwich 17/12/44.
Yarmouth 30/12/45.
Norwich 23/2/46.
Yarmouth 29/6/47.
Melton Constable 13/8/47.
Norwich 5/10/47.
March 16/10/49.

RENUMBERED:
8878 ?/6/24.
2529 23/6/46.
ᴇ**2529** 3/3/48.
62529 22/4/50.

CONDEMNED: 23/11/59.
Cut up at Stratford.

8879

To traffic 6/1902.

REPAIRS:
Str. 29/12/08—28/4/09.**G.**
Str. 8/1—22/4/14.**G.**
Str. 7/12/17—12/7/18.**G.**
Str. 17/2—2/6/22.**G.**
Str. 30/1—30/5/23.**G.**
Str. 3/5—30/7/24.**G.**
Str. 7/9/25—12/2/26.**G.**
Str. 6/10—31/12/27.**G.**
Rebuilt to D15/2.
Superheated boiler fitted.
Coal guard on tender.
Str. 22/6—22/8/29.**G.**
Str. 2/5—23/6/32.**G.**
Str. 14/3—8/6/34.**G.**
Str. 18/3—24/4/36.**G.**
Str. 11—18/6/36.**L.**
Str. 28/2—29/4/38.**G.**
Rebuilt to D16/3.
Str. 23/5—10/6/39.**G.**
Str. 4/3—27/4/40.**G.**
Str. 2/2—1/3/41.**L.**
Str. 10/5—24/7/43.**G.**
Str. 14/1—21/2/45.**G.**
Str. 27/6—14/9/46.**G.**
Str. 19/9—28/10/48.**G.**
Str. 22/10—18/11/50.**G.**
Str. 26/3—17/4/52.**C/L.**
Str. 18/9—25/10/52.**G.**
Str. 17/5—12/6/54.**G.**
Str. 20/4—1/6/56.**G.**

BOILERS:
1879.
1879 *(new)* 28/4/09.
3251 *(new)* 22/4/14.
1880 *(ex8880)* 12/7/18.
1899 *(ex8899)* 2/6/22.
3661 *(ex8871)* 31/12/27.
3634 *(ex8882)* 22/8/29.
1269 *(exJ18 8248)* 23/6/32.
3624 *(ex8799)* 8/6/34.
3678 *(ex8877)* 24/4/36.
4202 *(ex8848)* 29/4/38.
4219 *(ex8823)* 27/4/40.
4215 *(exJ19 8245)* 24/7/43.
4211 *(ex8848)* 21/2/45.
4213 *(ex8866)* 14/9/46.
4229 *(ex8786)* 28/10/48.
23316 *(ex ?)* 18/11/50.
23415 *(ex ?)* 25/10/52.

23404 (ex8838) 12/6/54.
23424 (ex8825) 1/6/56.

SHEDS:
Norwich.
Peterborough East 15/9/32.
Norwich 30/6/36.
Yarmouth 1/8/37.
Norwich 12/5/38.
Yarmouth 25/9/38.
Norwich 7/5/40.
Yarmouth 5/3/41.
Norwich 18/5/41.
Yarmouth 23/11/41.
Norwich 7/12/41.
Yarmouth 9/1/44.
Norwich 2/12/45.
Yarmouth 10/12/45.
Stratford 7/10/46.
Cambridge 12/11/47.
King's Lynn 2/10/49.
Cambridge 31/10/49.
March 24/11/57.

RENUMBERED:
8879 ?/7/24.
2530 23/6/46.
62530 23/10/48.

CONDEMNED: 22/9/58.
Cut up at Stratford.

8860

To traffic 5/1903.

REPAIRS:
Str. 29/12/11—26/3/12.**G**.
Str. 31/1—4/6/19.**G**.
Rebuilt to D15.
Superheated boiler fitted.
Str. 2/10—16/12/22.**G**.
Str. 19/2—24/6/24.**G**.
Vacuum brake added.
Str. 15/8—1/9/24.**L**.
Str. 31/3—31/7/26.**G**.
Str. 2/3—2/6/28.**G**.
Altered to D15/2.
Coal guard on tender.
Str. 20/2—24/4/30.**G**.
Str. 17/3—3/6/32.**G**.
Str. 26/3—21/6/34.**G**.
Rebuilt to D16/3 (14/2 to 5/36).
Str. 6—31/10/34.**L**.
Str. 26/3—29/5/36.**G**.
Str. 10/9—22/10/37.**G**.
Str. 28/12/39—12/3/40.**G**.
Str. 31/7—16/8/41.**L**.
Str. 3/8—2/10/42.**G**.
Str. 5/11—5/12/44.**G**.
Str. 19/7—1/10/46.**G**.

Str. 23/8—16/9/47.**C/L**.
Str. 22/6—28/8/48.**G**.
Str. 9/2—31/3/50.**G**.
Str. 4/8—2/9/50.**C/L**.
Str. 10/2—15/3/52.**G**.
W.P.U. gear removed.
Str. 25/9—7/11/53.**G**.

BOILERS:
1860.
1860 *(new)* 26/3/12.
3590 *(new)* 4/6/19.
3588 *(ex8888)* 24/6/24.
3636 *(ex8880)* 2/6/28.
4202 *(ex8866)* 21/6/34.
4206 *(ex8821)* 29/5/36.
4216 *(ex8869)* 22/10/37.
4232 *(ex8816)* 12/3/40.
4236 *(ex8865)* 2/10/42.
4269 *(ex8835)* 5/12/44.
4233 *(ex8851)* 1/10/46.
4239 *(ex8810)* 28/8/48.
4342 *(new)* 31/3/50.
23392 *(ex ?)* 15/3/52.
23371 *(exJ19 8267)* 7/11/53.

SHEDS:
Stratford.
Norwich 3/10/25.
Stratford 12/10/25.
Cambridge 2/6/28.
March 25/6/28.
Cambridge 29/3/31.
King's Lynn 21/3/43
Cambridge 8/8/43.

RENUMBERED:
8860 ?/6/24.
2531 2/6/46.
62531 28/8/48.

CONDEMNED: 21/3/55.
Cut up at Stratford.

8861

To traffic 6/1903.

REPAIRS:
Str. 19/10/12—10/4/13.**G**.
Str. 8/8/16—21/2/17.**G**.
Str. 2/9—23/11/21.**G**.
Rebuilt to D15 saturated.
Str. 24/4—7/7/23.**G**.
Str. 27/11/24—23/5/25.**G**.
Str. 25/2—23/6/27.**G**.
Vacuum brake added.
Str. 7/8—1/11/29.**G**.
Altered to D15/2.
Superheated boiler fitted.
Coal guard on tender.

Str. 22/9—20/11/31.**G**.
Str. 1/1—14/2/34.**G**.
Str. 9/3—21/3/34.**L**.
Str. 1/2—24/4/36.**G**.
Rebuilt to D16/3 (14/2 to 5/36).
Str. 22/8—4/9/36.**L**.
Str. 15—16/7/37.**L**.
Str. 29/8—8/10/37.**G**.
Str. 20/1—22/2/39.**L**.
Str. 21/4—6/5/39.**L**.
Str. 3/12/39—9/2/40.**G**.
Str. 11/2—27/4/43.**G**.
Str. 9/3—14/4/45.**G**.
Str. 1/10—12/11/46.**G**.
Dn. 5/5—16/7/48.**G**.
Str. 4—30/4/49.**C/L**.
Str. 4—17/11/49.**C/L**.
Str. 15/3—28/4/51.**G**.
Str. 7—17/10/53.**C/L**.
Str. 12—19/1/54.**C/L**.
Str. 7/9—23/10/54.**G**.
Str. 4—17/11/54.**N/C**.
Str. 3/4—18/5/56.**C/L**.
Str. 30/10/56. *Not repaired.*

BOILERS:
1861.
1861 *(new)* 10/4/13.
1881 *(ex8881)* 21/2/17.
3614 *(new)* 23/11/21.
3617 *(ex8886)* 1/11/29.
3584 *(ex8893)* 20/11/31.
3674 *(ex8872)* 14/2/34.
4244 *(new)* 24/4/36.
4234 *(exJ19 8252)* 8/10/37.
4237 *(ex8865)* 9/2/40.
4232 *(ex8860)* 27/4/43.
4255 *(ex8876)* 14/4/45.
4262 *(ex8857)* 12/11/46.
23342 *(ex ?)* 28/4/51.
23417 *(ex8820)* 23/10/54.

SHEDS:
Stratford.
Cambridge 24/6/27.
Stratford 4/5/36.
Colchester 10/3/40.
Stratford 8/9/40.
Trafford Park 11/6/50.
Cambridge 8/6/52.
Pbo (Spital Bridge) 12/10/52.
Cambridge 13/9/53.

RENUMBERED:
8861 ?/?/??.
2532 30/9/46.
62532 16/7/48.

CONDEMNED: 12/11/56.
Cut up at Stratford.

8862

To traffic 6/1903.

REPAIRS:
Str. 29/5—19/9/13.**G**.
Str. 24/2—21/5/20.**G**.
Str. 16/8—7/12/23.**G**.
Rebuilt to D15.
Superheated boiler fitted.
Str. 2/5—14/8/25.**G**.
Str. 3/3—26/5/27.**G**.
Vacuum brake added.
Str. 20/9—13/12/28.**G**.
Coal guard on tender.
Str. 21/3—23/5/30.**G**.
Altered to D15/2.
Str. 5/3—4/5/32.**G**.
Str. 27/12/33—1/2/34.**G**.
Str. 3/10—7/11/35.**G**.
Str. 6—10/7/36.**L**.
Str. 9—20/11/36.**H**.
Str. 2/1—5/2/38.**G**.
Str. 21/3—15/6/40.**G**.
Rebuilt to D16/3.
Str. 18/6—21/8/42.**G**.
Str. 13/11/43—15/1/44.**G**.
Str. 22/4—13/5/44.**L**.
Str. 19/11—9/12/44.**L**.
Str. 12/6—21/7/45.**G**.
Str. 1/3—21/5/47.**G**.
Str. 30/4—18/6/49.**G**.
Str. 24/6—8/9/50.**C/L**.
Str. 7/8—8/9/51.**G**.
Str. 17—22/9/51.**N/C**.
Str. 6—16/12/52.**C/L**.
Str. 21/4—27/5/54.**G**.
Str. 17/5—23/6/56.**C/L**.
Str. 7/9/57. *Not repaired.*

BOILERS:
1862.
1862 *(new)* 19/9/13.
1863 *(ex8863)* 21/5/20.
3577 *(ex8890)* 7/12/23.
3591 *(ex8882)* 26/5/27.
3588 *(ex8860)* 13/12/28.
3587 *(ex8881)* 4/5/32.
3585 *(ex8867)* 1/2/34.
3676 *(ex8872)* 7/11/35.
3261 *(ex8875)* 20/11/36.
3633 *(ex8897)* 5/2/38.
4207 *(ex8874)* 15/6/40.
4205 *(ex8878)* 21/8/42.
4224 *(ex8844)* 21/7/45.
4200 *(ex8814)* 21/5/47.
4226 *(ex8814)* 18/6/49.
4226 renum 23301 8/9/50.
23360 *(ex ?)* 8/9/51.
23462 *(new)* 27/5/54.

WORKS CODES:- Bd - Beardmore. Ca - Cambridge shed. Dn - Doncaster. Go - Gorton. Ips - Ipswich shed. Nr - Norwich shed. Str - Stratford.
REPAIR CODES:- **C/H** - Casual Heavy. **C/L** - Casual Light. **G** - General. **H** - Heavy. **H/I** - Heavy Intermediate. **L** - Light. **L/I** - Light Intermediate. **N/C** - Non-Classified.

When the number was applied to the cab, Stratford squeezed it between splasher beading and the side windows by means of using 9" shaded figures; although they did change to the standard 12" letters on the tender. No.8889 ex works 31st July 1929 had this style and is seen at Stratford 21st June 1931.

(centre) After deciding to dispense with the rear splasher beading and to move the number plate to the front splasher, Stratford could then adopt Group Standard style as on no.8899 here. This particular engine was a unique case but for a completely different reason however. After being a Part 2 engine from 5th July 1929 to 18th January 1933 it was ex works 13th April 1933 with a short smokebox thus reverting to Part 1. When it went into works 1st January 1935 it was the last example to have short smokebox and Part 1 was then extinct.

(below) Already superheated, no.8819 was ex works 27th January 1926 with its smokebox extended from the usual 3' 4¾" to 4' 10", as seen here on no.8848. Trials with the extended smokebox led to it being adopted as standard for all the engines with the 4' 9" diameter superheated boiler. Three more engines followed in 1927 and Part 2 was introduced for them. From no.8819 in January 1926 to no.8899 in March 1935, there were 58 rebuilt to Part 2 from Part 1. Ultimately some 80 engines were done in this style. *L.N.E.R.*

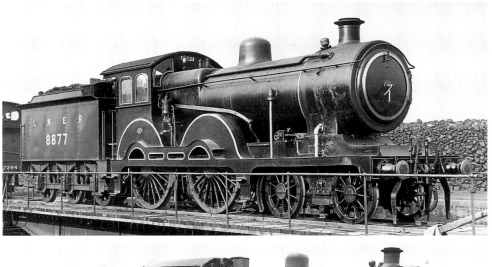

(left) Seven (nos.8865, 8868, 8875, 8876, 8877, 8879, 8881) became Part 2 by direct rebuilding from Class D14. No.8877 is seen here after general repair in October 1929 when it changed from green to black and vacuum brake was added. *W.L.Good.*

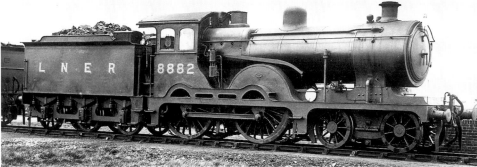

(second from top) Four washout plugs could be found on the left side with three more on the right opposite the spaces. All these plugs had covers at first, even those boilers built during the early years of the LNER but as time went on they gradually lost the covers. This 1924 built boiler on no.8882 (December 1934 to April 1936) had also lost the covers to the three plugs on the right hand side. The early conversions to Part 2 retained their chimney with brass cap but by 1929 the plain cast straight sided type was fitted as standard. *W.L.Good.*

(centre) Difficulties with steaming led to no.8836 being fitted in February 1930 (when it became Part 2) with the shorter variety of O2 class chimney with Doncaster pattern blast pipe and cowl. The chimney was also set 3⅝" further forward. 8836 reverted to GE type chimney in October 1935. However, in 1932 three more engines (nos.8811, 8855, 8798) had similar treatment. Then no.8799 got a GN chimney in 1934 but in 1935 when nos.8844 and 8872 also got GN chimney, their steeply sloping grate was made much flatter and this combination provided a satisfactory answer to the small coal and steaming problems. Having found the answer, Stratford then called in all Part 2 engines for fitting with GN O2 chimney (3½" taller than the LNER variety) and flatter grates, completing the process between 1st May and 10th July 1936. *W.L.Good.*

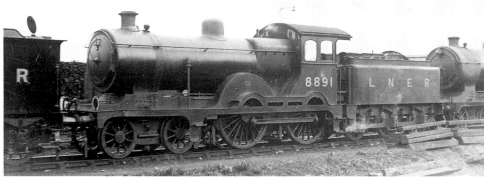

(second from bottom) Boilers built to 1925 had four-column Ramsbottom safety valves enclosed in a rectangular casing. Only the last eleven 4' 9" boilers (nos.3674 to 3685), built in 1926-28 had Ross 'pop' safety valves fitted.

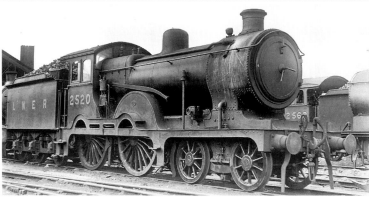

(left) For some curious reason the provision and fitting of sight screens on this class was very limited, and many never got this facility. When ex works 22nd May 1947, no.2520 (ex8889) was equipped with hinged glass sight screens, the only D15/2 so noted. However, no.8884 was recorded as being fitted with them at its 'general' repair in 1938.

8862 cont.
SHEDS:
Stratford.
Norwich 18/5/39.
Yarmouth Beach 23/6/39.
Melton Constable 22/10/39.
Norwich 23/7/40.
Yarmouth 24/11/40.
Yarmouth Beach 14/10/41.
Melton Constable 3/5/45.

RENUMBERED:
 1862ᴇ 7/12/23.
 8862 ?/?/25.
 2533 10/11/46.
 62533 18/6/49.

CONDEMNED: 23/9/57.
Cut up at Stratford.

8863

To traffic 6/1903.

REPAIRS:
Str. 14/4—12/6/13.**G.**
Str. 26/11/19—24/2/20.**G.**
Str. 23/8—9/12/21.**G.**
Rebuilt to D15 saturated.
Str. 24/11/22—29/3/23.**G.**
Str. 2/6—29/10/24.**G.**
Str. 9/3—18/6/26.**G.**
Superheated boiler fitted.
Str. 9/11/27—29/2/28.**G.**
Coal guard on tender.
Str. 6—20/4/29.**N/C.**
Vacuum brake added.
Str. 13/11/29—24/1/30.**G.**
Str. 8/4—29/5/31.**G.**
Str. 14/3—28/4/33.**G.**
Altered to D15/2.
Str. 5/1—6/4/35.**G.**
Rebuilt to D16/3 (14/2 to 5/36).
Str. 19/4—7/5/36.**L.**
Str. 31/10—11/12/36.**G.**
Str. 24/5—7/7/38.**G.**
Str. 12/12/40—6/2/41.**G.**
Str. 17/10—27/11/43.**G.**
Str. 24/3—28/4/44.**L.**
Str. 10/9—19/9/44.**L.**
Str. 25/12/44—17/2/45.**G.**
Str. 17/8—24/10/46.**G.**
Str. 27/10—18/12/48.**G.**
Str. 25/7—9/9/49.**C/L.**
Str. 20/9—20/10/51.**G.**
Str. 15/11—12/12/53.**G.**
Str. 29/1—16/3/56.**G.**

BOILERS:
 1863.
 1863 *(new)* 12/6/13.
 1882 *(ex8882)* 24/2/20.
 3615 *(new)* 9/12/21.
 3674 *(new)* 18/6/26.

3591 *(ex8862)* 24/1/30.
3663 *(ex8877)* 29/5/31.
3614 *(ex8873)* 28/4/33.
4228 *(new)* 6/4/35.
4229 *(ex8876)* 11/12/36.
4226 *(exJ19 8254)* 6/2/41.
4220 *(ex8875)* 27/11/43.
4211 *(ex8879)* 24/10/46.
4260 *(ex8869)* 18/12/48.
23370 *(ex ?)* 20/10/51.
23344 *(ex8780)* 12/12/53.
23319 *(ex8899)* 16/3/56.

SHEDS:
Norwich.
Stratford 18/6/26.
Ipswich 8/8/26.
Colchester ?/??
Stratford 24/1/30.
Colchester 12/11/39.
Stratford 10/3/40.
South Lynn 30/7/46.
King's Lynn 15/4/51.
Cambridge 7/4/57.
King's Lynn 18/8/57.
Cambridge 2/11/58.

RENUMBERED:
 8863 *after* 6/24.
 2534 1/12/46.
 62534 11/12/48.

CONDEMNED: 11/11/58.
Cut up at Stratford.

8864

To traffic 7/1903.

REPAIRS:
Str. 28/12/12—18/4/13.**G.**
Str. 28/11/19—17/4/20.**G.**
Str. 30/10/22—15/5/23.**G.**
Rebuilt to D15.
Superheated boiler fitted.
Str. 2/10—29/11/24.**G.**
Str. 11/3—23/7/26.**G.**
Str. 24/5/27. **L.**
Vacuum brake added.
Str. 13/1—3/5/28.**G.**
Coal guard on tender.
Str. 9/11/29—3/2/30.**G.**
Str. 2/1—2/3/32.**G.**
Altered to D15/2.
Str. 2/10—17/11/33.**G.**
Str. 3/3—26/4/35.**G.**
Str. 25—27/5/36.**L.**
Str. 16/8—22/10/36.**G.**
Rebuilt to D16/3.
Str. 8/6—7/7/37.**L.**
Str. 19/4—22/6/38.**G.**
Str. 8/4—25/5/40.**G.**
Str. 24/11/40—1/1/41.**L.**
Str. 23/5—31/7/43.**G.**

Str. 20—28/9/44.**L.**
Str. 21/5—20/6/45.**G.**
Str. 15/5—8/6/46.**L.**
Str. 17/11/46—10/1/47.**G.**
Str. 10/9—20/10/47.**H.**
Str. 1/7—20/8/48.**L.**
Str. 12/6—30/7/49.**G.**
Str. 11—13/10/49.**N/C.**
Str. 30/9—14/11/53.**G.**
Str. 21/4—17/6/55.**C/L.**
Str. 6/3—14/4/56.**G.**

BOILERS:
 1864.
 1864 *(new)* 18/4/13.
 1870 *(exJ16 8179)* 17/4/20.
 3635 *(new)* 15/5/23.
 3681 *(new)* 3/5/28.
 3680 *(ex8880)* 2/3/32.
 3256 *(ex8896)* 17/11/33.
 3660 *(ex8878)* 26/4/35.
 4248 *(new)* 22/10/36.
 4242 *(ex8900)* 25/5/40.
 4268 *(ex8859)* 31/7/43.
 4280 *(ex8887)* 20/6/45.
 4265 *(ex8886)* 10/1/47.
 4329 *(exJ19 8145)* 30/7/49.
 23357 *(exJ19 8265)* 14/11/53.
 23363 *(ex8841)* 14/4/56.

SHEDS:
Stratford.
Southend 16/8/30.
Stratford 23/8/30.
Norwich 6/8/35.
Yarmouth 25/6/47.
Norwich 2/7/47.
Gorton 19/10/49.
Trafford Park 21/10/49.
Cambridge 8/6/52.
Pbo. (Spital Bridge) 12/10/52.
Lincoln 24/3/57.

RENUMBERED:
 1864ᴇ ?/1/24.
 8864 29/11/24.
 2535 30/10/46.
 62535 20/8/48.

CONDEMNED: 25/11/57.
Cut up at Stratford.

8865

To traffic 9/1903.

REPAIRS:
Str. 5/10/11—2/2/12.**G.**
Str. 6/9/18—28/2/19.**G.**
Str. 25/9—22/12/20.**G.**
Str. 20/10/23—19/1/24.**G.**
Str. 19/11/25—22/5/26.**G.**
Coal guard on tender.
Str. 2/11/27—3/3/28.**G.**

Str. 24/9—2/10/28.**N/C.**
Vacuum brake added.
Str. 12/2—4/4/30.**G.**
Rebuilt to D15/2.
Superheated boiler fitted.
Str. 24/8—24/10/31.**G.**
Str. 22—26/8/32.**L.**
Str. 4/9—12/10/33.**G.**
Str. 25/10—5/12/34.**G.**
Str. 19/4—23/7/36.**G.**
Rebuilt to D16/3.
Str. 13/4—14/5/37.**L.**
Str. 6/2—25/3/38.**G.**
Cabside screens fitted.
Str. 9/9—3/11/39.**G.**
Str. 16/3—6/4/40.**L.**
Str. 26/2—29/4/42.**G.**
Str. 13—23/10/42.**L.**
Str. 12/3—27/4/44.**G.**
Str. 8/1—6/2/46.**G.**
Str. 6/5—25/6/46.**L.**
Str. 5—24/9/46.**L.**
Str. 3—13/12/47.**L.**
Str. 30/1—25/3/48.**G.**
Str. 8—21/6/48.**L.**
Str. 10—18/11/48.**L.**
Str. 25/11/49—13/1/50.**G.**
Str. 16—26/5/50.**L.**
Str. 14/1—6/2/53.**L.**
Str. 2/10—14/11/53.**G.**
Str. 13/7/55. *Not repaired.*

BOILERS:
 1865.
 1865 *(new)* 2/2/12.
 1871 *(ex8871)* 28/2/19.
 1863 *(ex8862)* 19/1/24.
 3253 *(ex8876)* 22/5/26.
 3674 *(ex8863)* 4/4/30.
 3591 *(ex8863)* 24/10/31.
 3255 *(ex8876)* 12/10/33.
 3662 *(ex8897)* 5/12/34.
 4241 *(new)* 23/7/36.
 4237 *(exJ19 8248)* 25/3/38.
 4236 *(exJ19 8145)* 3/11/39.
 4231 *(ex8816)* 29/4/42.
 4294 *(ex8811)* 27/4/44.
 4266 *(ex8816)* 6/2/46.
 4304 *(exJ19 8264)* 25/3/48.
 4336 *(new)* 13/1/50.
 4336 renum 23424 6/2/53.
 23327 *(ex8830)* 14/11/53.

SHEDS:
Stratford.
Norwich 5/7/26.
Cambridge 3/3/28.
Stratford 17/12/34.
Cambridge 31/1/35.
King's Lynn 19/8/45.
Cambridge 26/8/45.
King's Lynn 11/1/48.
Cambridge 18/1/48.
Trafford Park 7/4/50.

Cambridge 8/6/52.
Pbo. (Spital Bridge) 12/10/52.

RENUMBERED:
8865 ?/?/25.
2536 10/11/46.
62536 25/3/48.

CONDEMNED: 25/7/55.
In Septemebr 1955 no.62536
was made Stationery Boiler
no.3339, to supply steam at
Stratford Works. It was finally
condemned in December 1958
and was cut-up in April 1959 at
Stratford.

8866

To traffic 10/1903.

REPAIRS:
Str. 18/4—8/9/16.**G**.
Str. 24/3—14/5/21.**G**.
Str. 11/1—8/6/23.**G**.
Rebuilt to D15.
Superheated boiler fitted.
Str. 22/4—30/6/24.**G**.
Str. 6/3—21/7/26.**G**.
Str. 16/3—23/6/28.**G**.
Altered to D15/2.
Vacuum brake added.
Coal guard on tender.
Str. 29/10—11/12/30.**G**.
Str. 30/12/32—9/3/33.**G**.
Rebuilt to D16/3 (14/2 to 5/36).
Str. 4/4—4/5/34.**G**.
Str. 11/12/35—16/1/36.**G**.
Str. ?/?—3/12/37.**G**.
Str. ?/?—27/12/39.**G**.
Str. ?/?—9/12/41.**G**.
Str. ?/?—2/6/44.**G**.
Str. ?/?—18/5/45.**L**.
BOILERS:
1866.
1891 (ex8891) 8/9/16.
1867 (ex8878) 14/5/21.
3637 (new) 8/6/23.
3587 (ex8891) 21/7/26.
3683 (new) 23/6/28.
3616 (ex8874) 11/12/30.
4202 (new) 9/3/33.
4215 (new) 4/5/34.
4209 (exJ19 8254) 3/12/37.
4222 (ex8840) 27/12/39.
4208 (ex8815) 9/12/41.
4213 (ex8843) 2/6/44.

SHEDS:
Stratford.
Norwich 9/7/27.

Ipswich ?/??.
Parkeston 13/9/29.
Cambridge 11/12/30.
Peterborough East 12/1/31.
Cambridge 24/2/31.
March 24/10/40.
Cambridge 14/12/42.

RENUMBERED:
8866 ?/?/25.
2537 allocated but not carried.

CONDEMNED: 12/9/45.
Cut up at Stratford.

8867

To traffic 10/1903.

REPAIRS:
Str. 26/10/11—18/1/12.**G**.
Str. 13/10/13—12/3/14.**G**.
Str. 24/6/18—18/2/19.**G**.
Str. 27/10/22—23/5/23.**G**.
Rebuilt to D15.
Superheated boiler fitted.
Str. 1/10—30/12/24.**G**.
Str. 17/9/26—13/1/27.**G**.
Coal guard on tender.
Str. 29/1—11/2/27.**L**.
Vacuum brake added.
Str. 12/10/28—21/1/29.**G**.
Str. 4/12/30—23/2/31.**G**.
Str. 27/10—21/12/33.**G**.
Altered to D15/2.
Str. 3/7—30/8/35.**G**.
Str. 5—10/6/36.**L**.
Str. 14/2—25/3/37.**G**.
Str. 23/10—13/12/38.**G**.
Str. 26/4—6/6/41.**G**.
Str. 14/5—10/6/44.**G**.
Str. 26/1—9/4/47.**G**.
Str. 14/4—19/8/48.**H**.
Str. 1/1—18/2/50.**G**.
Str. 13—23/3/50.**N/C**.
Special painting only.
Str. 20/4/52. Not repaired.

BOILERS:
1867.
1867 (new) 18/1/12.
3253 (new) 12/3/14.
1872 (ex8872) 18/2/19.
3634 (new) 23/5/23.
3576 (ex8883) 13/1/27.
3585 (ex8883) 21/1/29.
3591 (ex8865) 21/12/33.
3256 (ex8864) 30/8/35.
3676 (ex8862) 25/3/37.
3636 (ex8899) 13/12/38.
3261 (ex8877) 6/6/41.

3255 (ex8881) 10/6/44.
3445 (ex8897) 9/4/47.
3518 (new) 19/8/48.

SHEDS:
Colchester.
Stratford 25/9/39.
Colchester 3/12/39.
Stratford 18/11/44.
Melton Constable 1/1/49.
Norwich 3/2/52.

RENUMBERED:
1867E ?/?/24.
8867 30/12/24.
2538 15/6/46.
62538 14/8/48.

CONDEMNED: 28/4/52.
Cut up at Stratford.

8868

To traffic 12/1903.

REPAIRS:
Str. 25/11/14—26/3/15.**G**.
Str. 26/11/20—12/2/21.**G**.
Str. 6/9/22—4/1/23.**G**.
Str. 16/5—24/9/24.**G**.
Str. 25/5—11/6/25.**L**.
Str. 6/11/25—17/4/26.**G**.
Str. 1/6/27.**N/C**.
Vacuum brake added.
Str. 6/1—28/4/28.**G**.
Coal guard on tender.
Str. 15/7—12/9/29.**G**.
Rebuilt to D15/2.
Superheated boiler fitted.
Str. 21/2—1/5/31.**G**.
Str. 25/5—2/6/32.**L**.
Str. 23/1—31/3/33.**G**.
Str. 9/10—23/11/34.**G**.
Str. 26/4—3/7/36.**G**.
Str. 22/5—23/7/38.**G**.
Str. 13/4—11/7/40.**G**.
Rebuilt to D16/3.
Str. 18/10/41—15/1/42.**L**.
Str. 26/11/42—5/2/43.**G**.
Str. 13/10—18/11/44.**G**.
Str. 19/12/46—26/1/47.**G**.
Str. 8/3—30/4/49.**G**.
Str. 1/6—22/7/49.**C/L**.
Str. 24/10—29/11/50.**C/L**.
Str. 23/2—22/3/52.**G**.
W.P.U. gear removed.
Str. 12/8—2/9/53.**C/L**.
Str. 15/8—25/9/54.**G**.
Str. 11/10—12/11/54.**N/C**.
Str. 5/3—14/4/56.**C/L**.

BOILERS:
1868.
1890 (ex8890) 26/3/15.
1874 (ex8874) 12/2/21.
3251 (ex8873) 4/1/23.
1860 (ex8886) 17/4/26.
3256 (new) 12/9/29.
3593 (ex8885) 1/5/31.
3262 (ex8870) 31/3/33.
3636 (ex8860) 23/11/34.
3659 (ex8882) 3/7/36.
3624 (ex8891) 23/7/38.
4216 (ex8860) 11/7/40.
4209 (ex8874) 5/2/43.
4210 (ex8844) 18/11/44.
4208 (ex8844) 26/1/47.
4217 (ex8848) 30/4/49.
4217 renum 23321 29/11/50.
23396 (ex ?) 22/3/52.
23375 (ex8821) 25/9/54.

SHEDS:
Ipswich.
Stratford 27/9/24.
Lincoln 28/4/28.
Cambridge 12/9/29.
King's Lynn 29/9/29.
March 21/11/42.
Cambridge 22/4/56.

RENUMBERED:
8868 24/9/24.
2539 15/6/46.
62539 30/4/49.

CONDEMNED: 28/10/57.
Cut up at Stratford.

8869

To traffic 11/1903.

REPAIRS:
Str. 14/1—8/6/10.**G**.
Str. 15/11/18—23/5/19.**G**.
Str. 11/11/21—26/1/22.**G**.
Rebuilt to D15.
Str. 25/9/23—5/2/24.**G**.
Superheated boiler fitted.
Str. 15/1—23/4/26.**G**.
Str. 11/4—20/7/28.**G**.
Altered to D15/2.
Vacuum brake added.
Coal guard on tender.
Str. 22/2—24/4/30.**G**.
Str. 13/3—26/5/32.**G**.
Str. 16/9—21/10/32.**L**.
Str. 12/3—8/6/34.**G**.
Rebuilt to D16/3 (14/2 to 5/36).
Str. 5/11—23/12/35.**G**.
Str. 7/6—27/7/37.**G**.

Str. 5/4—26/5/39.**G**.
Str. 1/4—22/5/42.**G**.
Str. 7/5—16/6/44.**G**.
Str. 3/5—28/6/46.**G**.
Str. 14—30/8/46.**L**.
Str. 28/9—12/10/46.**L**.
Str. 3/10—24/11/48.**G**.
Str. 3/1—8/2/51.**G**.
Str. 14/7—22/8/53.**G**.
Str. 17/3—12/4/55.**C/L**.
Str. 7/3—24/4/56.**G**.
Str. 10/5—7/6/56.**C/L**.
Str. 20/8/59. *Not repaired.*

BOILERS:
1869.
1869 *(new)* 8/6/10.
3253 *(ex8867)* 23/5/19.
3616 *(new)* 26/1/22.
3638 *(new)* 5/2/24.
3659 *(ex8872)* 20/7/28.
3681 *(ex8864)* 26/5/32.
4216 *(new)* 8/6/34.
4265 *(new)* 27/7/37.
4255 *(ex8808)* 26/5/39.
4286 *(ex8808)* 22/5/42.
4260 *(exJ19 8267)* 16/6/44.
4300 *(exJ19 8246)* 24/11/48.
23313 *(ex ?)* 8/2/51.
23353 *(ex8883)* 22/8/53.
23341 *(ex8830)* 24/4/56.

SHEDS:
Ipswich.
Norwich 2/8/33.
Yarmouth 3/11/34.
Norwich 21/11/34.
Yarmouth 16/10/38.
Norwich 13/8/39.
Yarmouth 7/3/40.
Norwich 19/5/40.
Yarmouth 24/11/40.
Norwich 15/2/42.
Yarmouth 15/3/42.
Norwich 1/4/42.
Yarmouth 5/6/42.
Norwich 11/1/49.
Yarmouth Beach 26/1/49.
Yarmouth 24/4/49.
Norwich 13/11/49.

RENUMBERED:
1869ᴇ 5/2/24.
8869 ?/?/??.
2540 27/6/46.
62540 20/11/48.

CONDEMNED: 24/8/59.
Cut up at Stratford.

When no.8885 was ex works 7th May 1931 the decorative valance over the coupling rods had been removed, probably in connection with the design of D16/3 Class then in progress. It was the only one so altered deliberately, and was itself rebuilt to D16/3 in July 1937.

The alteration on the other side also brought into view the Westinghouse train brake pipe. This was now on the outside of the angle with the running plate instead of behind it.

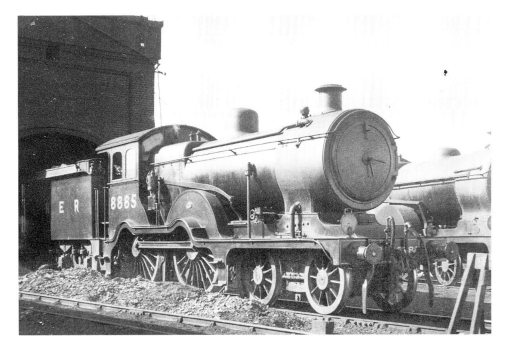

51

8850

To traffic 1/1904.

REPAIRS:
Str. 25/2—7/7/13.**G.**
Str. ?/?—?/5/20.**G.**
Str. ?/9/21—?/1/22.**G.**
Superheated boiler fitted.
Str. 9/4—23/6/23.**G.**
Str. 19/11/24—5/5/25.**G.**
Str. 23/2—3/6/27.**G.**
Str. 22/9—26/11/28.**G.**
Vacuum brake added.
Coal guard on tender.
Str. 12/3—14/5/30.**G.**
Str. 4/1—26/2/32.**G.**
Altered to D15/2.
Str. 25/4—2/6/33.**G.**
Str. 17/2—29/3/35.**G.**
Str. 15—19/6/36.**L.**
Str. 8/4—4/6/37.**G.**
Str. 1/4—15/7/39.**G.**
Rebuilt to D16/3.
Str. 23/9—25/10/41.**G.**
Str. 22/6—18/12/43.**G.**
Str. 27/1—10/2/45.**L.**
Str. 14/7—10/8/45.**L.**
Str. 16/12/45—26/1/46.**G.**
Str. 13/4—3/6/47.**G.**
Str. 5/3—16/4/49.**G.**
Str. 4/4—12/5/51.**G.**
Str. 14—28/5/52.**C/L.**
Str. 23/6—8/8/53.**G.**
Str. 15/11—24/12/54.**C/L.**

BOILERS:
1850.
1850 *(new)* 7/7/13.
1820 *(ex8806)* ?/5/20.
3603 *(new)* ?/1/22.
3572 *(ex8801)* 3/6/27.
3624 *(ex8807)* 26/11/28.
3612 *(ex8791)* 26/2/32.
3594 *(ex8809)* 2/6/33.
3464 *(ex8825)* 29/3/35.
3649 *(ex8815)* 4/6/37.
4294 *(new)* 15/7/39.
4296 *(exJ19 8249)* 25/10/41.
4277 *(exJ19 8243)* 18/12/43.
4237 *(exJ19 8148)* 26/1/46.
4248 *(ex8888)* 3/6/47.
4318 *(ex8780)* 16/4/49.
23349 *(ex ?)* 12/5/51.
23308 *(ex8831)* 8/8/53.

SHEDS:
Stratford.
Norwich 13/8/26.
Yarmouth 30/8/36.
Norwich 5/3/37.

Bury St Edmunds 9/3/52.
Cambridge 21/2/54.

RENUMBERED:
8850 ?/?/??.
2541 22/6/46.
62541 16/4/49.

CONDEMNED: 17/10/55.
Cut up at Stratford.

8851

To traffic 1/1904.

REPAIRS:
Str. 14/10/13—10/2/14.**G.**
Str. 31/5—6/12/18.**G.**
Superheated boiler fitted.
Str. 11/4—20/7/23.**G.**
Str. 31/10/24—20/3/25.**G.**
Str. 25/2—23/6/27.**G.**
Rebuilt to D16/2.
Vacuum brake added.
Str. 2/11/28—15/2/29.**G.**
Coal guard on tender.
Str. 26/11/31—22/1/32.**G.**
Str. 20/2—19/4/34.**G.**
Ash ejector fitted.
Str. 16/10—8/11/35.**L.**
Str. 24/4—19/6/36.**G.**
Str. 3—26/11/37.**L.**
Str. 8/5—28/6/38.**G.**
Rebuilt to D16/3.
Str. 23/9—21/11/40.**G.**
Str. 27/6/43—6/1/44.**G.**
Str. 7—27/2/45.**L.**
Str. 31/3—14/5/46.**G.**
Str. 12/9—26/10/48.**G.**
Str. 21/9—26/10/51.**G.**
Str. 18/2—14/3/52.**C/L.**
Str. 31/1—4/3/54.**G.**
Str. 1/10/56. *Not repaired.*

BOILERS:
1851.
1851 *(new)* 10/2/14.
3573 *(new)* 6/12/18.
3571 *(ex8799)* 20/7/23.
3908 *(new)* 23/6/27.
3901 *(ex8818)* 15/2/29.
3913 *(ex8792)* 22/1/32.
3918 *(ex8787)* 19/4/34.
3917 *(ex8838)* 19/6/36.
4275 *(new)* 28/6/38.
4235 *(ex8802)* 21/11/40.
4233 *(exJ19 8147)* 6/1/44.
4267 *(ex8817)* 14/5/46.
4296 *(ex8820)* 26/10/48.
23369 *(ex ?)* 26/10/51.
23334 *(ex8874)* 4/3/54.

SHEDS:
Stratford.
Cambridge 4/10/26.
Stratford 1/1/27.
Cambridge 23/5/29.
March 26/5/29.

RENUMBERED:
8851 20/3/25.
2542 10/5/46.
62542 23/10/48.

CONDEMNED: 15/10/56.
Cut up at Stratford.

8852

To traffic 1/1904.

REPAIRS:
Str. 12/11/13—6/4/14.**G.**
Str. 12/10/17—5/3/18.**G.**
Str. 17/3—6/7/22.**G.**
Superheated boiler fitted.
Str. 18/9—12/12/33.**G.**
Str. 8/8—25/11/25.**G.**
Str. 21/6/27.**N/C.**
Vacuum brake added.
Str. 28/10/27—16/2/28.**G.**
Rebuilt to D16/2.
Coal guard on tender.
Str. 5/3—29/6/29.**G.**
Str. 15/11/30—6/2/31.**G.**
Str. 10/10—2/12/32.**G.**
Str. 28/8—3/10/34.**G.**
Str. 28/2—17/4/36.**G.**
Str. 29/12/37—4/2/38.**G.**
Str. 22/5—15/8/39.**G.**
Str. 18/3—11/5/40.**G.**
Str. 14—16/5/40.**N/C.**
Str. 12/9—12/10/42.**G.**
Str. 9—28/10/44.**G.**
Str. 19/5—25/7/46.**G.**
Str. 5—22/5/48.**L.**
Str. 7/11/48—8/2/49.**G.**
Rebuilt to D16/3.
Str. 31/12/50—3/2/51.**G.**
Str. 28/12/52—31/1/53.**G.**
Str. 29/7—12/8/54.**C/L.**
Str. 20/3—30/4/55.**G.**
Str. 6/3—24/4/57.**G.**
Str. 10/10/58. *Not repaired.*

BOILERS:
1852.
1852 *(new)* 6/4/14.
1805 *(ex8805)* 5/3/18.
3624 *(new)* 6/7/22.
3566 *(ex8848)* 25/11/25.
3912 *(new)* 16/2/28.
3914 *(ex8839)* 2/12/32.

3901 *(ex8822)* 3/10/34.
3905 *(ex8853)* 17/4/36.
3921 *(ex8833)* 4/2/38.
3904 *(ex8813)* 11/5/40.
1788 *(ex8786)* 12/10/42.
3922 *(ex8847)* 28/10/44.
3919 *(ex8781)* 25/7/46.
4245 *(ex8849)* 8/2/49.
23328 *(ex ?)* 3/2/51.
23455 *(new)* 31/1/53.
23302 *(exJ19 8261)* 30/4/55.
23464 *(ex8842)* 24/4/57.

SHEDS:
Stratford.
Yarmouth 3/10/28.
Lowestoft 14/10/28.
Stratford 30/10/28.
Southend 8/11/30.
Stratford 15/11/30.
Cambridge 29/12/32.
King's Lynn 2/3/39.
Cambridge 10/9/39.
South Lynn 9/8/46.
King's Lynn 5/11/50.
Cambridge 19/11/50.
Bury St Edmunds 10/8/52.
March 24/11/57.

RENUMBERED:
8852 *after* 17/1/25.
2543 23/9/46.
62543 22/5/48.

CONDEMNED: 13/10/58.
Cut up at Stratford.

8853

To traffic 1/1904.

REPAIRS:
Str. 4/6—31/7/13.**G.**
Str. 5/11/15—2/3/16.**G.**
Str. 26/11/20—2/2/21.**G.**
Str. ?/?—?/8/22.**G.**
Str. 31/10/23—28/3/24.**G.**
Str. 14/1—29/5/26.**G.**
Rebuilt to D16/1.
Superheated boiler fitted.
Coal guard on tender.
Str. 9/10/27—4/2/28.**G.**
Str. 10—24/10/28.**N/C.**
Vacuum brake added.
Str. 17/9—14/11/29.**G.**
Altered to D16/2.
Str. 2/3—24/4/31.**G.**
Str. 27/9—3/11/32.**G.**
Str. 26/3—18/5/34.**G.**
Str. 17/2—8/4/36.**G.**
Str. 30/3—2/6/38.**G.**

WORKS CODES:- Bd - Beardmore. Ca - Cambridge shed. Dn - Doncaster. Go - Gorton. Ips - Ipswich shed. Nr - Norwich shed. Str - Stratford.
REPAIR CODES:- **C/H** - Casual Heavy. **C/L** - Casual Light. **G** - General. **H**- Heavy. **H/I** - Heavy Intermediate. **L** - Light. **L/I** - Light Intermediate. **N/C** - Non-Classified.

52

Str. 10/9—8/11/40.**G.**
Str. 12/4—19/6/43.**G.**
Str. 1—30/4/45.**G.**
Str. 17/9/46—17/3/47.**G.**
Rebuilt to D16/3.
Str. 30/5—3/7/48.**H.**
Str. 7/5—4/6/49.**G.**
Str. 27/1—5/3/52.**G.**
W.P.U. gear removed.
Str. 18/6—3/7/53.**C/L.**
Str. 26/3—6/5/55.**G.**
Str. 1—2/7/59.**N/C.**
Tender change only.

BOILERS:
  1853.
  1853 *(new)* 31/7/13.
  1843 *(ex8843)* 2/3/16.
  1842 *(ex8842)* 2/2/21.
  3904 *(new)* 29/5/26.
  3932 *(new)* 24/4/31.
  1783 *(ex8788)* 3/11/32.
  3905 *(ex8794)* 18/5/34.
  3901 *(ex8852)* 8/4/36.
  3929 *(ex8792)* 2/6/38.
  3928 *(ex8827)* 8/11/40.
  3901 *(ex8839)* 19/6/43.
  3932 *(ex8805)* 30/4/45.
  4257 *(ex8794)* 17/3/47.
  4278 *(exJ19 8269)* 4/6/49.
23391 *(ex ?)* 5/3/52.
23416 *(ex8834)* 6/5/55.

SHEDS:
Stratford.
Norwich 19/6/26.
Yarmouth *by* 5/32.
Norwich 18/2/37.
Yarmouth 24/11/40.
Norwich 2/6/57.

RENUMBERED:
  1853ᴇ 28/3/24.
  8853 ?/?/??.
  2544 9/11/46.
  62544 3/7/48.

CONDEMNED: 24/11/59.
Cut up at Stratford.

8854

To traffic 1/1904.

REPAIRS:
Str. 24/3—26/6/16.**G.**
Superheated boiler fitted.
Str. 7/9—13/12/21.**G.**
Str. 29/1—21/4/23.**G.**
Str. 12/4—6/7/24.**G.**
Str. 17/8—25/9/25.**L.**
Str. 20/9/26—1/1/27.**G.**
Coal guard on tender.
Str. 3/9—6/10/27.**L.**

Str. 5/1—11/5/29.**G.**
Vacuum brake added.
Str. 19/2—17/4/31.**G.**
Str. 12/1—17/3/33.**G.**
Rebuilt to D16/3.
Str. 17/7—24/8/34.**G.**
B17 tender axleboxes fitted.
Str. 16/3—24/4/36.**G.**
Str. 8/4—17/6/37.**G.**
Str. 13/6—5/8/39.**G.**
Str. 9—26/6/40.**L.**
Str. 18/8—19/9/42.**G.**
Str. 1/10—1/11/44.**G.**
Str. 11/6—13/8/46.**G.**
Str. 21/9—12/10/46.**L.**
Str. 11/1—14/2/48.**H.**
Str. 26/2—9/3/48.**L.**
Str. 2/1—28/2/49.**G.**
Str. 1/4—13/5/49.**N/C.**
Str. 26/4—9/5/51.**C/L.**
Str. 25/10—1/12/51.**G.**
W.P.U. gear removed.
Str. 25/4—29/5/54.**G.**
Str. 12/2—17/3/56.**G.**

BOILERS:
  1854.
  3567 *(new)* 26/6/16.
  3559 *(ex8807)* 13/12/21.
  3580 *(ex8832)* 1/1/27.
  3625 *(ex8811)* 11/5/29.
  3576 *(ex8886)* 17/4/31.
  4203 *(new)* 17/3/33.
  4218 *(new)* 24/8/34.
  4204 *(ex8900)* 24/4/36.
  4220 *(ex8878)* 17/6/37.
  4206 *(ex8849)* 5/8/39.
  4227 *(ex8823)* 19/9/42.
  4229 *(ex8815)* 1/11/44.
  4225 *(ex8815)* 13/8/46.
  4214 *(ex8821)* 14/2/48.
  4214 *renum* 23352 9/5/51.
23304 *(ex8782)* 1/12/51.
23463 *(new)* 29/5/54.
23420 *(ex8793)* 17/3/56.

SHEDS:
Stratford.
Ipswich 3/7/24.
Norwich 27/5/31.
Yarmouth 1/8/37.
Norwich 5/2/39.
Yarmouth 25/3/45.
Norwich 30/12/45.
Yarmouth Beach 2/2/46.
Norwich 16/2/46.
Yarmouth 9/5/48.
Norwich 4/8/48.
Melton Constable 15/8/48.
Norwich 27/10/48.
Lowestoft 19/12/48.
Norwich 2/1/49.
Lowestoft 29/6/52.
Norwich 14/9/52.

Bury St Edmunds 7/6/53.
Cambridge 21/2/54.
King's Lynn 13/3/55.
Cambridge 7/4/57.
King's Lynn 13/10/57.

RENUMBERED:
  8854 6/7/24.
  2545 9/8/46.
  62545 26/2/49.

CONDEMNED: 22/9/58.
Cut up at Stratford.

8855

To traffic 3/1904.

REPAIRS:
Str. 9/9—1/12/14.**G.**
Superheated boiler fitted.
Str. 24/10/19—26/3/20.**G.**
Str. 5/10/22—21/2/23.**G.**
Str. 6/6—11/9/24.**G.**
Str. 25/3—4/8/26.**G.**
Str. 2/9—22/10/27.**G.**
Str. 6/7—19/9/28.**G.**
Altered to D15/2.
Vacuum brake added.
Coal guard on tender.
Str. 9/4—4/7/30.**G.**
Str. 15/2—1/4/32.**G.**
Str. 16/11/33—18/1/34.**G.**
Rebuilt to D16/3.
Str. 13/6—26/7/35.**G.**
Str. 1/1—3/3/37.**G.**
Str. 5/3—6/5/39.**G.**
Str. 11/9—24/10/39.**L.**
Str. 2/2—27/3/42.**G.**
Str. 14—30/4/43.**L.**
Str. 23/7—26/8/44.**G.**
Str. 10/7—3/8/45.**L.**
Str. 2—20/3/46.**L.**
Str. 16/7—4/10/46.**G.**
Str. 28/9—10/11/48.**G.**
Str. 30/9—22/10/49.**C/L.**
Str. 9/12/51—31/1/52.**G.**
W.P.U. gear removed.
Str. 8/4—1/5/53.**N/C.**
Str. 23/10—4/12/54.**G.**

BOILERS:
  1855.
  3564 *(new)* 1/12/14.
  3582 *(new)* 26/3/20.
  3569 *(ex8824)* 21/2/23.
  3613 *(ex8814)* 19/9/28.
  3568 *(ex8814)* 4/7/30.
  3648 *(ex8816)* 1/4/32.
  4209 *(new)* 18/1/34.
  4213 *(ex8828)* 26/7/35.
  4205 *(ex8809)* 3/3/37.
  4287 *(new)* 6/5/39.
  4265 *(exJ19 8269)* 27/3/42.

4330 *(new)* 26/8/44.
4264 *(ex8884)* 10/11/48.
23384 *(ex ?)* 31/1/52.
23340 *(exJ19 8264)* 4/12/54.

SHEDS:
Colchester.
Ipswich 10/6/32.
Stratford 29/9/45.
Norwich 21/10/46.
Yarmouth 11/6/47.

RENUMBERED:
  8855 11/9/24.
  2546 27/9/46.
  62546 30/10/48.

CONDEMNED: 18/6/57.
Cut up at Stratford.

8856

To traffic 3/1904.

REPAIRS:
Str. 24/2—22/5/14.**G.**
Str. 26/6—7/12/17.**G.**
Str. 21/5—21/8/20.**G.**
Str. 27/4—26/9/23.**G.**
Superheated boiler fitted.
Str. 31/10/24—3/3/25.**G.**
Str. 5/2—21/5/27.**G.**
Rebuilt to D16/2.
Str. 7—27/8/28.**N/C.**
Vacuum brake added.
Str. 6/2—1/5/29.**G.**
Coal guard on tender.
Str. 17/2—24/4/31.**G.**
Str. 3/1—17/2/33.**G.**
Str. 9/3—16/5/35.**G.**
Str. 27/2—24/6/38.**G.**
Str. 12—20/10/38.**L.**
Str. 11/12/40—6/2/41.**G.**
Str. 27/4—3/7/43.**G.**
Str. 3/9—6/10/45.**G.**
Str. 26—31/10/45.**N/C.**
Str. 16—31/1/46.**L.**
Str. 26/4—17/6/48.**G.**
Str. 12/1/51. *Not repaired.*

BOILERS:
1856.
3551 *(new)* 22/5/14.
1824 *(ex8824)* 7/12/17.
1835 *(ex8835)* 21/8/20.
3647 *(new)* 26/9/23.
3906 *(new)* 21/5/27.
1787 *(ex8787)* 1/5/29.
3900 *(ex8801)* 24/4/31.
3916 *(ex8783)* 17/2/33.
3928 *(ex8784)* 16/5/35.
3918 *(ex8805)* 24/6/38.
3917 *(ex8795)* 6/2/41.
3928 *(ex8853)* 3/7/43.

On 27th November 1934 no.8896 suffered damage in an accident at Wormley and this is how it was received at Stratford for repair. When ex works 15th February 1935, it too was without the valance over the coupling rods. *L.N.E.R.*

(above) **During the 1939-45 War, the front side windows of the cab were removed and replaced by a steel plate on many D15/2, and the glass was never put back.** *L.R.Peters.*

(above) Whilst buffers with hollow spindle were general, some had them combined with a tapered shank. More usual was the shank stepped in two parallel portions, similar to the later Group Standard type, but with circular base flange, and small diameter head. 8893 is at Peterborough 29th May 1937. *H.C.Casserley.*

(below) Standard lubrication for the front end was by Wakefield mechanical type and no other types, or changes, were noted. The engines also had forced lubrication provided for their bogie slides.

8856 cont.
3914 (*ex8801*) 6/10/45.

SHEDS:
Stratford.
Cambridge 23/11/26.
March 26/5/29.

RENUMBERED:
8856 3/3/25.
2547 15/6/46.
62547 12/6/48.

CONDEMNED: 5/2/51.
Cut up at Stratford.

8857

To traffic 4/1904.

REPAIRS:
Str. 6/7—28/11/16.**G.**
Superheated boiler fitted.
Str. 30/8/19—5/2/20.**G.**
Str. 25/10/22—27/1/23.**G.**
Str. 10/9—9/12/24.**G.**
Str. 31/3—29/7/26.**G.**
Str. 21/6/27.**N/C.**
Vacuum brake added.
Str. 24/2—14/6/28.**G.**
Coal guard on tender.
Str. 7/10/29—3/1/30.**G.**
Str. 13/5—22/7/31.**G.**
Str. 14/9—27/10/33.**G.**
Altered to D15/2.
Str. 17—29/3/34.**L.**
Str. 2/4—7/6/35.**G.**
Str. 29/6—3/7/36.**L.**
Str. 10/1—26/2/37.**G.**
Str. 3/5—22/7/39.**G.**
Rebuilt to D16/3.
Str. 9—11/8/39.**L.**
Str. 12/10—15/11/41.**G.**
Str. 13/11—16/12/42.**L.**
Str. 7/12/43—22/1/44.**G.**
Str. 8—19/10/44.**L.**
Str. 27/2—19/4/46.**G.**
Str. 2/5—9/6/48.**G.**
Str. 17/9—28/10/50.**G.**
Str. 13/10—15/11/52.**G.**
Str. 7/3—16/4/55.**G.**

BOILERS:
1857.
3568 (*new*) 28/11/16.
1798 (*ex8798*) 5/2/20.
3583 (*ex8844*) 9/12/24.
3565 (*ex8813*) 29/7/26.
3573 (*ex8839*) 14/6/28.
3567 (*ex8849*) 22/7/31.
3582 (*ex8814*) 27/10/33.
3679 (*ex8870*) 7/6/35.
4292 (*new*) 22/7/39.
4262 (*ex8809*) 15/11/41.

4295 (*ex8788*) 22/1/44.
4273 (*ex8832*) 19/4/46.
4232 (*ex8809*) 9/6/48.
23309 (*ex ?*) 28/10/50.
23331 (*ex8826*) 15/11/52.
23322 (*ex8788*) 16/4/55.

SHEDS:
Stratford.
Southend 18/1/30.
Stratford 15/3/30.
Southend 12/4/30.
Stratford 19/4/30.
Colchester 20/10/45.
March 14/8/46.

RENUMBERED:
8857 9/11/24.
7727 16/12/42.
2548 4/5/46.
62548 5/6/48.

CONDEMNED: 8/10/57.
Cut up at Stratford.

8858

To traffic 6/1904.

REPAIRS:
Str. 7/1—16/5/13.**G.**
Str. 5/10/15—18/2/16.**G.**
Str. 17/4—15/7/20.**G.**
Str. 19/3—9/6/23.**G.**
Str. 7/3—30/6/24.**G.**
Str. 7/9—27/11/25.**G.**
Str. 28/1—26/5/27.**G.**
Superheated boiler fitted.
Coal guard on tender.
Str. 20/9—30/11/28.**G.**
Str. 26/2—7/5/30.**G.**
Altered to D15/2.
Str. 16/2—12/4/32.**G.**
Str. 24/10—14/12/33.**G.**
Str. 14/10/35—6/1/36.**G.**
Str. 18—21/5/36.**L.**
Str. 10/1—18/3/38.**G.**
Rebuilt to D16/3.
Str. 13—24/5/39.**L.**
Str. 9/2—18/4/40.**G.**
Str. 22/10/42—6/1/43.**G.**
Str. 5/11—9/12/44.**G.**
Str. 18/3—6/4/45.**L.**
Str. 21/7—13/10/46.**G.**
Str. 2/6—4/8/47.**L.**
Str. 19/1—13/2/48.**L.**
Str. 20/12/48—18/2/49.**G.**
Str. 4—19/5/50.**C/L.**
Str. 19/9—21/10/50.**G.**
Str. 17/6—1/8/52.**G.**
Str. 1—10/10/52.**N/C.**
Str. 5/4—8/5/54.**G.**

BOILERS:
1858.
1858 (*new*) 16/5/13.
1848 (*ex8848*) 18/2/16.
3550 (*ex8828*) 15/7/20.
3622 (*ex8811*) 26/5/27.
3639 (*ex8791*) 30/11/28.
3570 (*ex8797*) 12/4/32.
3573 (*ex8797*) 14/12/33.
4273 (*new*) 18/3/38.
4223 (*ex8875*) 18/4/40.
4212 (*ex8848*) 6/1/43.
4217 (*ex8878*) 9/12/44.
4207 (*ex8878*) 13/10/46.
4220 (*ex8796*) 18/2/49.
23310 (*ex ?*) 21/10/50.
23411 (*ex ?*) 1/8/52.
23387 (*ex8887*) 8/5/54.

SHEDS:
Ipswich.
Norwich 26/5/27.
Yarmouth 3/10/30.
Norwich 7/6/31.
Yarmouth 8/2/42.
Norwich 15/3/42.
Yarmouth 11/11/45.
Melton Constable 30/11/45.
Norwich 12/12/45.
Yarmouth 3/5/46.
Norwich 9/5/46.
Stratford 15/10/46.
Cambridge 23/11/47.
King's Lynn 23/4/48.
Cambridge 13/5/48.

RENUMBERED:
8858 30/6/24.
7728 6/1/43.
2549 31/3/46.
62549 18/2/49.

CONDEMNED: 12/12/55.
Cut up at Stratford.

8859

To traffic 6/1904.

REPAIRS:
Str. 12/11/12—11/3/13.**G.**
Str. 20/3—1/7/20.**G.**
Str. 8/3—4/7/24.**G.**
Str. 24/6—19/11/26.**G.**
Coal guard on tender.
Str. ?/?—?/2/29.**G.**
Str. 8/4—22/5/31.**G.**
Altered to D15/2.
Superheated boiler fitted.
Str. 7/3—3/5/34.**G.**
Rebuilt to D16/3.
Str. 10/12/35—24/1/36.**G.**
Str. ?/?—13/1/38.**G.**
Str. ?/?—?/?/??.**G.**

New cylinders.
Str. ?/?—9/4/40.**G.**
Str. ?/?—21/5/43.**G.**
Str. 15/9—6/10/45.**G.**

BOILERS:
1859.
1859 (*new*) 11/3/13.
3554 (*ex8834*) 1/7/20.
1817 (*ex8837*) 4/7/24.
3555 (*ex8841*) ?/2/29.
3579 (*ex8821*) 22/5/31.
4214 (*new*) 3/5/34.
4215 (*ex8866*) 13/1/38.
4268 (*exJ19 8149*) 9/4/40.
4263 (*ex8825*) 21/5/43.
4320 (*ex8875*) 6/10/45.

SHEDS:
Ipswich.
Peterborough East 1/3/29.
Norwich 18/11/29.
Yarmouth 20/7/30.
Norwich 10/10/30.
Lowestoft 12/6/31.
Norwich 29/4/33.
Yarmouth 5/10/35.
Norwich 30/11/35.
Yarmouth 3/3/36.
Norwich 1/11/36.
Yarmouth 5/3/37.
Norwich 8/8/37.
Yarmouth 27/4/38.
Norwich 8/1/39.
Yarmouth 12/3/39.
Norwich 10/12/39.
Yarmouth Beach 14/6/46.

RENUMBERED:
8859 ?/7/24.
2550 24/9/46.

CONDEMNED: 13/11/46.
Cut up at Stratford.

8840

To traffic 11/1906.

REPAIRS:
Str. 25/11/15—14/4/16.**G.**
Str. 18/3—9/9/21.**G.**
Str. 23/3—28/8/23.**G.**
Superheated boiler fitted.
Str. 13/2—19/6/25.**G.**
Str. 11/3—4/6/27.**G.**
Str. 24/10/28—28/2/29.**G.**
Altered to D15/2.
Vacuum brake added.
Coal guard on tender.
Str. 22/10/30—16/1/31.**G.**
Str. 13/12/32—7/2/33.**G.**
Str. 29/12/34—7/3/35.**G.**
Rebuilt to D16/3.

No.8877 was the first one transferred to work on the Midland & Great Northern line (29th January 1939) for which it was fitted with tablet exchanging apparatus. Here in March 1939 it heads a train at Norwich City terminus. *H.C.Casserley.*

(*right*) By the time they reached Part 2 all were dual fitted with Westinghouse and vacuum brakes. No D15/2 seems to have acquired the larger 8/8½" Westinghouse pump, the 6/6½" being standard. The Westinghouse pump also provided compressed air for sanding the leading coupled wheels in both directions of movement. Cab roofs remained the traditional Stratford type of wood planking covered by canvas and with rain strips which had been added about 1922/23. No.62509 lost its rain strips at sometime during the transition from LNER to BR as it certainly had them as late as October 1945. Cambridge 1st July 1952. *C.Major.*

The narrow bunker of the 'Watercart' tender restricted adding to the amount of coal carried even by piling it up. Some of the sheds got round this problem by adding wooden planking above the coal guard, as seen on this engine shedded at March. The six which remained D15/2 to withdrawal (nos.8891, 8892, 8893, 8895, 8896, 8897) continued with 'Watercart' tenders.

Str. 17/1—5/3/37.**G.**
Str. 12/7—6/8/38.**L.**
Str. 23/5—1/7/39.**G.**
Str. 3—23/5/40.**L.**
Str. 26/6—22/8/41.**G.**
Str. 18/10—17/12/43.**G.**
Str. 27/8—29/9/45.**G.**
Blow-down gear fitted.
Str. 6/6—16/8/47.**G.**
Str. 12—24/12/48.**L.**
Str. 24/3—23/4/49.**G.**
Str. 4/3—7/4/51.**G.**
Str. 22/3—24/4/53.**G.**
Str. 26/5—4/6/53.**N/C.**
Str. 25/5—23/7/55.**G.**
Str. 26/5/56. *Not repaired.*

BOILERS:
  1840.
  1810 *(ex8810)* 14/4/16.
  3551 *(ex8804)* 9/9/21.
  3648 *(new)* 28/8/23.
  3647 *(ex8856)* 4/6/27.
  3606 *(ex8832)* 16/1/31.
  3647 *(ex8835)* 7/2/33.
  4227 *(new)* 7/3/35.
  4222 *(ex8870)* 5/3/37.
  4293 *(new)* 1/7/39.
  4290 *(ex8849)* 22/8/41.
  4241 *(exJ19 8148)* 17/12/43.
  4249 *(ex8830)* 29/9/45.
  4256 *(ex8887)* 16/8/47.
  4293 *(ex8822)* 23/4/49.
23339 *(ex ?)* 7/4/51.
23456 *(new)* 24/4/53.
23371 *(ex8860)* 23/7/55.

SHEDS:
Cambridge.
Peterborough East 24/2/29.
March 30/4/39.
Cambridge 23/10/40.
King's Lynn 2/10/49.
Cambridge 9/10/49.
King's Lynn 27/4/52.
Cambridge 18/5/52.
King's Lynn 3/8/52.
Cambridge 26/10/52.
Pbo. (Spital Bridge) 20/12/53.

RENUMBERED:
  8840 19/6/25.
  2551 2/6/46.
  62551 23/4/49.

CONDEMNED: 16/7/56.
Cut up at Stratford.

8841

To traffic 11/1906.

REPAIRS:
Str. 20/3—11/9/17.**G.**

Str. 21/5—9/9/20.**G.**
Str. 11/11/21—10/2/22.**G.**
Str. 4/7—4/12/23.**G.**
Str. 4/5—8/8/25.**G.**
Str. 17/9/26—25/1/27.**G.**
Str. 27/9/28—30/1/29.**G.**
Rebuilt to D16/2.
Superheated boiler fitted.
Coal guard on tender.
Str. 24/4/29.**N/C.**
Vacuum brake added.
Str. 8/9—14/11/31.**G.**
Str. 8/12/33—1/2/34.**G.**
Str. 18/11—24/12/35.**G.**
Str. 14/4—4/6/37.**G.**
Str. 22/5—23/6/39.**G.**
Str. 19/1—27/2/41.**L.**
Str. 16/1—10/3/42.**G.**
Str. 4/6—22/7/44.**G.**
Str. 30/1—18/3/46.**G.**
Str. 21/3—15/5/47.**L.**
Str. 25/11/48—3/2/49.**G.**
Rebuilt to D16/3.
Str. 25/3—5/5/51.**G.**
Str. 13/9—17/10/53.**G.**
Str. 22/4—7/5/54.**C/L.**
Str. 20/10/55. *Not repaired.*

BOILERS:
  1841.
  1806 *(ex8806)* 11/9/17.
  1814 *(ex8843)* 9/9/20.
  3555 *(ex8820)* 8/8/25.
  3922 *(new)* 30/1/29.
  3931 *(ex8795)* 1/2/34.
  1782 *(ex8801)* 24/12/35.
  3934 *(ex8794)* 4/6/37.
  3907 *(ex8781)* 23/6/39.
  3935 *(ex8785)* 10/3/42.
  3927 *(ex8795)* 22/7/44.
  3931 *(ex8795)* 18/3/46.
  4295 *(exJ19 8253)* 3/2/49.
23346 *(ex ?)* 5/5/51.
23363 *(ex8787)* 17/10/53.

SHEDS:
Ipswich.
Norwich 23/4/50.
Ipswich 3/2/52.
Norwich 7/6/53.
Ipswich 13/6/54.

RENUMBERED:
  1841E 4/12/23.
  8841 8/8/25.
  2552 18/8/46.
  62552 29/1/49.

CONDEMNED: 24/10/55.
Cut up at Stratford.

8842

To traffic 12/1906.

REPAIRS:
Str. 14/11/19—12/3/20.**G.**
Str. 23/12/21—10/6/22.**G.**
Str. 22/8—8/11/23.**G.**
Str. 9/5—20/6/24.**L.**
Str. 7/9/25—3/2/26.**G.**
Str. 3/2—16/5/28.**G.**
Coal guard on tender.
Str. 17/11—13/12/28.**N/C.**
Vacuum brake added.
Str. 26/6—12/9/30.**G.**
Rebuilt to D16/2.
Superheated boiler fitted.
Str. 21/4—8/6/32.**G.**
Str. 6/2—12/4/34.**G.**
Ash ejector fitted.
Str. 8—30/7/35.**H.**
Str. 1/9—9/10/36.**G.**
Str. 22/5—5/7/38.**G.**
Str. 15/5—27/7/40.**G.**
Str. 17/10—21/12/42.**G.**
Str. 12/11—9/12/44.**G.**
Str. 25/1—18/4/47.**G.**
Str. 23/7—22/8/47.**L.**
Str. 1/4—14/5/48.**L.**
Str. 18/7—9/9/49.**G.**
Rebuilt to D16/3.
Str. 1/2—12/3/52.**G.**
W.P.U. gear removed.
Str. 30/8—2/10/54.**G.**
Str. 6—28/1/56.**C/L.**

BOILERS:
  1842.
  1796 *(ex8801)* 12/3/20.
  1850 *(ex8806)* 10/6/22.
  1796 *(ex8806)* 3/2/26.
  1781 *(ex8789)* 12/9/30.
  3926 *(ex8845)* 8/6/32.
  3927 *(ex8846)* 12/4/34.
  3916 *(ex8856)* 30/7/35.
  3919 *(ex8826)* 9/10/36.
  3901 *(ex8853)* 5/7/38.
  3905 *(ex8790)* 27/7/40.
  3936 *(ex8819)* 21/12/42.
  3925 *(ex8818)* 9/12/44.
  3909 *(ex8826)* 18/4/47.
  4265 *(ex8864)* 9/9/49.
23394 *(ex ?)* 12/3/52.
23464 *(new)* 2/10/54.

SHEDS:
Ipswich.
Norwich 11/11/45.
Ipswich 4/12/45.
Yarmouth 14/9/47.
Norwich 26/12/48.
Yarmouth 6/2/49.
Norwich 27/2/49.
Yarmouth 1/5/49.

Norwich 15/7/49.
Cambridge 2/10/55.

RENUMBERED:
  8842 20/6/24.
  7712 21/12/42.
  2553 23/3/46.
  62553 14/5/48.

CONDEMNED: 1/1/57.
Cut up at Stratford.

8843

To traffic 12/1906.

REPAIRS:
Str. 31/8—22/12/15.**G.**
Str. 24/4—19/8/20.**G.**
Str. 27/1—21/7/22.**G.**
Str. 19/2—13/5/24.**G.**
Str. 25/7—10/12/25.**G.**
Str. 8/3—9/7/27.**G.**
Rebuilt to D16/2.
Superheated boiler fitted.
Str. 3—12/10/28.**N/C.**
Vacuum brake added.
Str. 25/1—29/4/29.**G.**
Coal guard on tender.
Str. 16/3—18/7/31.**G.**
Str. 13/3—28/4/33.**G.**
Str. 9/10—17/11/34.**G.**
Str. 30/8—8/10/36.**G.**
Str. 17/9—17/11/38.**G.**
Rebuilt to D16/3.
Str. 22/9—22/10/41.**G.**
Str. 26/12/43—12/2/44.**G.**
Str. 7/10—7/11/45.**G.**
Str. 20/4—10/6/47.**G.**
Str. 19/5—25/6/49.**G.**
Str. 22/4—26/5/51.**G.**
Str. 26/10—13/11/52.**C/L.**
Str. 19/8—12/9/53.**G.**

BOILERS:
  1843.
  1814 *(ex8814)* 22/12/15.
  1804 *(ex8817)* 19/8/20.
  1819 *(ex8837)* 10/12/25.
  3907 *(new)* 9/7/27.
  3925 *(new)* 29/4/29.
  3900 *(ex8856)* 28/4/33.
  1783 *(ex8853)* 17/11/34.
  3906 *(ex8805)* 8/10/36.
  4201 *(ex8804)* 17/11/38.
  4213 *(exJ19 8140)* 22/10/41.
  4203 *(ex8823)* 12/2/44.
  4202 *(ex8814)* 7/11/45.
  4209 *(ex8885)* 10/6/47.
  4221 *(ex8836)* 25/6/49.
23451 *(new)* 26/5/51.
23312 *(ex8844)* 12/9/53.

SHEDS:
Yarmouth.
Norwich 2/4/28.
Yarmouth 13/10/28.
Lowestoft 17/8/30.
Norwich 23/8/30.
Yarmouth 1/4/35.
Norwich 25/11/35.
Yarmouth 16/2/36.
Norwich 30/8/36.
Yarmouth 16/10/46.
Norwich 31/3/47.

RENUMBERED:
8843 13/5/24.
2554 7/10/46.
62554 25/6/49.

CONDEMNED: 28/11/55.
Cut up at Stratford.

8844

To traffic 12/1906.

REPAIRS:
Str. 22/8—19/11/14.**G.**
Superheated boiler fitted.
Str. 12/10—11/12/20.**G.**
Str. 30/8—25/11/22.**G.**
Str. 13/3—28/6/24.**G.**
Str. 18/6—28/10/26.**G.**
Vacuum brake added.
Coal guard on tender.
Str. 13/8—13/11/28.**G.**
Altered to D15/2.
Str. 12/10/30—2/1/31.**G.**
Str. 23/2—22/4/33.**G.**
Str. 22/4—23/7/35.**G.**
Str. 6—20/3/36.**L.**
Str. 26/8—14/9/36.**H.**
Str. 18/2—8/4/37.**G.**
Str. 27/5—4/6/37.**L.**
Str. 27/12/38—3/3/39.**G.**
Rebuilt to D16/3.
Str. 29/11/41—2/1/42.**G.**
Str. 1—29/1/43.**L.**
Str. 21/6—4/8/44.**G.**
Str. 7/4—21/5/46.**G.**
Str. 11/4—14/5/48.**G.**
Str. 1/10—4/11/50.**G.**
Str. 10/6—3/7/53.**G.**
Str. 3/8—3/9/55.**G.**

BOILERS:
1844.
1794 *(ex8794)* 19/11/14.
3583 *(new)* 11/12/20.
1793 *(ex8849)* 28/6/24.
3581 *(ex8825)* 13/11/28.
3613 *(ex8855)* 2/1/31.
3576 *(ex8854)* 22/4/33.
3616 *(ex8873)* 23/7/35.
4224 *(ex8876)* 3/3/39.

4210 *(ex8885)* 2/1/42.
4208 *(ex8866)* 4/8/44.
4228 *(ex8870)* 21/5/46.
4204 *(ex8837)* 14/5/48.
23312 *(ex ?)* 4/11/50.
23330 *(ex8899)* 3/7/53.
23379 *(ex8801)* 3/9/55.

SHEDS:
Parkeston.
Ipswich 21/4/28.
Norwich 30/6/34.
Yarmouth 25/7/34.
Norwich 8/9/34.
Stratford 23/7/35.
Colchester 1/12/39.
Parkeston 2/1/43.
Stratford 16/1/43.
Norwich 2/9/46.
Melton Constable 9/3/47.
Norwich 24/7/47.
Yarmouth 11/2/48.
Norwich 25/2/48.

RENUMBERED:
8844 28/6/24.
2555 7/10/46.
62555 8/5/48.

CONDEMNED: 24/3/58.
Cut up at Stratford.

8845

To traffic 1/1907.

REPAIRS:
Str. 9/7—23/10/14.**G.**
Superheated boiler fitted.
Str. 10/10/21—14/1/22.**G.**
Str. 18/2—16/3/22.**H.**
New cylinders.
Str. 16/2—9/6/23.**G.**
Str. 19/7—10/9/24.**L.**
Str. 12/1—6/6/25.**G.**
Str. 15/12/25—8/1/26.**L.**
Str. 3/12/26—1/4/27.**G.**
Coal guard on tender.
Str. 17/1—13/5/29.**G.**
Rebuilt to D16/2.
Vacuum brake added.
Str. 23/9/30—2/1/31.**G.**
Str. 14/3—28/4/32.**G.**
Str. 1/1—1/3/34.**G.**
Str. 6/4—28/6/35.**G.**
Str. 20/4—24/6/37.**G.**
Str. 22/8—6/10/39.**G.**
Str. 3/6—17/7/42.**G.**
Str. 23—30/7/42.**N/C.**
Str. 23/7—2/9/44.**G.**
Str. 3/3—9/4/46.**G.**
Rebuilt to D16/3.
Str. 4/4—8/5/48.**H.**
Str. 30/1—16/3/49.**G.**

Str. 29/4—15/6/51.**G.**
Str. 26/10—13/11/52.**C/L.**
Str. 26/1—5/3/53.**C/L.**
Str. 13/12/53—16/1/54.**G.**

BOILERS:
1845.
3563 *(new)* 23/10/14.
3594 *(ex8821)* 14/1/22.
1799 *(ex8793)* 6/6/25.
3926 *(new)* 13/5/29.
3902 *(ex8846)* 28/4/32.
3903 *(ex8788)* 1/3/34.
1782 *(ex8841)* 24/6/37.
3900 *(ex8780)* 6/10/39.
3908 *(ex8831)* 17/7/42.
3934 *(ex8819)* 2/9/44.
4218 *(exJ19 8261)* 9/4/46.
4216 *(ex8878)* 8/5/48.
23454 *(new)* 15/6/51.
23370 *(ex8863)* 16/1/54.

SHEDS:
Norwich.
Yarmouth 31/1/35.
Norwich 1/4/35.
Yarmouth 5/9/43.
Norwich 10/10/43.
Yarmouth 30/9/45.
Ipswich 14/11/45.
Norwich 9/6/46.
Ipswich 20/6/46.
Norwich 16/4/50.
Lowestoft 29/10/50.
Norwich 29/4/51.

RENUMBERED:
8845 6/6/25.
2556 29/9/46.
62556 8/5/48.

CONDEMNED: 1/1/57.
Cut up at Stratford.

8846

To traffic 1/1907.

REPAIRS:
Str. 10/10/17—6/2/18.**G.**
Str. 15/10/19—16/1/20.**G.**
Str. 26/7/21—20/1/22.**G.**
Ips. 13/4—27/8/23.**H.**
Str. 14/8—19/12/24.**G.**
Rebuilt to D16/1.
Superheated boiler fitted.
Go. 22/5—16/9/26.**G.**
Str. 2/11/28—22/2/29.**G.**
Vacuum brake added.
Coal guard on tender.
Str. 24/11/31—12/2/32.**G.**
Str. 26/1—15/3/34.**G.**
Altered to D16/2.
Str. 30/1—20/3/36.**G.**

Str. 26/11—10/12/36.**L.**
Str. 22/10—26/11/37.**G.**
Str. 23/5—14/7/39.**G.**
Str. 28/10—29/11/41.**G.**
Str. 24/2—1/4/44.**G.**
Rebuilt to D16/3.
Str. 22/7—7/9/45.**G.**
Str. 18/3—8/8/47.**G.**
Str. 2/5—3/6/49.**G.**
Str. 2/9—13/10/51.**G.**
Str. 29/3—9/5/53.**C/L.**
Str. 8/11—5/12/53.**G.**

BOILERS:
1846.
1841 *(ex8841)* 6/2/18.
1818 *(ex8818)* 16/1/20.
3902 *(new)* 19/12/24.
3927 *(ex8805)* 12/2/32.
3904 *(ex8780)* 15/3/34.
3931 *(ex8841)* 20/3/36.
1788 *(ex8783)* 26/11/37.
3913 *(ex8838)* 14/7/39.
3912 *(ex8838)* 29/11/41.
4300 *(ex8783)* 1/4/44.
4321 *(ex8797)* 7/9/45.
4320 *(ex8859)* 8/8/47.
4231 *(ex8784)* 3/6/49.
23301 *(ex8862)* 13/10/51.
23392 *(ex8860)* 5/12/53.

SHEDS:
Colchester.
Cambridge 18/3/39.
Stratford 22/3/39.
Cambridge 18/9/39.
King's Lynn 10/2/52.
Cambridge 26/10/52.

RENUMBERED:
8846 19/12/24.
2557 15/12/46.
62557 3/6/49.

CONDEMNED: 31/10/55.
Cut up at Stratford.

8847

To traffic 1/1907.

REPAIRS:
Str. 26/4—1/8/16.**G.**
Str. 17/12/20—14/5/21.**G.**
Superheated boiler fitted.
Str. 2/10/22—6/1/23.**G.**
Str. 3/4—28/6/24.**G.**
Str. 11/3—27/7/26.**G.**
Rebuilt to D16/1.
Str. 9/3—21/6/28.**G.**
Coal guard on tender.
Str. 16/9—4/12/30.**G.**
Str. 31/8—20/10/33.**G.**
Altered to D16/2.

Str. 21/1—27/2/36.**G.**
B17 tender axleboxes fitted.
Str. 15/2—7/4/38.**G.**
Str. 26/2—9/5/40.**G.**
Str. 18/5—21/6/41.**L.**
Str. 20/6—7/8/42.**G.**
Str. 16—20/8/42.**L.**
Str. 8—20/2/43.**L.**
Str. 23/7—9/9/44.**G.**
Str. 14/4—31/5/46.**G.**
Str. 19/7—7/9/48.**G.**
Rebuilt to D16/3.
Str. 19/2—17/3/51.**G.**
Str. 28/3—11/4/51.**C/L.**
Str. 2/4—10/5/52.**C/L.**
Str. 21/6—15/8/53.**G.**
Str. 12/4—14/5/55.**G.**

BOILERS:
 1847.
 3556 *(new)* 1/8/16.
 3598 *(new)* 14/5/21.
 3905 *(new)* 27/7/26.
 3930 *(new)* 4/12/30.
 3933 *(ex8818)* 20/10/33.
 3925 *(ex8829)* 27/2/36.
 3926 *(ex8822)* 7/4/38.
 1785 *(ex8833)* 9/5/40.
 3922 *(ex8790)* 7/8/42.
 3929 *(ex8785)* 9/9/44.
 3930 *(ex8800)* 31/5/46.
 4205 *(ex8815)* 7/9/48.
 23335 *(ex8826)* 17/3/51.
 23333 *(ex8789)* 15/8/53.
 23403 *(ex8833)* 14/5/55.

SHEDS:
Stratford.
Norwich 7/10/25.
Stratford 16/1/26.
March 7/6/29.
Cambridge 24/10/40.
March 13/10/44.
Cambridge 31/12/44.
South Lynn 19/6/46.
Cambridge 15/4/51.
King's Lynn 7/10/51.
Cambridge 2/3/52.
King's Lynn 18/5/52.
Cambridge 26/10/52.
King's Lynn 6/11/55.

RENUMBERED:
 8847 28/6/24.
 2558 3/11/46.
 62558 4/9/48.

CONDEMNED: 6/5/57.
Cut up at Stratford.

8848

To traffic 3/1907.

REPAIRS:
Str. 29/9/14—25/1/15.**G.**
Str. 24/5—1/10/18.**G.**
Superheated boiler fitted.
Str. 27/1—24/6/22.**G.**
Str. 10/7—10/10/23.**G.**
Str. 2/5—28/7/25.**G.**
Str. 11/3—20/7/27.**G.**
Str. 23/11/28—11/4/29.**G.**
Altered to D15/2.
Coal guard on tender.
Str. 10/1—13/3/31.**G.**
Str. 16—29/7/31.**L.**
Str. 3—9/3/32.**L.**
Str. 21/4—27/5/32.**L.**
Str. 17/11/32—20/1/33.**G.**
Rebuilt to D16/3.
Str. 4/10—24/11/34.**G.**
Str. 21/4—19/6/36.**G.**
Str. 27/12/37—4/2/38.**G.**
Str. 12/9—20/12/39.**G.**
Str. 26/6—18/8/42.**G.**
Str. 20/6—5/8/44.**G.**
Str. 20/10—4/12/46.**G.**
Str. 17/2—26/3/49.**G.**
Str. 14/6—11/8/51.**G.**
Str. 2—26/9/53.**G.**
Str. 31/8—16/9/54.**C/L.**
Str. 31/1—4/3/55.**N/C.**

BOILERS:
 1848.
 1839 *(ex8839)* 25/1/15.
 3570 *(new)* 1/10/18.
 3566 *(ex8831)* 24/6/22.
 3594 *(ex8845)* 28/7/25.
 3581 *(ex8844)* 13/3/31.
 4201 *(new)* 20/1/33.
 4207 *(ex8821)* 24/11/34.
 4202 *(ex8860)* 19/6/36.
 4211 *(ex8849)* 4/2/38.
 4212 *(ex8885)* 20/12/39.
 4211 *(ex8836)* 18/8/42.
 4226 *(ex8863)* 5/8/44.
 4217 *(ex8858)* 4/12/46.
 4211 *(ex8863)* 26/3/49.
 23358 *(ex8843)* 11/8/51.
 23428 *(ex ?)* 26/9/53.

SHEDS:
Stratford.
Southend ?/??.
Stratford 7/12/29.
Southend 21/12/29.
Stratford 4/1/30.
Southend 25/1/30.
Stratford 29/3/30.
Southend 25/10/30.
Stratford 15/11/30.
Cambridge 26/3/31.

Stratford 29/12/32.
South Lynn 30/7/46.
King's Lynn 21/8/49.

RENUMBERED:
 8848 28/7/25.
 2559 22/6/46.
 62559 19/3/49.

CONDEMNED: 12/12/55.
Cut up at Stratford.

8849

To traffic 3/1907.

REPAIRS:
Str. 25/2—15/6/14.**G.**
Str. 7/2—23/5/19.**G.**
Superheated boiler fitted.
Str. 21/3—30/6/22.**G.**
Str. 8/1—12/4/24.**G.**
Str. 11/2—23/7/26.**G.**
Str. 17/2—25/5/28.**G.**
Altered to D15/2.
Coal guard on tender.
Str. 28/4—12/6/31.**G.**
Str. 26/1—5/4/33.**G.**
Rebuilt to D16/3.
Str. 9—11/7/34.**L.**
Str. 25/10—5/12/34.**G.**
Str. 30/3—8/5/36.**G.**
Str. ?/?—28/7/37.**G.**
Str. ?/?—16/2/38.**G.**
Str. ?/?—10/6/39.**G.**
Str. ?/?—?/8/41.**G.**
Str. ?/?—?/9/43.**G.**
Str. ?/?—20/5/44.**L.**
Str. 6/10—3/11/45.**G.**
Str. 6/1—15/2/46.**C/L.**
Str. 28/12/46—25/1/47.**L.**
Str. 22/3—31/5/47.**L.**
Str. 11/9/48. *Not repaired.*

BOILERS:
 1849.
 1828 *(ex8828)* 15/6/14.
 1793 *(ex8793)* 23/5/19.
 3601 *(ex8821)* 12/4/24.
 3606 *(ex8814)* 23/7/26.
 3567 *(ex8819)* 25/5/28.
 3598 *(ex8815)* 12/6/31.
 4204 *(new)* 5/4/33.
 4201 *(ex8848)* 5/12/34.
 4211 *(ex8816)* 8/5/36.
 4206 *(ex8860)* 16/2/38.
 4290 *(new)* 10/6/39.
 4276 *(exJ19 8268)* ?/8/41.
 4278 *(ex8793)* ?/9/43.
 4245 *(exJ19 8263)* 3/11/45.

SHEDS:
Stratford.
Norwich 6/10/25.

Stratford ?/??.
Cambridge 25/5/28.
Stratford 5/1/30.
Southend 29/3/30.
Stratford 20/9/30.
Colchester 10/3/40.
Stratford 8/9/40.
Ipswich 4/3/47.
Norwich 11/1/48.
Yarmouth 6/2/48.
Norwich 28/3/48.
Melton Constable 7/4/48.
Norwich 9/6/48.
Melton Constable 15/8/48.
Norwich 4/9/48.

RENUMBERED:
8849 12/4/24.
2560 1/12/46.

CONDEMNED: 24/9/48.
Cut up at Stratford.

(opposite, top) **When painted black, Stratford also covered the brass beading of the splashers therefore necessitating the use of 9" figures when the numbers were moved to the cab side. From 1931 the beading was discarded and the number plate moved to the leading splasher enabling 12" figures to be used.** *L.N.E.R.*

(opposite, centre) **Shed crews which took a pride in their engine, such as no.8868 at King's Lynn, soon removed the black paint from the brasswork and then kept it polished.**

(opposite, bottom) **The prominence of the red lining on no.8892 is probably due to a panchromatic film being used. The picture was taken 18th March 1939, the day the engine was ex works from a general repair. Note brasswork painted over. From November 1941 the red lining was discarded and from July 1942 only NE appeared on the tender.** *G.W.Powell.*

From January 1946 LNER was restored and during that year re-numbering to 2500-2620 took place. By then only thirteen D15/2 remained and no.2538 (ex8867) was the highest number. After a shed renumbering on 15th June 1946, it was out from a 'general' on 9th April 1947 with shaded transfers still used for numbers and restored LNER. *Photomatic.*

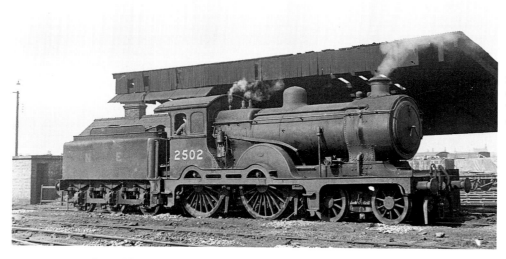

No.8891 was re-numbered to 2502 at King's Lynn shed on Sunday 6th October 1946, the local painter faithfully copying the size and style of the former number but without the shading. The NE on the tender dated from its previous repair, out 13th July 1945. *H.C.Casserley.*

No.2504 was withdrawn in LNER lettering but nos.62509 (ex-works 8th April 1948) and 62512 (25th May 1948) got BRITISH RAILWAYS on the tender and 12" numbers in Gill Sans style but with the modified 6 and 9, and with number painted on the front buffer beam. 62512 is at King's Lynn 30th July 1949. *J.F.Henton.*

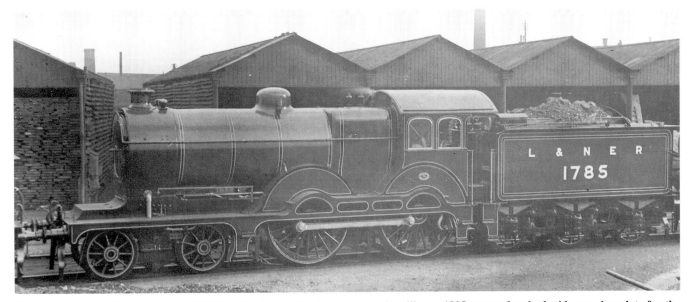

From 21st June to 29th September 1923 Stratford turned out ten new engines like no.1805 except they had wide running plate for the full length and they had exhaust steam injector fitted on the left hand side. They were all painted green, with L&NER on the tender. The first six were nos.1780 to 1785, but on 24th August 1923 the next out, no.1786, had an 'E' suffix, as did the final three as they left the paint shop.

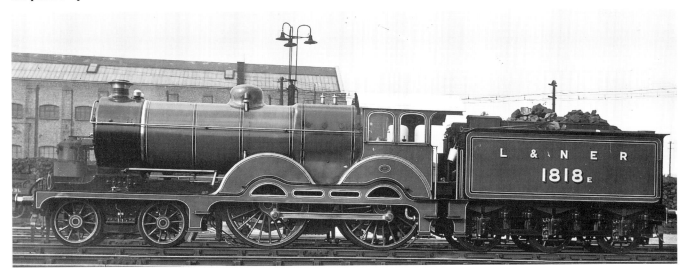

(above) At the same time as they were building the new engines, no.1818 was being rebuilt like no.1805. It was ex works 9th June 1923 but later in the year was given white cab roof, polished brass rim to chimney, and had 'E' suffix added, in preparation for it to take up a Royal train working to or from a Sandringham visit. Three more, nos.8846 (19th December 1924), 8853 (29th May 1926), 8847 (27th July 1926), were similarly rebuilt and also received green livery, so the class totalled fifteen.

(right) Very soon after building, the first six nos.1780-1785 had the area suffix 'E' added, this being done at their shed.

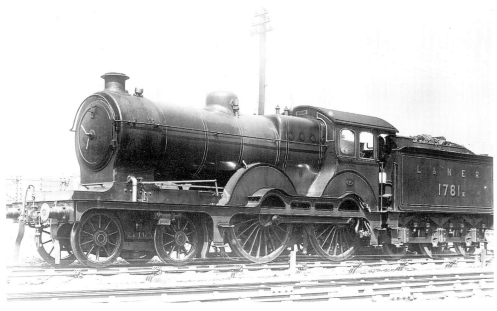

8830

To traffic 3/1908.

REPAIRS:
Str. 9/5—4/12/18.**G.**
Str. 28/4—11/7/23.**G.**
Str. 20/10/24—29/1/25.**G.**
Superheated boiler fitted.
Vacuum brake added.
Gor. 21/5—6/9/26.**G.**
Str. 1—22/10/27.**L.**
Str. 1/3—24/5/29.**G.**
Altered to D15/2.
Coal guard on tender.
Str. 30/9—11/12/30.**G.**
Str. 14/6—9/8/32.**G.**
Str. 14/2—11/4/34.**G.**
Ash ejector fitted.
Str. 28/11/35—17/1/36.**G.**
Str. 25—27/5/36.**L.**
Str. 30/11—29/12/37.**G.**
Str. 9/5—3/6/38.**L.**
Str. 7/12/39—16/3/40.**G.**
Rebuilt to D16/3.
Str. 8/2—20/3/42.**G.**
Str. 10/10—4/12/43.**G.**
Str. 16/2—3/4/45.**G.**
Str. 19/7—6/10/46.**G.**
Str. 15/12/48—1/2/49.**G.**
Str. 18—25/7/50.**C/L.**
Str. 21/12/50—27/1/51.**G.**
Str. 16/11—13/12/52.**C/L.**
Str. 1—31/10/53.**G.**
Str. 29/11—2/12/53.**N/C.**
Str. 26/8—2/10/54.**C/L.**
Str. 25/4—8/6/55.**C/L.**
Str. 2/2—24/5/56.**G.**

BOILERS:
1830.
1802 *(ex8802)* 4/12/18.
1810 *(ex8840)* 11/7/23.
3652 *(new)* 29/1/25.
3622 *(ex8858)* 24/5/29.
3562 *(ex8797)* 11/12/30.
3639 *(ex8858)* 9/8/32.
3595 *(ex8798)* 11/4/34.
3437 *(exJ17 8235)* 17/1/36.
3625 *(ex8811)* 29/12/37.
4307 *(new)* 16/3/40.
4315 *(new)* 20/3/42.
4249 *(ex8828)* 4/12/43.
4302 *(ex8820)* 3/4/45.
4331 *(ex8812)* 6/10/46.
4313 *(ex8832)* 1/2/49.
23327 *(ex ?)* 27/1/51.
23341 *(exJ19 8247)* 31/10/53.
23309 *(exJ19 8245)* 24/5/56.

SHEDS:
March.
Cambridge 26/5/29.
King's Lynn 11/6/39.

March 21/11/42.
Yarmouth Beach 18/7/43.
Norwich 3/10/48.
Lowestoft 31/10/48.
Yarmouth Beach 16/2/49.
Norwich 7/9/52.
Melton Constable 26/9/55.

RENUMBERED:
8830 ?/?/??.
2561 27/10/46.
62561 29/1/49.

CONDEMNED: 10/2/58.
Cut up at Stratford.

8831

To traffic 4/1908.

REPAIRS:
Str. 22/12/15—6/4/16.**G.**
Superheated boiler fitted.
Str. 21/12/21—11/5/22.**G.**
Str. 17/3—11/5/23.**G.**
Str. 26/7—14/10/24.**G.**
Str. 15/9—23/10/25.**L.**
Str. 10/3—8/7/26.**G.**
Str. 31/12/27—19/4/28.**G.**
Rebuilt to D16/2.
Coal guard on tender.
Str. 24/7—17/8/28.**L.**
Vacuum brake added.
Str. 8/11/29—21/1/30.**G.**
Str. 7/5—2/7/31.**G.**
Str. 6/3—13/4/33.**G.**
Str. 14/10—26/11/34.**G.**
Str. 23/9—29/10/36.**G.**
Str. 9/5—1/7/38.**G.**
Str. 5/6—16/8/40.**G.**
Str. 20/4—12/6/42.**G.**
Str. 16/4—18/5/44.**G.**
Str. 30/12/45—9/2/46.**G.**
Rebuilt to D16/3.
Str. 1/2—30/7/47.**L.**
Str. 14/3—15/5/48.**G.**
Str. 12/10—18/11/50.**G.**
Str. 9/4—30/5/53.**G.**
Str. 19/4—21/5/55.**G.**

BOILERS:
1831.
3566 *(new)* 6/4/16.
3568 *(ex8807)* 11/5/22.
3915 *(new)* 19/4/28.
3906 *(ex8784)* 2/7/31.
3923 *(ex8784)* 13/4/33.
3929 *(ex8819)* 26/11/34.
3916 *(ex8842)* 29/10/36.
3908 *(ex8805)* 16/8/40.
3920 *(ex8792)* 12/6/42.
3912 *(ex8846)* 18/5/44.
4333 *(ex8873)* 9/2/46.
4306 *(ex8798)* 15/5/48.

23308 *(ex ?)* 18/11/50.
23336 *(ex8785)* 30/5/53.
23331 *(ex8857)* 21/5/55.

SHEDS:
Norwich.
Yarmouth 27/3/35.
Norwich 21/12/35.
Yarmouth 26/1/36.
Norwich 27/9/36.
Yarmouth 18/2/37.
Norwich 8/5/38.
Yarmouth 7/7/38.
Norwich 6/5/40.
Yarmouth 6/6/43.
Norwich 25/7/43.
Lowestoft 20/10/45.
Norwich 18/11/45.
Melton Constable 2/12/45.
Norwich 23/3/52.
Cambridge 29/6/52.
King's Lynn 3/8/52.
Cambridge 7/9/52.
Pbo. Spital Bridge 4/10/52.
Cambridge 12/10/52
March 21/2/54.

RENUMBERED:
8831 14/10/24.
2562 18/8/46.
62562 15/5/48.

CONDEMNED: 22/10/57.
Cut up at Stratford.

8832

To traffic 5/1908.

REPAIRS:
Str. 8/3—15/7/19.**G.**
Superheated boiler fitted.
Str. 23/8—28/10/21.**G.**
Str. 17/8/22—28/2/23.**G.**
Str. 24/4—12/7/24.**G.**
Str. 13/8—3/12/26.**G.**
Str. ?/?—?/12/28.**G.**
Vacuum brake added.
Coal guard on tender.
Str. ?/?—?/11/30.**G.**
Altered to D15/2.
Str. 16/11—15/12/32.**G.**
Str. 22/6—26/7/34.**G.**
Str. 17/4—10/7/36.**G.**
Rebuilt to D16/3.
Str. ?/?—4/2/38.**G.**
Str. ?/?—19/12/40.**G.**
Str. ?/?—19/10/43.**G.**
Str. 13—30/10/45.**G.**
Str. 16/3—2/4/46.**L.**
Str. 25/5—27/7/46.**L.**
Str. 23/11—3/12/46.**L.**
Str. 1/2—13/3/47.**L.**
Str. 23/2—6/3/48.**L.**

BOILERS:
1832.
3580 *(new)* 15/7/19.
3582 *(ex8855)* 28/2/23.
3580 *(ex8824)* 12/7/24.
3598 *(ex8847)* 3/12/26.
3606 *(ex8849)* ?/12/28.
3566 *(ex8817)* ?/11/30.
3643 *(ex8793)* 15/12/32.
3569 *(ex8811)* 26/7/34.
4240 *(new)* 10/7/36.
4243 *(ex8900)* 4/2/38.
4244 *(exJ19 8247)* 19/12/40.
4273 *(exJ19 8260)* 19/10/43.
4313 *(ex8811)* 30/10/45.

SHEDS:
Ipswich.
Norwich 26/1/29.
Peterborough East 26/7/34.
Ipswich 13/11/34.
Norwich 19/10/41.
Yarmouth 4/6/44.
Norwich 9/7/44.

RENUMBERED:
8832 12/7/24.
2563 29/10/46.

CONDEMNED: 6/8/48.
Cut up at Stratford.

8833

To traffic 5/1908.

REPAIRS:
Str. 22/10/20—28/1/21.**G.**
Str. 26/10/23—6/3/24.**G.**
Str. 24/8/25—9/3/26.**G.**
Vacuum brake added.
Str. 9/12/27—24/3/28.**G.**
Coal guard added.
Str. 9/11/29—30/1/30.**G.**
Rebuilt to D16/2.
Superheated boiler fitted.
Str. 8/4—10/6/31.**G.**
Str. 24/4—2/6/33.**G.**
Str. 27/11/34—9/1/35.**G.**
Str. 28/4—17/6/36.**G.**
Str. 18/12/37—28/1/38.**G.**
Str. 21/9—21/12/39.**G.**
Str. 27/8—9/10/43.**G.**
Str. 24/5—22/7/44.**G.**
Str. 17/12/45—19/1/46.**G.**
Str. 19/11/47—22/1/48.**G.**
Rebuilt to D16/3.
Str. 14/1—24/2/50.**G.**
Str. 23/3—1/5/52.**G.**
W.P.U. gear removed.
Str. 27/2—2/4/55.**G.**
Str. 29/12/55—21/1/56.**C/L.**
Str. 14/2/58. *Not repaired.*

BOILERS:
1833.
1795 (ex8795) 28/1/21.
1786 (ex8786) 30/1/30.
1784 (ex8838) 2/6/33.
3914 (ex8852) 9/1/35.
3921 (ex8786) 17/6/36.
1785 (ex8786) 28/1/38.
3931 (ex8822) 21/12/39.
3917 (ex8856) 9/10/43.
3921 (ex8838) 19/1/46.
4253 (ex8808) 22/1/48.
4340 (new) 24/2/50.
4340 reno. 23403 1/5/52.
23396 (ex8868) 2/4/55.

SHEDS:
Cambridge.
Stratford 5/6/26.
Southend 22/2/30.
Stratford 26/7/30.
Southend 9/8/30.
Stratford 8/11/30.
Colchester 8/9/40.
Stratford 2/1/43.
Norwich 4/8/45.
Yarmouth 10/10/45.
Yarmouth Beach 19/3/46.
Norwich 30/3/46.
Yarmouth Beach 8/5/46.
Melton Constable 22/9/46.
Yarmouth Beach 24/10/46.
Norwich 27/11/46.
Yarmouth 22/5/47.
Norwich 8/6/47.
Yarmouth Beach 13/7/47.
Norwich 21/9/47.
Yarmouth Beach 4/2/48.
Norwich 7/9/52.
Melton Constable 18/4/54.
Norwich 11/7/54.
Melton Constable 26/12/54.
Yarmouth Beach 2/1/55.
Norwich 3/4/55.
Yarmouth Beach 13/11/55.
Norwich 18/12/55.
Cambridge 6/1/57.
Lincoln 24/3/57.

RENUMBERED:
1833ᴇ 6/3/24.
8833 after 12/24.
2564 27/10/46.
62564 24/2/50.

CONDEMNED: 24/3/58.
Cut up at Stratford.

8834

To traffic 5/1908.

REPAIRS:
Str. 29/9—23/12/14.**G.**

Str. 10/10/19—30/1/20.**G.**
Str. 18/3—28/7/21.**G.**
Str. 20/11/22—24/2/23.**G.**
Str. 10/9/24—13/1/25.**G.**
Str. 19/2—14/6/27.**G.**
Vacuum brake added.
Str. 21/12/28—22/3/29.**G.**
Rebuilt to D16/2.
Superheated boiler fitted.
Coal guard on tender.
Str. 12—28/11/29.**L.**
Str. 14/10/30—15/1/31.**G.**
Str. 27/7—10/9/31.**H.**
Str. 24/9—24/11/33.**G.**
Str. 9—17/4/34.**L.**
Str. 22/2—8/3/35.**L.**
Str. 15/3—1/5/36.**G.**
Str. 24/4—11/6/38.**G.**
Str. 8/3—24/4/41.**G.**
Str. 12/2—6/4/43.**G.**
Str. 13/5—21/6/45.**G.**
Rebuilt to D16/3.
Str. 8/10/46—21//1/47.**G.**
Str. 5/6—14/7/47.**L.**
Str. 8/6—6/8/49.**G.**
Str. 20—28/9/49.**N/C.**
Str. 4/8—13/9/52.**G.**
Str. 22/3/54. Weigh.
Str. 3/10—6/11/54.**G.**
Str. 26/3—5/5/56.**C/L.**

BOILERS:
1834.
3554 (new) 23/12/14.
1808 (ex8836) 30/1/20.
1818 (ex8846) 13/1/25.
3924 (new) 22/3/29.
1789 (ex8829) 24/11/33.
3933 (ex8847) 1/5/36.
1786 (ex8813) 11/6/38.
3914 (ex8839) 24/4/41.
3905 (ex8842) 6/4/43.
4236 (ex8860) 21/6/45.
4328 (exJ19 8149) 21/1/47.
4292 (exJ19 8265) 6/8/49.
23416 (ex ?) 13/9/52.
23380 (exJ19 8143) 6/11/54.

SHEDS:
Stratford.
Cambridge 5/10/26.
Stratford 1/1/27.
Cambridge 15/4/29.
March 26/5/29.
Norwich 21/9/39.
Yarmouth 6/3/40.
Norwich 19/5/40.
Yarmouth 18/6/44.
Norwich 2/7/44.
Yarmouth Beach 14/1/45.
Stratford 10/8/45.
Colchester 17/8/46.
Stratford 7/12/46.
Colchester 28/12/46.

Stratford 16/5/48.
Cambridge 20/5/51.
King's Lynn 5/8/51.

RENUMBERED:
8834 13/1/25.
2565 13/9/46.
62565 6/8/49.

CONDEMNED: 1/1/57.
Cut up at Stratford.

8835

To traffic 5/1908.

REPAIRS:
Str. 25/3—24/7/20.**G.**
Str. 12/10/21—9/2/22.**G.**
Ca. 14/4—25/5/23.**H.**
Str. 3/11/24—6/3/25.**G.**
Superheated boiler fitted.
Str. 17/12/26—3/5/27.**G.**
Coal guard on tender.
Str. 5/12/28—16/5/29.**G.**
Altered to D15/2.
Str. 14/1—20/3/31.**G.**
Str. 22/11/32—6/1/33.**G.**
Str. 1/12/34—25/1/35.**G.**
Str. 2—5/6/36.**L.**
Str. 28/9—30/10/36.**G.**
Str. 23/10/38—27/1/39.**G.**
Rebuilt to D16/3.
Str. 16/6—26/7/40.**G.**
Str. 15/7—31/8/42.**G.**
Str. 8—14/9/42.**L.**
Str. 13/8—30/9/44.**G.**
Str. 20/3—21/5/46.**G.**
Str. 21/8—5/10/48.**G.**
Str. 16/7—19/8/50.**G.**
Str. 30/6—16/8/52.**G.**
Str. 4—24/1/53.**C/L.**
Str. 29/6—21/8/54.**G.**
Str. 1/10—17/11/56.**G.**

BOILERS:
1835.
1859 (ex8859) 24/7/20.
3656 (new) 6/3/25.
1798 (ex8798) 16/5/29.
3647 (ex8840) 20/3/31.
3583 (ex8817) 6/1/33.
3675 (ex8887) 25/1/35.
3652 (ex8806) 30/10/36.
4284 (new) 27/1/39.
4261 (ex8825) 26/7/40.
4269 (ex8812) 31/8/42.
4314 (exJ19 8251) 30/9/44.
4311 (ex8787) 21/5/46.
4310 (exJ19 8148) 5/10/48.
4322 (ex8838) 19/8/50.
23413 (ex ?) 16/8/52.
23429 (ex ?) 21/8/54.
23460 (ex8878) 17/11/56.

SHEDS:
March.
Cambridge 26/5/29.
King's Lynn 5/7/31.
Cambridge 6/12/31.
King's Lynn 16/5/37.
Cambridge 31/10/37.
King's Lynn 23/3/39.
Cambridge 14/6/39.
Bury St Edmunds 10/12/39.
King's Lynn 9/6/57.

RENUMBERED:
8835 6/3/25.
2566 27/10/46.
62566 2/10/48.

CONDEMNED: 2/12/58.
Cut up at Stratford.

8836

To traffic 6/1908.

REPAIRS:
Str. 16/4—14/9/15.**G.**
Str. 14/8/18—11/2/19.**G.**
Str. 25/6—16/11/20.**G.**
Str. 19/7/22—3/3/23.**G.**
Str. 12/7—31/12/24.**G.**
Str. 19/2—16/6/26.**G.**
Str. 1/6/27.**N/C.**
Vacuum brake added.
Str. 2/3—29/6/28.**G.**
Superheated boiler fitted.
Coal guard on tender.
Str. 19/12/29—20/2/30.**G.**
Altered to D15/2.
Str. 7/9—30/10/31.**G.**
Str. 19/10—11/12/33.**G.**
Str. 10/9—18/10/35.**G.**
Str. 22—26/6/36.**L.**
Str. 23/8—15/10/37.**G.**
Rebuilt to D16/3.
Str. 6/2—30/3/40.**G.**
Str. 26/3—12/5/42.**G.**
Str. 28/9—8/10/42.**L.**
Str. 3/8—2/9/44.**G.**
Str. 11—25/1/45.**L.**
Str. 4/6—16/7/45.**L.**
Str. 24/7—13/8/45.**L.**
Str. 3/9—18/12/46.**G.**
Str. 30/11—24/12/47.**L.**
Str. 28/1—8/2/48.**L.**
Str. 7/2—10/4/49.**G.**
Str. 22/4—2/6/51.**G.**
Str. 17/2—20/3/53.**G.**
Str. 24/9—17/10/53.**C/L.**
Str. 14/11—18/12/54.**G.**
Str. 3/12/56. Not repaired.

BOILERS:
1836.
1808 (ex8808) 14/9/15.

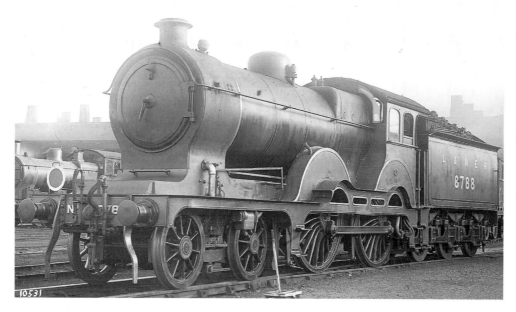

Some time between 17th and 28th January 1925 this engine was changed from 1788ᴇ to 8788, probably at the shed by a Stratford works painter. It then entered works 19th March 1925 for a 'general' and when out on 2nd July it had lost the ampersand. No.8818 was another which had L&NER combined with its 1924 number. When ex works 16th January 1925 from a 'general', the tender was not painted, the number being patched from 1818ᴇ to 8818.

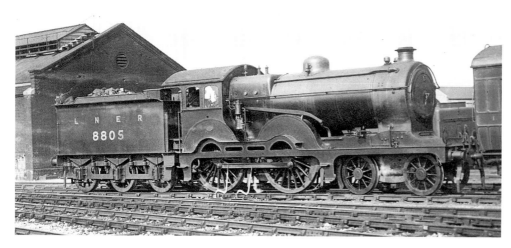

At Grouping nos.1818 and 1847 already had dual braking and the 1923-built engines had the Westinghouse and vacuum ejector when new. The other three had vacuum ejector added, 8805 (June 1927), 8853 (October 1928), 8846 (February 1929). Ex works 14th December 1928, no.8805 was in black livery with single red lining and still with number on the tender, but now carrying LNER for the first time. When ex works 5th July 1924 this engine had got its small LNER numberplate but it kept the grey paint until 14th September 1928 so never had green livery unlike the rest of the class.

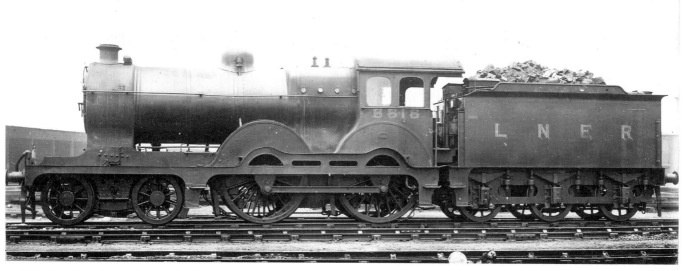

In 1927 class Part 1 was given to the fifteen engines with short smokebox. When no.8818 had number put on its cab, 22nd November 1929, only four other Part 1 engines remained: 8782, 8805, 8846, 8847. Note that none of the tenders had coal guards on them when first D16/1. No.8818 received its coal guard 26th May 1928. *L.N.E.R.*

On 9th April 1926, no.8813 was ex works rebuilt with the 5' 1⅛" boiler, but also including a new feature which, by 1935, had been applied to all 121 of the 'Clauds' - this was the extended smokebox, from 3' 4¾" to 4' 10". Note also that the tender was fitted with copings which Stratford referred to as coal guards. In 1927, engines with extended smokebox became Part 2. No.8813 is at Colchester shed in 1926. *H.Gordon Tidey.*

Whilst no.8813 was being assessed, two more D15's had been rebult to D16/1 i.e. with short smokebox, and further rebuilding to D16/2 did not get under way until May 1927. From then until April 1931, twenty-four were dealt with. Eleven were rebuilt to D16/2 direct from D15NS, between July 1927 and April 1931. Eleven were rebuilt from D15/1 superheater, from May 1927 to May 1929. Two which had been fitted with extended smokebox to their 4' 9" boiler (making them D15/2) were also changed to D16/2, these were no.8819 (19th January 1928) and 8790 (26th April 1929). The frames of those built as D14 (nos.8860 to 8900) were not suitable for carrying the 5' 1⅛" diameter boiler with Belpaire firebox so none of them could become either D16/1 or D16/2. 8819 is at Felistowe, August 1933.

On the ten engines built as Part 1, nine got longer smokebox between 1st June 1928 (8783) and 10th June 1929 (8784). For some reason no.8782 came out 23rd June 1928 and 27th January 1930 from general repairs still with short box and did not become Part 2 until 29th May 1931. Between 14th November 1929 (no.8853) and 15th March 1934 (no.8846) the five rebuilt to D16/1 were fitted with longer smokebox, and Part 1 was then extinct and Part 2 then reached a total of 40 engines. 8846 is also at Colchester, 25th March 1937.

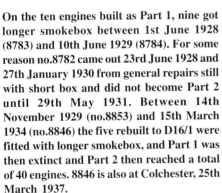

The normal frames had the concave curve at the front end under the smokebox. No.8781, however, had convex curves on the front end of its frame when ex works in May 1931. It was the only D16/2 to have such and resulted from accident damage when 8781 was in collision with B12 no.8578 which was running tender first and in error on the Clacton instead of the Walton line where it should have been.

8836 cont.
  1827 *(ex8827)* 11/2/19.
  1806 *(ex8841)* 16/11/20.
  3649 *(ex8817)* 29/6/28.
  3551 *(ex8824)* 20/2/30.
  3627 *(ex8809)* 30/10/31.
  3465 *(ex8803)* 11/12/33.
  3463 *(ex8807)* 18/10/35.
  4204 *(ex8854)* 15/10/37.
  4211 *(ex8848)* 30/3/40.
  4222 *(ex8866)* 12/5/42.
  4221 *(ex8871)* 2/9/44.
  4219 *(exJ19 8261)* 10/4/49.
  23452 *(new)* 2/6/51.
  23316 *(ex8879)* 20/3/53.
  23366 *(ex8870)* 18/12/54.

SHEDS:
  Norwich.
  Stratford 16/6/26.
  Ipswich 29/6/28.
  Cambridge 20/2/30.
  King's Lynn 18/2/37.
  Cambridge 16/5/37.

RENUMBERED:
  8836 31/12/24.
  2567 11/10/46.
  62567 9/4/49.

CONDEMNED: 17/12/56.
Cut up at Stratford.

8837

To traffic 7/1908.

REPAIRS:
  Str. 13/7/18—13/3/19.**G.**
  Str. 6/6—15/11/22.**G.**
  Str. 13/3—6/7/24.**G.**
  Str. 19/8/25—5/1/26.**G.**
  Str. 12/9/27—4/1/28.**G.**
  Coal guard on tender.
  Str. 22/6—17/10/29.**G.**
  Vacuum brake added.
  Str. 7/5—14/7/31.**G.**
  Altered to D15/2.
  Superheated boiler fitted.
  Str. 14/2—5/5/33.**G.**
  Rebuilt to D16/3.
  Str. 14/8—14/9/34.**G.**
  Str. 10/2—27/3/36.**G.**
  Str. 1/11—3/12/37.**G.**
  Str. 14/6—5/8/39.**G.**
  Str. 28/3—13/4/40.**L.**
  Str. 19/9—2/11/42.**G.**
  Str. 18/3—3/4/43.**L.**
  Str. 9/5—17/6/44.**G.**
  Str. 27/1—7/2/45.**L.**
  Str. 29/10—1/12/45.**G.**
  Str. 18/1—9/2/46.**L.**
  Str. 5/4—6/5/46.**L.**
  Str. 8/10—26/12/46.**L.**

  Str. 13/5—30/7/47.**L.**
  Str. 11/2—22/4/48.**G.**
  Str. 23/11—31/12/49.**G.**
  Str. 18/9—10/11/50.**C/H.**
  Str. 15—27/1/51.**C/L.**
  Str. 14/8—6/9/52.**C/L.**
  Str. 16/3—6/6/53.**G.**
  Str. 10/2—5/3/54.**C/L.**
  Str. 5/8—5/10/54.**C/H.**
  Str. 29/8—21/10/55.**G.**
  Str. 14/4/58. *Not repaired.*

BOILERS:
  1837.
  1817 *(ex8808)* 13/3/19.
  1819 *(ex8817)* 6/7/24.
  1804 *(ex8843)* 5/1/26.
  3463 *(new)* 14/7/31.
  4206 *(new)* 5/5/33.
  4219 *(new)* 14/9/34.
  4242 *(new)* 27/3/36.
  4231 *(exJ19 8149)* 3/12/37.
  4298 *(new)* 5/8/39.
  4284 *(ex8820)* 2/11/42.
  4325 *(new)* 17/6/44.
  4204 *(ex8871)* 1/12/45.
  4225 *(ex8854)* 22/4/48.
  4335 *(new)* 31/12/49.
  4335 reno. 23319 10/11/50.
  23306 *(ex8810)* 6/6/53.
  23410 *(exJ19 8141)* 21/10/55.

SHEDS:
  Yarmouth.
  Norwich 28/4/29.
  Yarmouth 13/7/30.
  Norwich 5/4/31.
  Yarmouth 19/7/31.
  Norwich 29/1/33.
  Stratford 2/10/33.
  Norwich 17/10/33.
  Yarmouth 8/2/42.
  Norwich 15/3/42.
  Stratford 30/9/45.
  Norwich 6/5/46.
  Yarmouth 25/7/46.
  Melton Constable 23/3/47.
  Norwich 13/5/47.
  Trafford Park 9/4/50.
  Norwich 8/6/52.
  Cambridge 22/6/52.
  South Lynn 22/9/52.
  Pbo. Spital Bridge 19/10/52.
  Lincoln 24/3/57.

RENUMBERED:
  8837 ?/?/??.
  7707 7/11/42.
  2568 6/4/46.
  62568 17/4/48.

CONDEMNED: 28/4/58.
Cut up at Stratford.

8838

To traffic 7/1908.

REPAIRS:
  Str. 26/1—25/5/16.**G.**
  Str. 28/12/17—10/5/18.**G.**
  Str. 26/6—7/11/22.**G.**
  Str. 10/10/23—24/1/24.**G.**
  Str. 21/8/25—21/1/26.**G.**
  Str. 4/11/27—10/2/28.**G.**
  Coal guard on tender.
  Str. 26/9—20/11/29.**G.**
  Rebuilt to D16/2.
  Superheated boiler fitted.
  Str. 28/2—1/5/31.**G.**
  Str. 10/12/32—26/1/33.**G.**
  Str. 8/4—29/6/34.**G.**
  Str. 9/3—7/5/36.**G.**
  Str. 2/1—16/1/37.**L.**
  Str. 5/2—6/4/39.**G.**
  Str. 26/6—15/7/39.**L.**
  Str. 29/5—18/7/41.**G.**
  Str. 17—27/3/42.**L.**
  Str. 16/10—10/11/42.**L.**
  Str. 22/1—15/2/43.**L.**
  Str. 8/12/43—17/2/44.**G.**
  Str. 3—16/3/44.**L.**
  Str. 22/11/45—5/1/46.**G.**
  Str. 21/5—26/8/46.**L.**
  Str. 14/3—1/5/48.**G.**
  Rebuilt to D16/3.
  Str. 14/5—17/6/50.**G.**
  Str. 6/4—6/5/52.**G.**
  W.P.U. gear removed.
  Str. 14/3—1/5/54.**G.**
  Str. 11/11/56. *Not repaired.*

BOILERS:
  1838.
  1858 *(ex8858)* 25/5/16.
  1838 *(ex-spare)* 10/5/18.
  1811 *(ex8802)* 7/11/22.
  1851 *(ex8827)* 21/1/26.
  1784 *(ex8784)* 20/11/29.
  3907 *(ex8801)* 26/1/33.
  3917 *(ex8827)* 29/6/34.
  3913 *(ex8837)* 7/5/36.
  3912 *(ex8795)* 6/4/39.
  3918 *(ex8856)* 18/7/41.
  3921 *(ex8805)* 17/2/44.
  3903 *(ex8829)* 5/1/46.
  4322 *(exJ19 8240)* 1/5/48.
  4234 *(ex8808)* 17/6/50.
  23404 *(ex ?)* 6/5/52.
  23381 *(ex8822)* 1/5/54.

SHEDS:
  Stratford.
  Southend 7/12/29.
  Stratford 31/5/50.
  Southend 14/6/30.
  Stratford 27/9/30.
  Southend 25/10/30.

  Stratford 1/11/30.
  March 7/5/36.
  Cambridge 15/8/41.
  King's Lynn 10/11/46.
  Cambridge 27/11/46.
  Bury St Edmunds 1/12/46.
  Cambridge 4/5/47.
  King's Lynn 13/5/47.

RENUMBERED:
  8838 *after 1/25.*
  7708 14/11/42.
  2569 24/3/46.
  62569 24/4/48.

CONDEMNED: 26/11/56.
Cut up at Stratford.

8839

To traffic 8/1908.

REPAIRS:
  Str. 24/3—17/7/14.**G.**
  Str. 28/2—18/6/20.**G.**
  Str. 3/11/21—4/3/22.**G.**
  Superheated boiler fitted.
  Str. 8/5—3/11/23.**G.**
  Str. 13/6—22/8/24.**G.**
  Str. 19/12/35—30/3/26.**G.**
  Str. 11/1—4/4/28.**G.**
  Rebuilt to D16/2.
  Coal guard on tender.
  Str. 30/1—12/4/30.**G.**
  Str. 8/11—17/12/30.**L.**
  Str. 11/4—27/5/32.**G.**
  Str. 20/9—24/10/34.**G.**
  Str. 10/9—20/10/36.**G.**
  Str. 12/5—12/7/38.**G.**
  Str. 20/7—29/10/40.**G.**
  Str. 30/11/42—26/1/43.**G.**
  Str. 21/1—17/2/45.**G.**
  Str. 29/8—11/10/45.**L.**
  Str. 16/3—30/5/47.**G.**
  Str. 20/8—29/9/49.**G.**
  Rebuilt to D16/3.
  Str. 14/11—19/12/51.**G.**
  W.P.U. gear removed.
  Str. 2/2—12/3/54.**G.**
  Str. 31/5—6/8/55.**C/L.**
  Str. 20/5—21/7/56.**G.**

BOILERS:
  1839.
  1815 *(ex8815)* 17/7/14.
  1839 *(ex8848)* 18/6/20.
  3613 *(new)* 4/3/22.
  3573 *(ex8821)* 30/3/26.
  3914 *(new)* 4/4/28.
  3919 *(ex8796)* 27/5/32.
  3907 *(ex8838)* 24/10/34.
  3914 *(ex8833)* 20/10/36.
  3901 *(ex8842)* 29/10/40.
  3904 *(ex8852)* 26/1/43.

Until November 1931 all D16/2 boilers had top feed clack boxes on the sides of the dome but in that month no.8841 came out of shops minus the top feed and with the clack boxes placed on the side of the boiler with a vertical pipe from under the running plate. This modification was eventually applied to all as shown on 8851. Later on, the feed pipes on no.8841 were modified again, this time arranged to run horizontally through the leading splasher before curving upward to the clack box; the only engine to have this unusual pipe run which it kept until rebuilt to Part 3 in 1948. *W.L.Good.*

The ten LNER built engines nos.8780 to 8789 came out equipped with exhaust steam injector on the left hand side, and this was also put on nos.8841 (30th January 1929) and 8834 (22nd March 1929). All were of the Davies & Metcalfe pattern, the pipe from the base of the smokebox and the grease separator under the running plate being in view.

Apart from the ten built in 1923, Wakefield type mechanical lubricator was fitted, mounted on the top edge of the right hand frame. The 1923 engines had Detroit sight feed lubricators in the cab, and kept these until the early 1930's. Starting with no.8783 in June 1928 these ten were gradually changed over to Wakefield lubricators. However, no.8788 kept its Detroit equipment until January 1937 at least.

On 1st June 1928 no.8783 was ex works as Part 2 and specially painted, also polished, to act as selected engine to work Royal trains between King's Cross and King's Lynn for Sandringham visits. Before each duty the cab roof received a coat of white paint. Few of the D16/2 engines got hinged glass sight screens fitted and those that did got them fairly late on, even 8783 and 8787, the Royal train duo did not receive them until 1934 at the earliest.

8839 cont.
   3915 *(ex8784)* 17/2/45.
   3925 *(ex8842)* 30/5/47.
   4202 *(ex8870)* 29/9/49.
   23352 *(ex8854)* 19/12/51.
   23382 *(exJ19 8266)* 12/3/54.
   23458 *(exJ19 8252)* 21/7/56.

SHEDS:
Parkeston.
Ipswich 13/9/29.
Yarmouth 24/8/47.
Norwich 26/10/47.
Cambridge 7/6/53.
Yarmouth 30/6/57.
March 21/6/59.

RENUMBERED:
   1839ᴇ 3/11/23.
   8839 *after* 1/25.
   2570 3/11/46.
   62570 29/9/49.

CONDEMNED: 26/11/59.
Cut up at Stratford.

8820

To traffic 7/1909.

REPAIRS:
Str. 27/6—24/11/16.**G.**
Bd. 14/1—10/9/20.**G.**
Str. 27/5—20/7/21.**G.**
Str. 18/1—8/5/23.**G.**
Str. 13/6—6/11/24.**G.**
Go. 6/12/26—16/5/27.**G.**
Str. 29/1—29/3/30.**G.**
Vacuum brake added.
Coal guard on tender.
Str. 4/4—25/5/32.**G.**
Altered to D15/2.
Superheated boiler fitted.
Str. 28/5—13/7/35.**G.**
Str. 11—15/5/36.**L.**
Str. 7/3—23/4/37.**G.**
Str. 30/6—15/7/37.**L.**
Str. 8/3—17/5/39.**G.**
Rebuilt to D16/3.
Str. 21/8—1/11/40.**G.**
Str. 2/5—17/6/42.**G.**
Str. 16/12/42—23/1/43.**G.**
Str. 19/3—17/4/43.**L.**
Str. 24/7—21/8/43.**L.**
Str. 29/10—25/11/44.**G.**
Str. 12/8—22/10/46.**G.**
Str. 12/4—19/5/47.**L.**
Str. 17/8—27/9/48.**G.**
Str. 11/11—16/12/50.**G.**
Str. 10/8—12/9/52.**G.**
Str. 30/7—14/8/53.**C/L.**
Str. 16/8—18/9/54.**G.**
Str. 10/6—24/8/56.**G.**

BOILERS:
   1820.
   1809 *(ex8809)* 24/11/16.
   3555 *(ex8805)* 8/5/23.
   3556 *(ex8804)* 6/11/24.
   3550 *(ex8858)* 16/5/27.
   3557 *(ex8829)* 29/3/30.
   3656 *(ex8799)* 25/5/32.
   3685 *(ex8791)* 13/7/35.
   4289 *(new)* 17/5/39.
   4284 *(ex8835)* 1/11/40.
   4287 *(ex8855)* 17/6/42.
   4302 *(ex8900)* 23/1/43.
   4251 *(ex8812)* 25/11/44.
   4296 *(ex8788)* 22/10/46.
   4233 *(ex8860)* 27/9/48.
   23324 *(ex ?)* 16/12/50.
   23417 *(ex ?)* 12/9/52.
   23314 *(ex8872)* 18/9/54.
   23312 *(ex8843)* 24/8/56.

SHEDS:
Ipswich.
Colchester 9/8/34.
Ipswich 15/9/34.
Cambridge 13/7/35.
King's Lynn 14/9/47.
Bury St Edmunds 19/10/47.
Cambridge 26/10/47.
King's Lynn 22/2/48.
Cambridge 29/2/48.
South Lynn 7/11/48.
Cambridge 22/12/48.
Lincoln 24/3/57.

RENUMBERED:
   8820 6/11/24.
   2571 17/10/46.
   62571 25/9/48.

CONDEMNED: 1/1/59.
Cut up at Stratford.

8821

To traffic 7/1909.

REPAIRS:
Str. 21/2—14/5/20.**G.**
Superheated boiler fitted.
Str. 24/3—5/7/21.**G.**
Str. 14/11/23—18/2/24.**G.**
Vacuum brake added.
Str. 21/11/25—24/2/26.**G.**
Str. 4/1—25/4/28.**G.**
Coal guard on tender.
Str. 12/10—21/12/29.**G.**
Str. 15/12/30—24/2/31.**G.**
Str. 14/2—5/5/33.**G.**
Rebuilt to D16/3.
Str. 26/9—2/11/34.**G.**
Str. 27/3—15/5/36.**G.**
Str. 2/1—11/2/38.**G.**
Str. 29/12/39—1/3/40.**G.**

Str. 4/2—17/4/43.**G.**
Str. 23/4—20/5/43.**L.**
Str. 10/10—2/11/44.**L.**
Str. 17/7—24/8/45.**G.**
Str. 15/4—3/6/47.**G.**
Str. 8/6—10/8/49.**G.**
Str. 14/12/50—13/1/51.**C/H.**
Str. 22/11—29/12/51.**G.**
W.P.U. gear removed.
Str. 2/7—9/8/52.**C/L.**
Str. 27/6—14/8/54.**G.**
Str. 24/2—11/4/57.**G.**
Str. 14—29/9/57.**G.**

BOILERS:
   1821.
   3594 *(new)* 14/5/20.
   3601 *(new)* 5/7/21.
   3573 *(ex8851)* 18/2/24.
   3579 *(ex8824)* 24/2/26.
   3601 *(ex8812)* 24/2/31.
   4207 *(new)* 5/5/33.
   4206 *(ex8837)* 2/11/34.
   4218 *(ex8854)* 15/5/36.
   4214 *(ex8859)* 11/2/38.
   4225 *(exJ19 8140)* 1/3/40.
   4223 *(ex8858)* 17/4/43.
   4214 *(exJ19 8245)* 24/8/45.
   4222 *(ex8871)* 3/6/47.
   4228 *(ex8794)* 10/8/49.
   23329 *(ex ?)* 13/1/51.
   23375 *(ex ?)* 29/12/51.
   23347 *(ex8886)* 14/8/54.
   23415 *(ex8811)* 11/4/57.

SHEDS:
Ipswich.
Cambridge 12/1/27.
King's Lynn 14/5/28.
Cambridge 25/8/29.
Stratford 25/7/30.
Cambridge 9/8/30.
Stratford 9/10/30.
Colchester 12/11/39.
Stratford 10/3/40.
Colchester 8/9/40.
Stratford 2/1/43.
Cambridge 22/7/46.
King's Lynn 20/7/47.
Cambridge 3/8/47.
March 13/10/47.
Cambridge 18/10/47.
South Lynn 31/10/47.
Stratford 22/8/48.
Colchester 11/6/50.
Stratford 26/11/50.
Cambridge 20/5/51.
King's Lynn 1/7/51.
March 12/9/51.

RENUMBERED:
   1821ᴇ 18/2/24.
   8821 ?/?/??.
   2572 3/11/46.

62572 10/8/49.

CONDEMNED: 28/7/58.
Cut up at Stratford.

8822

To traffic 10/1909.

REPAIRS:
Str. 8/10/14—20/1/15.**G.**
Str. 1/11/18—11/4/19.**G.**
Str. 10/2—8/7/22.**G.**
Str. 4/1—24/6/24.**G.**
Str. 11/3—29/7/26.**G.**
Str. 10/11/27—25/1/28.**G.**
Coal guard on tender.
Str. 22/4—17/5/29.**N/C.**
Vacuum brake added.
Str. 29/3—13/6/30.**G.**
Rebuilt to D16/2.
Superheated boiler fitted.
Str. 8/2—31/3/32.**G.**
Str. 2/1—8/2/34.**G.**
Str. 20/2—23/4/36.**G.**
Str. 30/11/37—7/1/38.**G.**
Str. 23/5—24/6/39.**G.**
Str. 3/10—8/12/42.**G.**
Str. 7/2—2/3/45.**G.**
Str. 13/1—11/3/47.**G.**
Rebuilt to D16/3.
Str. 21/2—9/4/49.**G.**
Str. 19/11/51—12/1/52.**G.**
W.P.U. gear removed.
Str. 6/12/53—8/1/54.**G.**
Str. 23/10/55. *Not repaired.*

BOILERS:
   1822.
   3555 *(new)* 20/1/15.
   3552 *(ex8815)* 11/4/19.
   3558 *(ex8829)* 25/1/28.
   3929 *(new)* 13/6/30.
   3901 *(ex8851)* 31/3/32.
   1780 *(ex8792)* 8/2/34.
   3926 *(ex8819)* 23/4/36.
   3931 *(ex8846)* 7/1/38.
   3910 *(ex8796)* 24/6/39.
   1785 *(ex8847)* 8/12/42.
   3933 *(ex8813)* 2/3/45.
   4293 *(exJ19 8253)* 11/3/47.
   4246 *(exJ19 8263)* 9/4/49.
   23381 *(ex ?)* 12/1/52.
   23361 *(ex8814)* 8/1/54.

SHEDS:
Ipswich.
Stratford 8/8/26.
Ipswich 22/8/26.
Colchester *by* 1932.
Stratford 26/3/39.
Colchester 8/9/40.
Stratford 2/1/43.
Colchester 20/10/45.

South Lynn 14/8/46.
Bury St Edmunds 19/11/50.
King's Lynn 30/3/52.

RENUMBERED:
  8822 24/6/24.
  7692 8/12/42.
  2573 13/4/46.
62573 9/4/49.

CONDEMNED: 24/10/55.
Cut up at Stratford.

8823

To traffic 12/1909.

REPAIRS:
Str. 17/2—6/7/16.**G.**
Str. 23/9—23/12/21.**G.**
Superheated boiler fitted.
Ca. 5/3—30/4/23.**H.**
Str. 27/9/24—1/1/25.**G.**
Vacuum brake added.
Go. 21/5—8/10/26.**G.**
Str. 15/2—6/6/28.**G.**
Coal guard on tender.
Str. 4/10—19/12/29.**G.**
Altered to D15/2.
Str. 19/10—18/12/31.**G.**
Str. 19/9—27/10/33.**G.**
Str. 15/9—1/11/35.**G.**
Str. 30/4—6/5/36.**L.**
Str. 21/1—1/4/38.**G.**
Rebuilt to D16/3.
Str. 19/11/39—7/2/40.**G.**
Str. 21/1—21/3/42.**G.**
Str. 26/11/43—5/2/44.**G.**
Str. 10/12/45—18/1/46.**G.**
Str. 5/10—19/11/47.**G.**
Str. 5/3—25/4/48.**L.**
Str. 30/3—23/4/49.**C/L.**
Str. 23/3—29/4/50.**G.**
Str. 24/2—27/3/52.**G.**
W.P.U. gear removed.
Str. 12/10—1/11/52.**C/L.**
Str. 28/12/53—13/2/54.**G.**

BOILERS:
  1823.
  1840 *(ex8840)* 6/7/16.
  3612 *(new)* 23/12/21.
  3582 *(ex8832)* 1/1/25.
  3595 *(ex8793)* 19/12/29.
  3467 *(new)* 18/12/31.
  3625 *(ex8808)* 27/10/33.
  3630 *(exJ17 8187)* 1/11/35.
  4219 *(ex8816)* 1/4/38.
  4227 *(exJ19 8243)* 7/2/40.
  4203 *(ex8817)* 21/3/42.
  4240 *(exJ19 8247)* 5/2/44.
  4252 *(ex8809)* 18/1/46.
  4309 *(ex8900)* 19/11/47.
  4249 *(ex8811)* 29/4/50.

23397 *(ex ?)* 27/3/52.
23332 *(ex8828)* 13/2/54.

SHEDS:
Cambridge.
March 3/5/29.
Cambridge 7/6/29.
Bury St Edmunds *after* 6/6/38.
Cambridge 3/1/43.

RENUMBERED:
  8823 1/1/25.
  2574 10/11/46.
62574 24/4/48.

CONDEMNED: 5/12/55.
Cut up at Stratford.

8824

To traffic 12/1909.

REPAIRS:
Str. 26/5—19/8/16.**G.**
Str. 4/1—29/4/18.**G.**
Superheated boiler fitted.
Str. 21/8/22—2/2/23.**G.**
Str. 8/3—20/6/24.**G.**
Vacuum brake added.
Str. 7/9—3/12/25.**G.**
*Boiler 3551 had been altered
from saturated to superheater.*
Str. 26/8—21/12/27.**G.**
Coal guard on tender.
Str. 13/3—26/4/28.**L.**
Str. 5/11/29—17/1/30.**G.**
Altered to D15/2.
Str. 18/9—10/12/31.**G.**
Str. 16/10—7/12/33.**G.**
Str. 22/2—7/3/34.**G.**
Str. 30/4—12/5/34.**L.**
Str. 21/9—3/12/35.**G.**
Str. 15—17/6/36.**L.**
Str. 30/8—30/9/37.**G.**
Str. 18/10/39—2/2/40.**G.**
Rebuilt to D16/3.
Str. 26/4—6/6/42.**G.**
Str. 27/8—22/9/44.**G.**
Str. 3—14/11/44.**L.**
Str. 27/1—10/2/45.**L.**
Str. 10/11—20/12/46.**G.**
Str. 2/11—17/12/48.**G.**
Str. 2/1—18/2/50.**C/L.**
Str. 8/4—25/5/51.**G.**
Str. 25/7—13/8/52.**N/C.**
Tender change only.
Str. 13/4—29/5/53.**G.**
Str. 28/3—7/5/55.**G.**

BOILERS:
  1824.
  1853 *(ex8853)* 19/8/16.
  3569 *(new)* 29/4/18.
  3580 *(ex8832)* 2/2/23.

3579 *(ex8819)* 20/6/24.
3551 *(ex8796)* 3/12/25.
3652 *(ex8830)* 17/1/30.
3466 *(new)* 10/12/31.
3467 *(ex8823)* 7/12/33.
3466 *(ex8811)* 3/12/35.
3653 *(ex8793)* 30/9/37.
4303 *(new)* 2/2/40.
4305 *(exJ19 8142)* 6/6/42.
4334 *(new)* 22/9/44.
4269 *(ex8860)* 20/12/46.
23348 *(ex ?)* 25/5/51.
23307 *(ex8876)* 29/5/53.
23455 *(ex8852)* 7/5/55.

SHEDS:
March.
Cambridge 14/5/31.
King's Lynn 18/2/37.
Cambridge 26/6/37.
Ipswich 20/1/38.
Cambridge 30/3/38.
King's Lynn 4/7/39.

RENUMBERED:
  8824 20/6/24.
  2575 10/11/46.
62575 11/12/48.

CONDEMNED: 29/5/57.
Cut up at Stratford.

8825

To traffic 12/1909.

REPAIRS:
Str. 3/2—31/5/22.**G.**
Superheated boiler fitted.
Nr. 25/5—5/7/23.**H.**
Nr. 25—29/8/24.**L.**
Str. 16/10/24—20/2/25.**G.**
Str. 20/3—31/7/26.**G.**
Str. 24/5/27.**N/C.**
Vacuum brake added.
Str. 9/3—28/6/28.**G.**
Altered to D15/2.
Coal guard on tender.
Str. 31/10/29—8/1/30.**G.**
Str. 25/6—16/10/31.**G.**
Str. 13/11/34—16/1/35.**G.**
Str. 22—26/6/36.**L.**
Str. 24/12/36—12/3/37.**G.**
Rebuilt to D16/3.
Str. 12/4—26/5/38.**G.**
Str. 13/5—20/6/40.**G.**
Str. 29/6—10/7/40.**N/C.**
Str. 16/10—19/12/42.**G.**
Str. 5—27/2/43.**L.**
Str. 26/11/44—5/1/45.**G.**
Str. 14—28/6/45.**L.**
Str. 13/9/46—31/10/46.**G.**
Str. 12/4—29/6/47.**L.**
Str. 16/7—14/8/47.**L.**

Str. 6/5—19/6/48.**L.**
Str. 18/1—1/4/49.**G.**
Str. 25/2—21/4/50.**C/L.**
Str. 16/7—10/8/50.**C/L.**
Str. 12/8—15/9/51.**G.**
Str. 19—23/11/51.**C/L.**
Str. 4—23/2/52.**C/L.**
Str. 1—28/11/53.**G.**
Str. 15—18/3/54.**N/C.**
Str. 27/2—19/3/55.**C/L.**
Str. 21/3—12/5/56. **G.**

BOILERS:
  1825.
  3595 *(ex8816)* 31/5/22.
  3612 *(ex8823)* 20/2/25.
  3581 *(ex8817)* 31/7/26.
  3685 *(new)* 28/6/28.
  3464 *(new)* 16/10/31.
  3643 *(ex8832)* 16/1/35.
  4261 *(new)* 12/3/37.
  4263 *(exJ19 8142)* 20/6/40.
  4306 *(ex8886)* 19/12/42.
  4283 *(exJ19 8244)* 5/1/45.
  4290 *(ex8785)* 31/10/46.
  4268 *(exJ19 8250)* 1/4/49.
  23362 *(ex ?)* 15/9/51.
  23424 *(ex8865)* 28/11/53.
  23343 *(exJ19 8262)* 12/5/56.

SHEDS:
Norwich.
Stratford 8/8/26.
Norwich 28/6/28.
Peterborough East 22/11/32.
Norwich 26/6/36.
Lowestoft 4/10/36.
Norwich 23/5/57.
Yarmouth 30/12/45.
Norwich 16/1/46.
Yarmouth 9/6/46.
Norwich 19/6/46.
Yarmouth 17/4/49.
Cambridge 7/6/53.
Bury St Edmunds 21/2/54.

RENUMBERED:
  8825 20/2/25.
  7695 19/12/42.
  2576 13/4/46.
62576 12/6/48.

CONDEMNED: 9/9/57.
Cut up at Stratford.

8826

To traffic 12/1909.

REPAIRS:
Str. 15/6—11/9/17.**G.**
Str. 17/3—29/7/22.**G.**
Superheated boiler fitted.
Nr. 5/10—11/12/23.**H.**

Str. 3—25/7/24.**L.**
Str. 11/4—22/7/25.**G.**
Str. 28/9/26—29/1/27.**G.**
Vacuum brake added.
Str. 5/1—15/4/29.**G.**
Rebuilt to D16/2.
Coal guard on tender.
Str. 27/3—5/6/30.**G.**
Str. 31/1—18/3/32.**G.**
Str. 19/12/34—22/2/35.**G.**
Str. 8/6—16/7/36.**G.**
Str. 21/2—14/4/38.**G.**
Str. 4/3—9/5/40.**G.**
Str. 17—20/5/40.**N/C.**
Str. 13/1—27/2/43.**G.**
Str. 19/11/44—5/1/45.**G.**
Str. 14/1—18/4/47.**G.**
Str. 5/4—20/5/49.**G.**
Rebuilt to D16/3.
Str. 11/1—24/2/51.**G.**
Str. 23—24/3/51.**N/C.**
Str. 21/10—2/11/51.**C/L.**
Str. 15/9—11/10/52.**G.**
Str. 21/8—5/9/53.**C/L.**
Str. 2/11—4/12/54.**G.**
Str. 6/1—2/2/56.**C/L.**

BOILERS:
  1826.
  1823 (ex8823) 11/9/17.
  3625 (new) 29/7/22.
  3563 (ex8810) 29/1/27.
  1788 (ex8788) 15/4/29.
  3920 (ex8785) 18/3/32.
  3919 (ex8839) 22/2/35.
  3922 (ex8790) 16/7/36.
  3925 (ex8847) 14/4/38.
  3915 (ex8818) 9/5/40.
  3910 (ex8822) 27/2/43.
  3909 (ex8789) 5/1/45.
  3933 (ex8822) 18/4/47.
  4208 (ex8868) 20/5/49.
  23331 (ex ?) 24/2/51.
  23383 (exJ19 8149) 11/10/52.
  23328 (ex8852) 4/12/54.

SHEDS:
Norwich.
Yarmouth 5/8/33.
Norwich 6/12/34.
Yarmouth 23/2/35.
Norwich 27/4/38.
Yarmouth 14/5/39.
Norwich 19/5/40.
Yarmouth 9/8/42.
Norwich 30/8/42.
Melton Constable 9/1/44.
Norwich 23/1/44.
Yarmouth Beach 15/6/47.
Norwich 25/6/47.

RENUMBERED:
  8826 25/7/24???.
  2577 17/11/46.

62577 20/5/49.

CONDEMNED: 29/10/56.
Cut up at Stratford.

8827

To traffic 1/1910.

REPAIRS:
Str. 1/3—10/9/18.**G.**
Str. 1/5—1/11/23.**G.**
Str. 4/6—4/11/25.**G.**
Str. 25/3—20/7/27.**G.**
Rebuilt to D16/2.
Superheated boiler fitted.
Vacuum brake added.
Coal guard on tender.
Str. 16/11/28—26/2/29.**G.**
Str. 1/5—25/6/31.**G.**
Str. 2/11—2/12/31.**G.**
Str. 31/12/33—15/2/34.**G.**
Str. 12/2—3/4/36.**G.**
Str. 13/3—29/4/38.**G.**
Str. 28/3—20/6/40.**G.**
Str. 26—28/6/40.**N/C.**
Str. 13/7—3/9/42.**G.**
Str. 30/7—16/9/44.**G.**
Rebuilt to D16/3.
Str. 21/4—8/6/46.**G.**
Str. 24/11/46—10/1/47.**L.**
Str. 24/2—14/4/48.**G.**
Str. 11/12/49—27/1/50.**G.**
Str. 16/12/51—1/2/52.**G.**
W.P.U. gear removed.
Str. 6/1—5/2/55.**G.**

BOILERS:
  1827.
  3558 (new) 10/9/18.
  1851 (exJ17 8222) 1/11/23.
  1837 (ex8809) 4/11/25.
  3909 (new) 20/7/27.
  3917 (ex8818) 25/6/31.
  3913 (ex8851) 15/2/34.
  3908 (ex8786) 3/4/36.
  3928 (ex8856) 29/4/38.
  3926 (ex8847) 20/6/40.
  3900 (ex8845) 3/9/42.
  4332 (new) 16/9/44.
  4314 (ex8835) 8/6/46.
  4266 (ex8865) 14/4/48.
  4338 (new) 27/1/50.
  23386 (ex ?) 1/2/52.
  23378 (exJ19 8241) 5/2/55.

SHEDS:
Norwich.
Stratford 5/5/24.
March 26/5/29.
Yarmouth Beach 20/7/43.
Melton Constable 8/10/44.
Norwich 11/11/45.
Melton Constable 18/11/45.

Norwich 2/12/45.
Melton Constable 11/12/45.

RENUMBERED:
  8827 *after* 17/1/25.
  2578 24/11/46.
  62578 10/4/48.

CONDEMNED: 21/10/57.
Cut up at Stratford.

8828

To traffic 2/1910.

REPAIRS:
Str. 27/11/13—30/3/14.**G.**
Str. 1/11/18—9/4/19.**G.**
Str. 10/1—27/5/22.**G.**
Str. 27/12/23—13/5/24.**G.**
Str. 5/3—23/7/26.**G.**
Str. 24/2—8/6/28.**G.**
Altered to D15/2.
Superheated boiler fitted.
Ashcroft cut-off control fitted.
Coal guard on tender.
Str. 16/11/29—24/1/30.**G.**
Str. 24/11/31—13/2/32.**G.**
Str. 25/1—22/3/34.**G.**
Rebuilt to D16/3.
Ash ejector fitted.
Str. 29/5—19/7/35.**G.**
Str. 7/3—27/4/37.**G.**
Str. 29/6—15/8/38.**G.**
Str. 31/12/40—1/3/41.**G.**
Str. 18/7—16/9/43.**G.**
Str. 6/10—10/11/45.**G.**
Str. 30/5—22/8/47.**L.**
Str. 20/5--1/7/48.**G.**
Str. 22/1—24/2/51.**G.**
Str. 12/2—13/3/53.**G.**

BOILERS:
  1828.
  3550 (new) 30/3/14.
  1830 (ex8830) 9/4/19.
  1853 (ex8790) 13/5/24.
  3621 (ex8816) 8/6/28.
  4213 (new) 22/3/34.
  4210 (ex8804) 19/7/35.
  4221 (exJ19 8243) 27/4/37.
  4239 (ex8810) 15/8/38.
  4249 (ex8876) 1/3/41.
  4279 (exJ19 8240) 16/9/43.
  4263 (ex8859) 10/11/45.
  4275 (exJ19 8247) 1/7/48.
  23332 (ex ?) 24/2/51.
  23406 (exJ19 8250) 13/3/53.

SHEDS:
Stratford.
Colchester 24/1/30.
Stratford 12/11/39.
Colchester 1/12/39.

Stratford 10/3/40.
March 18/7/46.
King's Lynn 18/3/51.

RENUMBERED:
  8828 13/5/24.
  2579 10/11/46.
  62579 22/6/48.

CONDEMNED: 7/3/55.
Cut up at Stratford.

8829

To traffic 2/1910.

REPAIRS:
Str. 7/11/17—16/4/18.**G.**
Str. 31/10/19—19/3/20.**G.**
Str. 24/8—29/12/23.**G.**
Str. 14/9—22/12/25.**G.**
Str. 18/8—10/11/27.**G.**
Coal guard on tender.
Str. 16/11/29—21/2/30.**G.**
Rebuilt to D16/2.
Superheated boiler fitted.
Str. 16/9—27/11/31.**G.**
Str. 18/7—15/9/33.**G.**
Str. 29/5—11/7/35.**G.**
Str. 20/3—7/5/37.**G.**
Str. 25/9—20/12/39.**G.**
Str. 8/2—8/4/42.**G.**
Str. 13/11/43—1/1/44.**G.**
Str. 5/11—8/12/45.**G.**
Str. 8/2—9/4/48.**G.**
Rebuilt to D16/3.
Str. 25/8—7/10/50.**G.**
Str. 9/12/52—17/1/53.**G.**
Str. 8/4—4/5/54.**C/L.**
Str. 28/5—3/8/56.**G.**

BOILERS:
  1829.
  1846 (ex8846) 16/4/18.
  3557 (ex8805) 19/3/20.
  3558 (ex8827) 29/12/23.
  3557 (ex8795) 10/11/27.
  1789 (ex8789) 21/2/30.
  3909 (ex8827) 27/11/31.
  3925 (ex8843) 15/9/33.
  3924 (ex8813) 11/7/35.
  3920 (ex8788) 7/5/37.
  3924 (ex8783) 20/12/39.
  3907 (ex8841) 8/4/42.
  3903 (ex8796) 1/1/44.
  3913 (ex8789) 8/12/45.
  4305 (exJ19 8242) 9/4/48.
  23305 (ex ?) 7/10/50.
  23317 (ex8885) 17/1/53.
  23407 (ex8882) 3/8/56.

SHEDS:
Stratford.
Cambridge 31/10/24.

Norwich 6/10/26.
Cambridge 19/12/26.
Lincoln 29/3/28.
Ipswich 28/9/31.
Colchester 19/12/31.
Norwich 18/7/35.
Lowestoft 23/5/37.
Yarmouth 8/5/38.
Norwich 18/2/40.
Yarmouth 3/3/40.
Norwich 19/5/40.
Yarmouth 24/11/40.
Cambridge 6/1/57.
King's Lynn 12/5/57.

RENUMBERED:
 1829ᴇ 29/12/23.
 8829 *after* 1/11/24.
 2580 10/12/46.
62580 3/4/48.

CONDEMNED: 9/6/58.
Cut up at Stratford.

Unlike the first engine to be made Part 2, no.8827 in July 1927 retained its tender in original form and did not have the extra coal guards fitted. All the D16/2's did eventually get the coal guards, the last being no.8784 in June 1929. At the time the June 1928 'painting economies' took effect there were eleven Part 2 engines: 8792, 8800, 8813, 8819, 8827, 8831, 8839, 8843, 8851, 8852, 8856 and these had fully lined green livery.

From April 1929 all D16/2 were dual brake fitted and from 1927 twenty-two of them (8780-89, 8792, 8794, 8800, 8819, 8827, 8831, 8839, 8842, 8843, 8851, 8852, 8856) were changed to the larger 8/8½" Westinghouse pump to give quicker recharging of the air reservoir when used on stopping trains. The others retained the 6/6½" pump which was capable of operating the brakes, power reversing gear, sanding, and water pick-up scoop. 8831 is at Norwich, 2nd May 1931.

The usual buffer type was that with parallel shank and hollow spindle with circular flange having wood packing behind it. Alternatively, some had the type with stepped shank but with hollow spindle and circular flange. Around 1927-29 however, two engines nos.8784 and 8851 carried buffers with taper shanks as fitted to nos.1860-1900 when they were built, but both soon had them changed to a more modern type. All had carriage heater connection at the front end.

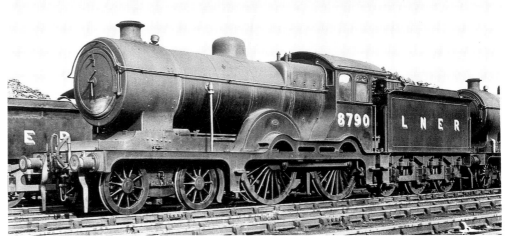

About 1939, a different buffer type was introduced. It was a hybrid, having the square base, and larger diameter head from the Group Standard design, with GER type parallel shank although longer. 2543 is at Leicester (London Road) 24th June 1947, with the 2 p.m. working to Lowestoft.

(centre) Ten Part 2 engines found their way on to M&GN workings, 8801 from 9th August 1942 and 8805 from 31st October 1943, being the first so allocated. Between 2nd December 1945 (8831) and 15th June 1947 (2577), nos.8822, 8833, 8847, 8852, 2613, 2620 also went to M&GN sheds. For use on the M&GN they required to be fitted with a tablet exchanger one of which can be seen fitted to the tender of 62543 (8852). Note the rare use of shaded transfers used for the BR number.

(below) The D16/2 boilers continued to have four washout plugs on the left hand side, complete with covers. *L.N.E.R.*

74

8810

To traffic 4/1910.

REPAIRS:
Str. 27/9—31/12/15.**G.**
Str. 25/11/21—12/4/22.**G.**
Superheated boiler fitted.
Str. 14/7—10/10/23.**G.**
Str. 28/11/24—19/2/25.**G.**
Str. 16/7—11/11/26.**G.**
Vacuum brake added.
Str. 9/11—30/12/27.**H.**
Str. 4/1—11/4/29.**G.**
Coal guard on tender.
Str. 17/12/30—4/3/31.**G.**
Altered to D15/2.
Str. 8/2—24/3/33.**G.**
Str. 1/10—8/11/34.**G.**
Str. 13/4—4/7/36.**G.**
Rebuilt to D16/3.
Str. 5—12/2/37.**L.**
Str. 12/6—23/7/38.**G.**
Str. 5/1—6/3/40.**G.**
Str. 6/11—19/12/41.**G.**
Str. 22/4—24/5/44.**G.**
Str. 5—28/4/45.**L.**
Str. 12/6—8/8/46.**G.**
Str. 16/9—1/10/46.**L.**
Str. 11/3—30/6/47.**L.**
Str. 9/5—7/8/48.**G.**
Str. 15/4—12/5/49.**C/L.**
Dn. 14/6—8/7/49.**C/L.**
Str. 20/8—16/9/50.**G.**
Str. 21/10—9/11/50.**C/L.**
Str. 20—28/9/51.**C/L.**
Str. 13/3—1/5/52.**C/H.**
W.P.U. gear removed.
Str. 1—17/9/52.**C/L.**
Str. 23/2/53. *Not repaired.*

BOILERS:
1810.
1836 (*ex8836*) 31/12/15.
3563 (*ex8845*) 12/4/22.
3612 (*ex8825*) 11/11/26.
3684 (*new*) 30/12/27.
3622 (*ex8830*) 4/3/31.
3606 (*ex8840*) 24/3/33.
3579 (*ex8859*) 8/11/34.
4239 (*new*) 4/7/36.
4233 (*exJ19 8268*) 23/7/38.
4234 (*ex8861*) 6/3/40.
4247 (*ex8803*) 19/12/41.
4282 (*exJ19 8144*) 24/5/44.
4239 (*ex8791*) 8/8/46.
4316 (*exJ19 8241*) 7/8/48.
23306 (*ex ?*) 16/9/50.

SHEDS:
March.

Cambridge 26/5/29.
Stratford 20/6/39.
Cambridge 10/6/40.
March 20/10/40.
Stratford 21/11/42.
Norwich 7/10/46.

RENUMBERED:
8810 ?/?/??.
2581 20/9/46.
62581 7/8/48.

CONDEMNED: 9/3/53.
Cut up at Stratford.

8811

To traffic 4/1910.

REPAIRS:
Bd. 31/10/19—26/4/20.**G.**
Str. 5/1—10/5/22.**G.**
Superheated boiler fitted.
Ca. 7/5—14/6/23.**H.**
Str. 24/11/24—31/3/25.**G.**
Str. 1/1—31/3/27.**G.**
Coal guard on tender.
Str. 18/10/28—23/3/29.**G.**
Vacuum brake added.
Str. 1/8—8/10/30.**G.**
Str. 8/2—23/3/32.**G.**
Altered to D15/2.
Str. 26—30/6/33.**N/C.**
Str. 23/11/33—12/1/34.**G.**
Str. 10/9—22/10/35.**G.**
Str. 18—21/5/36.**L.**
Str. 14/10—19/11/37.**G.**
Str. 1/10—16/12/39.**G.**
Rebuilt to D16/3.
Str. 13/1—5/2/40.**L.**
Str. 9/11—20/12/41.**G.**
Str. 12/12/43—5/2/44.**G.**
Str. 15/9—13/10/45.**G.**
Blow-down gear fitted.
Str. 21/6—17/9/47.**G.**
Str. 13/12/49—21/1/50.**G.**
Str. 30—31/1/50.**N/C.**
Str. 6—20/3/50.**N/C.**
Str. 20/4—23/5/52.**G.**
Str. 27/7—26/8/52.**N/C.**
Str. 12/6—31/7/54.**G.**
Str. 16/8/54.**N/C.**
Str. 14/11/56—12/1/57.**G.**

BOILERS:
1811.
1801 (*ex8802*) 26/4/20.
3622 (*new*) 10/5/22.
3625 (*ex8826*) 31/3/27.
3572 (*ex8850*) 23/3/29.
3558 (*ex8822*) 8/10/30.

3558 *fitted with superheater*
prior to installation.
3569 (*ex8804*) 23/3/32.
3466 (*ex8824*) 12/1/34.
3625 (*ex8823*) 22/10/35.
3464 (*ex8850*) 19/11/37.
4300 (*new*) 16/12/39.
4294 (*ex8850*) 20/12/41.
4313 (*ex8808*) 5/2/44.
4270 (*exJ19 8264*) 13/10/45.
4249 (*ex8840*) 17/9/47.
4339 (*new*) 21/1/50.
23407 (*ex ?*) 23/5/52.
23415 (*ex8879*) 31/7/54.
23339 (*exJ19 8263*) 12/1/57.

SHEDS:
Cambridge.
King's Lynn 1/6/47.
Cambridge 2/11/58.

RENUMBERED:
8811 after 14/6/24.
2582 27/10/46.
62582 21/1/50.

CONDEMNED: 1/1/59.
Cut up at Stratford.

8812

To traffic 4/1910.

REPAIRS:
Str. 27/10/21—11/3/22.**G.**
Superheated boiler fitted.
Str. ?/?—?/1/25.**G.**
Vacuum brake added.
Str. 1/10/26—20/1/27.**G.**
Str. ?/?—?/1/29.**G.**
Coal guard on tender.
Str. 1/10—14/11/30.**G.**
Str. 6/4—4/5/32.**G.**
Str. 12/3—13/4/34.**G.**
Altered to D15/2.
Str. 8/4—12/6/36.**G.**
Rebuilt to D16/3.
Str. 27—29/7/36.**N/C.**
Str. 12/4—12/5/38.**G.**
Str. ?/?—11/1/40.**G.**
Str. ?/?—29/6/42.**G.**
Str. ?/?—29/7/44.**G.**
Str. 1/6/46.**N/C.**
Str. 3/8—14/9/46.**G.**
Str. 2—22/11/46.**L.**
Str. 10—24/5/47.**L.**
Str. 26/7—13/8/47.**L.**
Str. 30/10/48. *Not repaired.*

BOILERS:
1812.

1797 (*ex8794*) 11/3/22.
3601 (*ex8849*) 20/1/27.
3572 (*ex8811*) 14/11/30.
3558 (*ex8811*) 4/5/32.
3570 (*ex8858*) 13/4/34.
4245 (*new*) 12/6/36.
4269 (*exJ19 8252*) 11/1/40.
4251 (*exJ19 8145*) 29/6/42.
4331 (*new*) 29/7/44.
4307 (*ex8799*) 14/9/46.

SHEDS:
Cambridge.
Peterborough East 30/5/34.
Norwich 1/7/34.
Lowestoft 7/7/34.
Norwich 1/1/36.
Lowestoft 12/1/36.
Norwich 29/3/36.
Yarmouth 1/11/36.
Norwich 15/12/37.
Stratford 21/11/42.
Norwich 11/1/47.

RENUMBERED:
8812 ?/1/25.
2583 6/9/46.

CONDEMNED: 23/11/48.
Cut up at Stratford.

8813

To traffic 5/1910.

REPAIRS:
Str. 2/3—28/7/14.**G.**
Superheated boiler fitted.
Str. 4/1—20/4/15.**G.**
After Ilford accident.
Str. 21/8/20—15/1/21.**G.**
Str. ?/?—?/5/22.**G.**
Str. 23/11/23—5/3/24.**G.**
Str. 14/12/25—9/4/26.**G.**
Rebuilt to D16/2.
Coal guard on tender.
Str. 16/12/27—17/3/28.**G.**
Str. 6/9/28.**N/C.**
Vacuum brake added.
Str. 15/2—12/4/30.**G.**
Str. 2/3—26/4/32.**G.**
Str. 4/1—22/2/34.**G.**
Str. 17/10—8/11/34.**L.**
Str. 10/4—20/6/35.**G.**
Str. 16/10—26/11/36.**G.**
Str. 17—26/11/37.**L.**
Str. 9/4—27/5/38.**G.**
Str. 8/11—30/12/39.**G.**
Str. 23/1—20/2/40.**L.**
Str. 26/4—6/6/42.**G.**
Str. 10/11—4/12/43.**L.**

WORKS CODES:- Bd - Beardmore. Ca - Cambridge shed. Dn - Doncaster. Go - Gorton. Ips - Ipswich shed. Nr - Norwich shed. Str - Stratford.
REPAIR CODES:- **C/H** - Casual Heavy. **C/L** - Casual Light. **G** - General. **H** - Heavy. **H/I** - Heavy Intermediate. **L** - Light. **L/I** - Light Intermediate. **N/C** - Non-Classified.

75

Str. 8/1—12/2/44.**L.**
Str. 15/10—17/11/44.**G.**
Str. 21/8—20/9/45.**G.**
Str. 13/9—30/10/46.**L.**
Str. 16/6—25/9/47.**G.**
Rebuilt to D16/3.
Str. 3—18/8/49.**C/L.**
Str. 12/2—27/4/50.**G.**
Str. 26/4—27/5/52.**G.**
Str. 4/8—17/9/53.**C/L.**
Str. 15/11—18/12/54.**G.**

BOILERS:
1813.
3560 *(new)* 28/7/14.
3565 *(new)* 20/4/15.
3903 *(new)* 9/4/26.
3928 *(new)* 12/4/30.
1788 *(ex8826)* 26/4/32.
3924 *(ex8834)* 22/2/34.
3930 *(ex8788)* 20/6/35.
1786 *(ex8782)* 26/11/36.
3904 *(ex8790)* 27/5/38.
3923 *(ex8800)* 30/12/39.
3933 *(ex8787)* 6/6/42.
3923 *(ex8780)* 17/11/44.
4321 *(ex8846)* 25/9/47.
4341 *(new)* 27/4/50.
23408 *(ex ?)* 27/5/52.
23430 *(ex ?)* 18/12/54.

SHEDS:
Colchester.
Cambridge 22/3/39.
March 18/3/40.
Cambridge 13/10/47.
March 18/10/47.
Norwich 16/10/49.
Cambridge 17/6/56.
King's Lynn 23/12/56.

RENUMBERED:
8813 5/3/24.
2584 8/9/46.
62584 27/4/50.

CONDEMNED: 23/12/57.
Cut up at Stratford.

8814

To traffic 5/1910.

REPAIRS:
Str. 27/3—26/6/15.**G.**
Str. 13/7—24/11/21.**G.**
Superheated boiler fitted.
Ca. 23/3—12/5/23.**H.**
Str. 31/3—6/7/24.**G.**
Str. 14/1—24/4/26.**G.**
Coal guard on tender.
Str. 28/6/27.**N/C.**
Vacuum brake added.
Str. 10/2—12/5/28.**G.**

Str. 23/1—15/3/30.**G.**
Str. 28/9—23/12/31.**G.**
Altered to D15/2.
Str. 27/4—7/7/33.**G.**
Str. 7/1—27/2/35.**G.**
Rebuilt to D16/3.
Str. 16/11/36—5/1/37.**G.**
Str. 24/5—15/7/38.**G.**
Str. 13/4—28/5/40.**G.**
Str. 6/1—27/3/43.**G.**
Str. 19/2—24/3/45.**G.**
Str. 11/1—29/3/47.**G.**
Str. 24/4—21/5/49.**G.**
Str. 5/8—8/9/51.**G.**
Str. 8/10—28/11/53.**G.**

BOILERS:
1814.
1790 *(ex8790)* 26/6/15.
3606 *(new)* 24/11/21.
3613 *(ex8839)* 24/4/26.
3568 *(ex8831)* 12/5/28.
3582 *(ex8823)* 15/3/30.
3649 *(ex8793)* 7/7/33.
4208 *(ex8809)* 27/2/35.
4228 *(ex8863)* 5/1/37.
4202 *(ex8879)* 28/5/40.
4200 *(ex8885)* 24/3/45.
4226 *(ex8848)* 29/3/47.
4210 *(ex8874)* 21/5/49.
23361 *(ex8848)* 8/9/51.
23323 *(ex8873)* 28/11/53.

SHEDS:
Cambridge.
Stratford 31/10/24.
Ipswich 12/5/28.
Parkeston 11/10/28.
Ipswich 11/12/28.
Norwich 13/7/34.
Yarmouth 20/10/34.
Norwich 6/11/34.
Yarmouth 8/8/37.
Norwich 3/4/38.
Yarmouth 8/1/39.
Norwich 18/2/40.
Yarmouth 15/3/42.
Norwich 5/6/42.
Yarmouth 10/11/45.
Norwich 12/12/45.
Melton Constable 1/5/46.
Norwich 13/7/46.
Cambridge 29/6/52.
Bury St Edmunds 3/8/52.
Cambridge 12/10/52.

RENUMBERED:
8814 6/7/24.
2585 21/9/46.
62585 7/5/49.

CONDEMNED: 11/4/55.
Cut up at Stratford.

8815

To traffic 5/1910.

REPAIRS:
Str. 8/1—5/5/14.**G.**
Str. 23/8—24/12/18.**G.**
Str. 2/6—14/11/22.**G.**
Superheated boiler fitted.
Str. 10—17/4/23.**L.**
Wheel change only.
Str. 23/5—29/8/24.**G.**
Gr. 22/10/26—21/4/27..**G.**
Str. 1/1—5/4/29.**G.**
Vacuum brake added.
Coal guard on tender.
Str. 20/3—18/5/31.**G.**
Altered to D15/2.
Str. 27/4—22/6/33.**G.**
Str. 18/3—16/5/35.**G.**
Str. 29/6—4/7/36.**L.**
Str. 5/3—21/4/37.**G.**
Str. 11/5—4/8/39.**G.**
Rebuilt to D16/3.
Str. 30/8—4/10/41.**G.**
Str. 17/8—6/11/43.**G.**
Str. 18/5—22/6/44.**L.**
Str. 24/9—20/10/45.**G.**
Str. 15/10—4/12/47.**G.**
Str. 25/6—12/8/50.**G.**
Str. 2/9—1/10/52.**G.**
Str. 26/12/54—5/2/55.**G.**

BOILERS:
1815.
3552 *(new)* 5/5/14.
1829 *(ex8829)* 24/12/18.
3627 *(new)* 14/11/22.
3598 *(ex8832)* 5/4/29.
3556 *(ex8795)* 18/5/31.
3556 converted to superheated
boiler prior to installation.
3571 *(ex8802)* 22/6/33.
3649 *(ex8814)* 16/5/35.
3582 *(ex8803)* 21/4/37.
4208 *(ex8870)* 4/8/39.
4229 *(ex8863)* 4/10/41.
4225 *(ex8821)* 6/11/43.
4205 *(ex8862)* 20/10/45.
4215 *(exJ19 8140)* 4/12/47.
4224 *(exJ19 8245)* 12/8/50.
4224 reno.23419 1/10/52.
23468 *(new)* 5/2/55.*
* *The last boiler made for a*
former GER 4-4-0.

SHEDS:
Ipswich.
Norwich 3/8/33.
Yarmouth 7/4/34.
Norwich 31/10/34.
Yarmouth 28/9/35.
Norwich 5/3/37.
Yarmouth 5/3/38.

Norwich 19/5/40.
Yarmouth 24/11/40.
Norwich 28/7/46.
Yarmouth 4/10/46.
Norwich 2/6/57.

RENUMBERED:
1815E ?/4/24.
8815 29/8/24.
2586 21/9/46.
62586 12/8/50.

CONDEMNED: 5/3/58.
Cut up at Stratford.

8816

To traffic 7/1910.

REPAIRS:
Str. 24/10/19—28/5/20.**G.**
Superheated boiler fitted.
Str. 18/1—6/5/22.**G.**
Ca. 17/4—10/5/23.**H.**
Str. 12/4—4/7/24.**G.**
Str. 11/2—18/6/26.**G.**
Str. 1/6/27.**N/C.**
Vacuum brake added.
Str. 23/12/27—31/3/28.**G.**
Coal guard on tender.
Str. 30/10—24/12/29.**G.**
Altered to D15/2.
Str. 2/1—5/3/32.**G.**
Str. 29/12/33—15/3/34.**G.**
Rebuilt to D16/3.
Ash ejector fitted.
Str. 4/3—9/4/36.**G.**
Str. 6/1—17/2/38.**G.**
Str. 9/9—14/12/39.**G.**
Str. 6/3—5/4/41.**H.**
Str. 13/9—20/10/41.**G.**
Str. 15/9—6/11/43.**G.**
Str. 30/8—23/9/44.**L.**
Str. 16/9—20/10/45.**G.**
Blow-down gear fitted.
Str. 5—15/2/46.**L.**
Str. 12/6—24/7/46.**L.**
Str. 18/7—2/8/47.**L.**
Str. 21/3—6/5/48.**G.**
Str. 26/1—18/3/50.**G.**
Str. 24/7—26/8/50.**C/L.**
Str. 10—27/11/52.**N/C.**
Str. 31/5—24/7/53.**C/L.**
Str. 4/4—13/5/54.**G.**
Str. 5/1—29/3/56.**C/L.**
Str. 27/11/56. *Not repaired.*

BOILERS:
1816.
3595 *(new)* 28/5/20.
3621 *(new)* 6/5/22.
3570 *(ex8797)* 31/3/28.
3648 *(ex8803)* 24/12/29.
3580 *(ex8807)* 5/3/32.

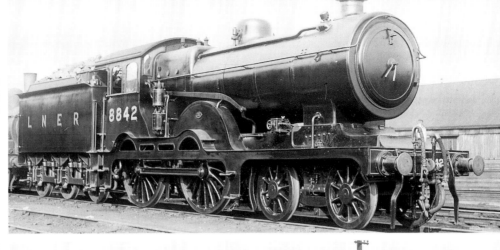

On the right hand side were three plugs. No.8842 was recorded as being fitted in April 1934 with ash ejector.

When the number was moved from the tender to the cab, starting with no.8838 in November 1929, the splasher beading was not at first removed so 9" numbers were squeezed between the splasher and the cab windows. This particular style persisted until June 1930 when finally the beading was removed, allowing 12" numbers to match the tenders letters. Apart from 8783 and 8787, this style was then standard until November 1941 when lining was discarded.

On 7th October 1930 the Royal engine no.8783 was transferred from Stratford to Cambridge followed on the 22nd by no.8787, which was nominated to act as reserve. No.8787 was in works 31st October to 30th December 1931 for specially painting green with white cab roof. Both 'Royal' engines remained green until after the War began.

From July 1942 only NE was used as a wartime economy. Note substitution of a steel plate for glass in the leading window space. 8847 reverses away from the Cambridge coaler in 1946.
L.R.Peters.

(left) **During 1946 the whole class was renumbered. No.8782 was renumbered to 2613 on 9th November during a 'general' repair, when it also re-gained LNER all in shaded transfers but on unlined black paint. Norwich circa 1947.** *P.Wilson.*

(second from top) **62553 got its BR number on 14th May 1948, at a light repair, and was in the Gill Sans style but with modified 6. Similar figures were used on the bufferbeam. Note the classification D16-2. Yarmouth South Town.** *P.Wilson.*

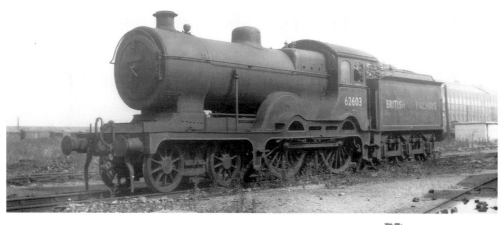

(third from top) **There were only four survivors to get BR livery. No.62547 was ex works 17th June 1948 in unlined black with BRITISH RAILWAYS on the tender and 10" numbers on the cab including a modified 6. No smokebox number plate was fitted. No.62591 had a 'casual/light' repair - at Doncaster - from which it was out 23rd April 1949 and was one of the first with BR emblem - the large size. No.62603 was ex Stratford from a 'general' on 1st February 1949 in black but with red, cream, and grey lining; correct Gill Sans figures had been applied on both the cab and smokebox plate. No.62590 was the last D16/2 to be repaired, ex works 1st September 1949, and also the last withdrawal on 28th January 1952. Unlike 62603 it was in unlined black but did get the large BR emblem on its tender and the correct 6 and 9 on cab and smokebox.**

(bottom) **The D16/1 and D16/2 engines had reached a total of 40 in April 1931 with the rebuilding of no.8795. The Belpaire design of boiler could not be fitted to the series 8860 to 8900 because of the frame design. In 1932 Stratford re-designed the 5' 1⅛" boiler with a round top firebox so that it could be used on all the Clauds. Slide valves and the corresponding frame front end were retained but the valance over the coupling rod, with its decorative splashers, was removed. For these rebuilds a new cab was provided 7' 11" wide, as on the Part 2 engines but now with vertical front edge to the side sheets and with separate narrow rear splasher. The first engine to be fitted with the new type of boiler was n.8848, ex works 20th January 1933. Down to 1943 a total of forty-eight were similarly rebuilt from classes D15/1 and D15/2. No.8828, ex works 22nd March 1934, was one of five to be fitted with ash ejector.** *Photomatic.*

8816 cont.
4211 *(new)* 15/3/34.
4219 *(ex8837)* 9/4/36.
4232 *(exJ19 8263)* 17/2/38.
4231 *(ex8837)* 14/12/39.
4239 *(ex8828)* 5/4/41.
4266 *(ex8802)* 6/11/43.
4323 *(exJ19 8260)* 20/10/45.
4274 *(ex8817)* 6/5/48.
4237 *(ex8806)* 18/3/50.
4237 reno. 23421 24/7/53.
23461 *(new)* 13/5/54.

SHEDS:
Cambridge.
Stratford 18/6/26.
Cambridge 29/3/28.
March 23/10/40.
Stratford 21/11/42.
Colchester 7/12/46.
Stratford 28/12/46.
Trafford Park 11/6/50.
Cambridge 8/6/52.
Pbo. Spital Bridge 12/10/52.

RENUMBERED:
8816 4/7/24.
2587 22/9/46.
62587 1/5/48.

CONDEMNED: 17/12/56.
Cut up at Stratford.

8817

To traffic 7/1910.

REPAIRS:
Str. 17/12/14—20/5/15.**G.**
Str. 21/2—8/5/20.**G.**
Str. 5/8/22—19/1/23.**G.**
Str. 26/2—31/5/24.**G.**
Superheated boiler fitted.
Str. 4/12/25—11/3/26.**G.**
Str. 28/6/27.**N/C.**
Vacuum brake added.
Str. 27/1—14/4/28.**G.**
Coal guard on tender.
Str. 27/2—8/5/30.**G.**
Altered to D15/2.
Str. 29/3—18/5/32.**G.**
Str. 24/3—6/7/34.**G.**
Rebuilt to D16/3.
Str. 24/9—14/11/35.**G.**
Str. 25/4—25/6/37.**G.**
Str. 22/5—1/7/39.**G.**
Str. 1/12/41—24/1/42.**G.**
Str. 5/12/43—26/1/44.**G.**
Str. 2/12/45—12/1/46.**G.**
Str. 18/11—23/12/47.**G.**
Str. 5/7—20/8/48.**L.**
Str. 19/10—10/12/49.**G.**
Dn. 3—16/11/50.**C/L.**
Str. 9/11—12/12/53.**G.**

Str. 23/12/53—2/1/54.**N/C.**
Str. 15/2—10/3/55.**C/L.**
Str. 3/5—23/6/56.**G.**
Str. 12—16/8/57.**C/L.**
Str. 16/12/57—1/2/58.**C/L.**

BOILERS:
1817.
1804 *(ex8804)* 20/5/15.
1819 *(ex8819)* 8/5/20.
3581 *(ex8801)* 31/5/24.
3649 *(ex8819)* 11/3/26.
3566 *(ex8852)* 14/4/28.
3583 *(ex8802)* 8/5/30.
3568 *(ex8855)* 18/5/32.
4217 *(new)* 6/7/34.
4210 *(ex8828)* 25/6/37.
4203 *(ex8809)* 1/7/39.
4201 *(ex8843)* 24/1/42.
4267 *(exJ19 8141)* 26/1/44.
4274 *(ex8804)* 12/1/46.
4252 *(ex8823)* 23/12/47.
4247 *(ex8801)* 10/12/49.
23362 *(ex8825)* 12/12/53.
23376 *(ex8805)* 23/6/56.

SHEDS:
Stratford.
Ipswich 14/4/28.
Parkeston 19/4/28.
Ipswich 9/7/28.
Hull Botanic Gardens 17/9/34.
Ipswich 15/10/34.
Stratford 7/10/45.
Norwich 9/1/47.
Yarmouth 2/7/47.
Norwich 7/1/48.
Trafford Park 23/4/50.
Norwich 8/6/52.
Cambridge 22/6/52.
March 6/7/52.
Bury St Edmunds 21/2/54.
King's Lynn 9/3/58.
Cambridge 8/6/58.

RENUMBERED:
8817 31/5/24.
2588 19/9/46.
62588 20/8/48.

CONDEMNED: 13/10/58.
*Used until June 1959 as a
temporary steam supply in the
works at Stratford.*
Cut up at Stratford.

8818

To traffic 7/1910.

REPAIRS:
Str. 5/7—24/12/18.**G.**
Str. 22/8—21/12/21.**G.**
Str. 13/3—9/6/23.**G.**

Rebuilt to D16/1.
Superheated boiler fitted.
Str. 9/10/24—16/1/25.**G.**
Str. 21/5—8/10/26.**G.**
Str. 2/3—26/5/28.**G.**
Coal guard on tender.
Str. 14/9—22/11/29.**G.**
Str. 9/3—12/5/31.**G.**
Str. 20/9—10/11/33.**G.**
Altered to D16/2.
Str. 19/10—29/11/35.**G.**
Str. 17/6—12/8/37.**G.**
Str. 24/1—19/4/40.**G.**
Str. 23/11—13/12/41.**L.**
Str. 20/6—1/8/42.**G.**
Str. 8/10—17/11/44.**G.**
Str. 10/1—26/3/47.**G.**
Rebuilt to D16/3.
Str. 30/12/48—17/2/49.**G.**
Str. 24/8—6/10/49.**C/L.**
Str. 24/8—29/9/51.**G.**
Str. 30/1—22/2/52.**C/L.**
Str. 23/11—21/10/53.**N/C.**
Str. 6/3—2/4/54.**G.**
Str. 11/12/56—16/2/57.**G.**

BOILERS:
1818.
1858 *(ex8838)* 24/12/18.
3901 *(new)* 9/6/23.
3917 *(new)* 26/5/28.
3933 *(new)* 12/5/31.
1785 *(ex8785)* 10/11/33.
3927 *(ex8842)* 29/11/35.
3915 *(ex8780)* 12/8/37.
3927 *(ex8786)* 19/4/40.
3925 *(ex8789)* 1/8/42.
3911 *(ex8787)* 17/11/44.
4334 *(ex8824)* 26/3/47.
4331 *(ex8830)* 17/2/49.
23365 *(ex ?)* 29/9/51.
23373 *(ex8880)* 2/4/54.
23305 *(exJ19 8265)* 16/2/57.

SHEDS:
Stratford.
Southend 7/12/29.
Stratford 14/6/30.
Southend 12/7/30.
Stratford 13/9/30.
Southend 20/9/30.
Cambridge 12/5/31.
March 14/12/42.

RENUMBERED:
1818E 9/6/23.
8818 16/1/25.
2589 8/9/46.
62589 12/2/49.

CONDEMNED: 18/5/59.
Cut up at Stratford.

8819

To traffic 7/1910.

REPAIRS:
Str. 7/3—24/6/19.**G.**
Superheated boiler fitted.
Str. 25/9/23—18/1/24.**G.**
Str. 23/10/25—27/1/26.**G.**
Altered to D15/2.
Str. 29/9/27—19/1/28.**G.**
Rebuilt to D16/2.
Coal guard on tender.
Str. 19/12/29—22/2/30.**G.**
Str. 4/5—15/6/32.**G.**
Str. 29/6—10/8/34.**G.**
Str. 3/2—8/4/36.**G.**
Str. 3/6—25/6/37.**G.**
Str. 5/1—18/2/38.**G.**
Str. 7/6—12/7/40.**G.**
Str. 9/9—16/10/42.**G.**
Str. 19/3—24/6/44.**G.**
Str. 29/12/46—10/2/47.**G.**
Str. 20/3—17/4/47.**L.**
Str. 1/2—8/3/48.**L.**
Str. 17/7—1/9/49.**G.**
Str. 15—28/10/49.**N/C.**
Str. 29/11—14/12/50.**C/L.**
Str. 11/1/52. *Not repaired.*

BOILERS:
1819.
3579 *(new)* 24/6/19.
3649 *(new)* 18/1/24.
3567 *(ex8807)* 27/1/26.
3911 *(new)* 19/1/28.
3929 *(ex8822)* 15/6/32.
3926 *(ex8842)* 10/8/34.
3932 *(ex8782)* 8/4/36.
3936 *(ex8794)* 12/7/40.
3934 *(ex8780)* 16/10/42.
3920 *(ex8831)* 24/6/44.
3936 *(ex8796)* 10/2/47.
3933 *(ex8826)* 1/9/49.
3933 reno. 23195 14/12/50.

SHEDS:
Stratford.
Cambridge 5/6/26.
Ipswich 12/1/27.
Pbo. Spital Bridge 1/4/51.
Ipswich 15/4/51.

RENUMBERED:
1819E 18/1/24.
8819 ?/?/??.
2590 8/9/46.
62590 1/9/49.

CONDEMNED: 28/1/52.
Cut up at Stratford.

8800

To traffic 8/1910.

REPAIRS:
Str. 11/11/14—2/3/15.**G.**
Str. 22/2—27/8/18.**G.**
Str. 5/5—11/11/22.**G.**
Nr. 12/12/23—16/2/24.**H.**
Str. 3/7—5/11/25.**G.**
Str. 20/4—27/7/27.**G.**
Rebuilt to D16/2.
Superheated boiler fitted.
Coal guard on tender.
Str. 30/7—9/8/28.**N/C.**
Vacuum brake added.
Str. 24/12/28—11/4/29.**G.**
Str. 29/3—5/6/30.**G.**
Str. 8/11—19/12/32.**G.**
Str. 1/10—9/11/34.**G.**
Str. 24/11/36—3/2/37.**G.**
Str. 6/6—28/7/39.**G.**
Str. 12/1—27/2/42.**G.**
Str. 30/1—11/3/44.**G.**
Str. 24/3—30/4/46.**G.**
Str. 13/9—26/11/47.**G.**
Dn. 21/3—23/4/49.**C/L.**
Str. 29/3/50. *Not repaired.*

BOILERS:
1800.
1801 *(ex8801)* 2/3/15.
1852 *(ex8852)* 27/8/18.
3910 *(new)* 27/7/27.
3932 *(ex8853)* 19/12/32.
3936 *(ex8783)* 9/11/34.
3923 *(ex8796)* 3/2/37.
3911 *(ex8784)* 28/7/39.
1783 *(ex8781)* 27/2/42.
3930 *(ex8801)* 11/3/44.
3934 *(ex8845)* 30/4/46.

SHEDS:
Yarmouth.
Norwich 13/7/30.
Yarmouth 7/6/31.
Norwich 7/2/32.
Yarmouth 29/4/33.
Norwich 17/3/34.
Yarmouth 1/9/34.
Norwich 29/9/34.
Yarmouth 8/6/35.
Norwich 14/2/37.
Yarmouth 10/12/39.
Norwich 19/5/40.
Yarmouth 24/11/40.
Norwich 28/5/46.
Yarmouth 7/6/46.

RENUMBERED:
8800 *after* 31/5/24.
2591 1/9/46.
62591 23/4/49.

CONDEMNED: 17/4/50.
Cut up at Stratford.

8801

To traffic 8/1910.

REPAIRS:
Str. 30/9—22/12/14.**G.**
Str. 14/2—13/6/19.**G.**
Superheated boiler fitted.
Str. 24/3—29/6/22.**G.**
Str. 22/9—28/12/23.**G.**
Nr. 30/6—3/7/24.**L.**
Str. 2/2—22/5/25.**G.**
Str. 19/1—7/4/27.**G.**
Coal guard on tender.
Str. 16/1—12/4/29.**G.**
Rebuilt to D16/2.
Vacuum brake added.
Str. 6/1—26/3/31.**G.**
Str. 18/5—10/6/32.**L.**
Str. 30/9—18/11/32.**G.**
Str. 16/7—1/9/33.**G.**
Str. 30/4—11/5/34.**L.**
Str. 8/4—4/6/35.**G.**
Str. 14/9—20/10/36.**G.**
Str. 19/9—3/11/38.**G.**
Str. 27/10—6/12/41.**G.**
Str. 3/10—16/11/43.**G.**
Str. 21/4—13/6/45.**G.**
Rebuilt to D16/3.
Str. 19/7—5/9/47.**G.**
Str. 15/10—26/11/49.**G.**
Str. 30/11—1/12/49.**N/C.**
Str. 15/5—2/6/51.**C/L.**
Str. 17/5—3/7/52.**G.**
Str. 3—29/9/53.**C/H.**
Str. 30/4—26/6/54.**C/H.**
Str. 10/5—25/6/55.**G.**
Str. 10—26/7/56.**N/C.**
Tender change only.

BOILERS:
1801.
1796 *(ex8796)* 22/12/14.
3581 *(new)* 13/6/19.
3572 *(ex8798)* 28/12/23.
3559 *(ex8854)* 7/4/27.
3900 *(ex8805)* 12/4/29.
3907 *(ex8786)* 26/3/31.
1782 *(ex8786)* 18/11/32.
3912 *(ex8805)* 4/6/35.
1780 *(ex8822)* 20/10/36.
3919 *(ex8842)* 3/11/38.
3930 *(ex8796)* 6/12/41.
3914 *(ex8834)* 16/11/43.
4301 *(ex8793)* 13/6/45.
4247 *(exJ19 8248)* 5/9/47.
4308 *(ex8887)* 26/11/49.
4308 reno. 23354 2/6/51.
23321 *(ex8868)* 3/7/52.
23321 had been reno. from 4217
prior to installation.

23379 *(ex8878)* 26/6/54.
23459 *(ex8787)* 25/6/55.

SHEDS:
Yarmouth.
Norwich 13/7/30.
Cambridge 11/11/33.
Norwich 20/8/38.
Yarmouth Beach 9/8/42.
Melton Constable 12/6/49.
Yarmouth Beach 1/1/50.
Norwich 7/9/52.
Melton Constable 21/6/53.
Norwich 30/8/53.
Melton Constable 23/1/55.
Norwich 18/2/55.
Yarmouth Beach 26/2/55.
Melton Constable 3/4/55.
Norwich 8/5/55.
Cambridge 6/1/57.
King's Lynn 24/3/57.

RENUMBERED:
8801 ?/?/??.
2592 1/9/46.
62592 26/11/49.

CONDEMNED: 1/4/58.
Cut up at Stratford.

8802

To traffic 9/1910.

REPAIRS:
Str. 22/3—7/10/18.**G.**
Bd. 30/1—22/7/20.**G.**
Str. 24/5/22—26/1/23.**G.**
Str. 8/5—9/8/24.**G.**
Str. 24/4—8/5/25.**L.**
Str. 9/11/25—9/3/26.**G.**
Vacuum brake added.
Str. 3/2—5/5/28.**G.**
Rebuilt to D15/2.
Superheated boiler fitted.
Coal guard on tender.
Str. 27/11/29—11/2/30.**G.**
Str. 10/6—15/8/31.**G.**
Str. 9/2—24/4/33.**G.**
Rebuilt to D16/3.
Str. 11/11—21/12/34.**G.**
Str. 8/6—10/7/36.**G.**
Str. 7/2—11/3/38.**G.**
Str. 26/7—21/12/40.**G.**
Str. 20/6—2/9/43.**G.**
Str. 7/10—3/11/45.**G.**
Str. 28/12/47—30/1/48.**G.**
Str. 17—20/2/48.**N/C.**
Str. ?/?—21/1/50.**G.**
Str. 12/3—23/4/52.**G.**
W.P.U. gear removed.
Str. 16/1—19/2/55.**G.**

BOILERS:
1802.
1801 *(ex8800)* 7/10/18.
1811 *(ex8811)* 22/7/20.
1838 *(ex8838)* 26/123.
3583 *(ex-spare)* 5/5/28.
3571 *(ex8807)* 11/2/30.
4205 *(new)* 24/4/33.
4200 *(ex8900)* 21/12/34.
4207 *(ex8848)* 10/7/36.
4235 *(exJ19 8242)* 11/3/38.
4266 *(exJ19 8143)* 21/12/40.
4253 *(exJ19 8262)* 2/9/43.
4212 *(ex8858)* 3/11/45.
4223 *(ex8870)* 30/1/48.
4225 *(ex8837)* 21/1/50.
23402 *(ex ?)* 23/4/52.
23419 *(ex8815)* 19/2/55.

SHEDS:
Cambridge.
Stratford 10/3/26.
Norwich 5/5/28.
Yarmouth 13/5/33
Norwich 30/12/33.
Yarmouth 7/11/35.
Norwich 11/3/36.
Yarmouth 12/4/36.
Norwich 17/5/36.
Lowestoft 8/5/38.
Norwich 6/11/38.
Yarmouth 6/3/46.
Norwich 19/4/46.
Yarmouth Beach 11/5/46.
Norwich 27/11/46.
Yarmouth Beach 2/2/47.
Norwich 20/4/47.
Lowestoft 5/12/47.
Norwich 22/2/48.

RENUMBERED:
8802 9/8/24.
2593 1/9/46.
ᴇ2593 30/1/48.
62593 21/1/50.

CONDEMNED: 7/10/57.
Cut up at Stratford.

8803

To traffic 9/1910.

REPAIRS:
Str. 13/8—23/12/20.**G.**
Str. ?/?—?/3/24.**G.**
Str. 24/9/25—25/2/26.**G.**
Str. 28/5—2/9/27.**G.**
Altered to D15/2.
Superheated boiler fitted.
Coal guard on tender.
Str. ?/?—?/5/29.**G.**
Vacuum brake added.
Str. 13/8—18/9/31.**G.**

Str. 11/10—17/11/33.**G.**
Str. ?/?—?/6/35.**G.**
Str. ?/?—16/4/37.**G.**
Rebuilt to D16/3.
Str. ?/?—3/2/39.**G.**
Str. ?/?—?/8/41.**G.**
Str. ?/?—11/10/43.**G.**
Str. ?/?—15/6/45.**G.**
Str. ?/?—21/6/47.**H.**
Str. ?/?—27/11/47.**L.**

BOILERS:
1803.
1850 *(ex8842)* 25/2/26.
3648 *(ex8840)* 2/9/27.
3603 *(ex8790)* ?/5/29.
3465 *(new)* 18/9/31.
3603 *(ex8791)* 17/11/33.
3582 *(ex8857)* ?/6/35.
4252 *(new)* 16/4/37.
4247 *(exJ19 8266)* 3/2/39.
4270 *(exJ19 8240)* ?/8/41.
4271 *(exJ19 8246)* 11/10/43.
4298 *(ex8872)* 15/6/45.
4280 *(ex8864)* 21/6/47.

SHEDS:
Ipswich.
Yarmouth 24/8/47.

RENUMBERED:
8803 *by* 10/10/24.
2594 7/4/46.

CONDEMNED: 24/3/49.
Cut up at Stratford.

8804

To traffic 9/1910.

REPAIRS:
Str. 17/9/14—11/1/15.**G.**
Str. 19/10/17—18/2/18.**G.**
Str. 11/2—28/5/21.**G.**
Str. ?/?—?/3/23.**G.**
Str. 30/5—28/10/24.**G.**
Str. 9/3—23/7/26.**G.**
Str. 27/5—2/6/27.**N/C.**
Vacuum brake added.
Str. ?/?—?/12/28.**G.**
Altered to D15/2.
Superheated boiler fitted.
Str. ?/??—2/32.**G.**
Str. 4/1—1/3/34.**G.**
Rebuilt to D16/3.
Str. 30/4—6/6/35.**G.**
Str. 22/9—23/10/36.**G.**
Str. ?/?—31/8/37.**H.**
New cylinders.
Str. ?/?—25/10/38.**G.**
Str. ?/?—4/1/41.**G.**
Str. ?/?—27/10/43.**G.**
Str. ?/?—23/4/45.**L.**

Str. ?/?—27/10/45.**G.**
Str. ?/?—27/4/46.**L.**
Str. ?/?—2/8/46.**L.**

BOILERS:
1804.
1813 *(ex8813)* 11/1/15.
3551 *(ex8856)* 18/2/18.
3556 *(ex8847)* 28/5/21.
3553 *(exJ17 8233)* 28/10/24.
3569 *(ex8855)* ?/12/28.
3652 *(ex8824)* ?/2/32.
4210 *(new)* 1/3/34.
4224 *(new)* 6/6/35.
4201 *(ex8849)* 23/10/36.
4258 *(ex8791)* 25/10/38.
4254 *(exJ19 8141)* 4/1/41.
4274 *(exJ19 8250)* 27/10/43.
4281 *(ex8899)* 27/10/45.

SHEDS:
Stratford.
Southend 7/12/29.
Stratford 4/1/30.
Southend 29/8/30.
Stratford 25/10/30.

RENUMBERED:
8804 28/10/24.
2595 1/11/46.

CONDEMNED: 13/11/46.
Cut up at Stratford.

8805

To traffic 9/1910.

REPAIRS:
Str. 7/6—6/9/17.**G.**
Str. 20/6—22/8/19.**G.**
Str. 11/10/22—28/3/23.**G.**
Rebuilt to D16/1.
Superheated boiler fitted.
Str. 24/4—5/7/24.**G.**
Str. 11/3—4/9/26.**G.**
Coal guard on tender.
Str. 21/6/27.**N/C.**
Vacuum brake added.
Str. 20/1—23/3/28.**H.**
Str. 14/9—14/12/28.**G.**
Str. 14/2--12/4/30.**G.**
Str. 12/8—4/11/31.**G.**
Altered to D16/2.
Str. 29/4—6/7/33.**G.**
Str. 31/1—1/3/35.**G.**
Str. 4/7—20/8/36.**G.**
Str. 15/5—4/7/38.**G.**
Str. 11/6—20/7/40.**G.**
Str. 31/3—12/6/43.**G.**
Str. 26/2—12/5/45.**G.**
Str. 7—27/7/45.**L.**
Str. 26/1—29/3/47.**G.**
Rebuilt to D16/3.

Str. 27/2—21/4/49.**G.**
Str. 23/3—27/4/50.**C/L.**
Str. 25/10—8/12/51.**G.**
W.P.U. gear removed.
Str. 8—24/12/52.**C/L.**
Str. 23/5—1/6/54.**C/L.**
Str. 19/9—23/10/54.**G.**

BOILERS:
1805.
3557 *(new)* 6/9/17.
3555 *(ex8822)* 22/8/19.
3900 *(new)* 28/3/23.
1783 *(ex8783)* 14/12/28.
3927 *(new)* 12/4/30.
3915 *(ex8831)* 4/11/31.
3912 *(ex8852)* 6/7/33.
3906 *(ex8782)* 1/3/35.
3918 *(ex8851)* 20/8/36.
3908 *(ex8827)* 4/7/38.
3921 *(ex8852)* 20/7/40.
3932 *(ex8795)* 12/6/43.
1785 *(ex8822)* 12/5/45.
4251 *(ex8820)* 29/3/47.
4297 *(ex8899)* 21/4/49.
23376 *(ex ?)* 8/12/51.
23465 *(new)* 23/10/54.

SHEDS:
Stratford.
Southend ?/??
Stratford 7/12/29.
Southend 14/12/29.
Stratford 15/2/30.
Southend 6/9/30.
Stratford 13/9/30.
Southend 18/10/30.
Stratford 8/11/30.
Norwich 2/3/39.
Yarmouth 10/3/40.
Norwich 5/5/40.
Yarmouth Beach 31/10/43.
Norwich 26/12/43.
Yarmouth Beach 23/7/44.
Norwich 13/8/44.
Melton Constable 11/8/45.
Yarmouth Beach 22/9/46.
Norwich 7/9/52.
Melton Constable 22/11/53.
Norwich 3/1/54.

RENUMBERED:
8805 5/7/24.
2596 3/11/46.
62596 21/4/49.

CONDEMNED: 28/10/57.
Cut up at Stratford.

8806

To traffic 11/1910.

REPAIRS:
Str. 2/12/16—29/6/17.**G.**
Str. ?/?—?/5/20.**G.**
Str. 14/12/21—1/4/22.**G.**
Str. 12/7—27/11/23.**G.**
Str. 20/6—29/10/25.**G.**
Str. 29/4—16/7/27.**G.**
Str. 22/6—30/8/29.**G.**
Altered to D15/2.
Superheated boiler fitted.
Vacuum brake added.
Coal guard on tender.
Str. 5/1—20/3/31.**G.**
Str. 13/11/32—18/1/33.**G.**
Str. 25/7—10/9/34.**G.**
Str. 18/5—26/6/36.**G.**
Str. 28/2—1/4/38.**G.**
Str. 21/10/39—5/1/40.**G.**
Rebuilt to D16/3.
Str. 8—16/11/40.**L.**
Str. 28/2—22/3/41.**L.**
Str. 21/7—10/9/42.**G.**
Str. 3/9—7/10/44.**G.**
Str. 18/3—4/5/46.**G.**
Str. 22/6—12/9/47.**G.**
Str. 4/12/49—7/1/50.**G.**
Str. 30/8—6/10/51.**G.**
Str. 21/9—17/10/53.**G.**
Str. 4/4—18/5/56.**G.**

BOILERS:
1806.
1820 *(ex8820)* 29/6/17.
1850 *(ex8850)* ?/5/20.
1796 *(ex8842)* 1/4/22.
1814 *(ex8841)* 29/10/25.
3643 *(ex8794)* 30/8/29.
3684 *(ex8810)* 20/3/31.
3572 *(ex8812)* 18/1/33.
3652 *(ex8804)* 10/9/34.
3627 *(ex8799)* 26/6/36.
3630 *(ex8823)* 1/4/38.
4301 *(new)* 5/1/40.
4308 *(ex8794)* 10/9/42.
4299 *(exJ19 8149)* 7/10/44.
4279 *(ex8828)* 4/5/46.
4237 *(ex8850)* 12/9/47.
4337 *(new)* 7/1/50.
23364 *(ex 8814)* 6/10/51.
23313 *(ex8869)* 17/10/53.
23365 *(ex8783)* 18/5/56.

SHEDS:
Ipswich.
Norwich 16/7/27.
Yarmouth 22/4/28.
Norwich 3/10/30.
Yarmouth 5/4/31.
Norwich 29/1/33.
Yarmouth 27/1/34.

Norwich 13/10/34.
Yarmouth 6/11/34.
Norwich 31/1/35.
Yarmouth 16/2/35.
Norwich 1/11/36.
Yarmouth 17/8/39.
Norwich 19/5/40.
Yarmouth 24/11/40.
Yarmouth Beach 14/10/56.
Melton Constable 5/5/57.
Norwich 1/3/59.
Pbo. Spital Bridge 12/4/59.

RENUMBERED:
1806E 27/11/23.
8806 29/10/25.
2597 27/10/46.
62597 7/1/50.

CONDEMNED: 4/1/60.
Cut up at Stratford.

8807

To traffic 11/1910.

REPAIRS:
Str. 17/2—27/7/14.**G**.
Superheated boiler fitted.
Str. 24/4—15/7/20.**G**.
Str. 11/11/21—18/3/22.**G**.
Str. 8/6—25/8/23.**G**.
Str. 7/9—11/12/25.**G**.
Str. 13/9—1/12/27.**G**.
Coal guard on tender.
Str. 30/12/28—9/1/29.**N/C**.
Vacuum brake added.
Str. 3/10—3/12/29.**G**.
Altered to D15/2.
Str. 17/8—3/10/31.**G**.
Str. 1/6—7/9/33.**G**.
Str. 10/7—13/9/35.**G**.
Str. 18—20/5/36.**L**.
Str. 12/3—29/4/37.**G**.
Str. 17/4—4/6/39.**G**.
Str. 14/10/41—1/1/42.**G**.
Rebuilt to D16/3.
Str. 6/6—4/9/43.**G**.
Str. 5/5—8/6/45.**G**.
Str. 15/3—14/5/47.**G**.
Str. 12/5—23/6/49.**G**.
Str. 30/4/52. *Not repaired.*

BOILERS:
1807.
3559 *(new)* 27/7/14.
3568 *(ex8857)* 15/7/20.
3567 *(ex8854)* 18/3/22.
3624 *(ex8852)* 11/12/25.
3571 *(ex8851)* 1/12/27.
3580 *(ex8854)* 3/12/29.
3685 *(ex8825)* 3/10/31.
3463 *(ex8837)* 7/9/33.
3576 *(ex8844)* 13/9/35.

3685 *(ex8820)* 4/6/39.
4310 *(new)* 1/1/42.
4238 *(ex-spare)* 8/6/45.
4236 *(ex8834)* 14/5/47.
4261 *(exJ19 8141)* 23/6/49.

SHEDS:
Ipswich.
Melton Constable 5/1/40.
Yarmouth Beach 12/6/41.
Norwich 15/10/41.
Yarmouth Beach 10/1/42.
Norwich 16/5/43.
Yarmouth Beach 26/9/43.
Melton Constable 3/5/45.
Stratford 11/8/45.
Colchester 17/8/46.
Norwich 20/5/51.

RENUMBERED:
8807 *after* 26/4/24.
2598 22/6/46.
62598 23/6/49.

CONDEMNED: 12/5/52.
Cut up at Stratford.

8808

To traffic 11/1910.

REPAIRS:
Str. 18/3—26/8/15.**G**.
Str. 17/8—18/10/18.**G**.
Str. 3/5—7/10/21.**G**.
Ca. 3/4—3/5/23.**H**.
Str. 7/7—18/12/24.**G**.
Vacuum brake added.
Str. 21/5/26. *Not repaired.*
Go. 22/5—7/10/26.**G**.
Str. 3/3—22/4/27.**G**.
Str. 19/4—12/7/29.**G**.
Altered to D15/2.
Superheated boiler fitted.
Coal guard on tender.
Str. 25/2—8/5/31.**G**.
Str. 28/3—2/6/33.**G**.
Str. 24/2—13/4/35.**G**.
Str. 8—12/6/36.**L**.
Str. 1/3—2/6/37.**G**.
Rebuilt to D16/3.
Str. 22—29/9/37. **L**.
Str. 4/3—29/4/39.**G**.
Str. 15/1—18/2/42.**G**.
Str. 31/10—11/12/43.**G**.
Str. 25/3—29/4/44.**L**.
Str. 11/11—12/12/45.**G**.
Str. 17/6—15/8/46.**L**.
Str. 21/1—17/3/47.**L**.
Str. 12/4—17/6/47.**G**.
Str. 12/10—19/11/49.**G**.
Str. 18/12/50—20/1/51.**C/L**.
Str. 23/6—22/8/52.**C/H**.
Str. 15/12/53—30/1/54.**G**.

Str. 26/3—12/5/56.**G**.
Str. 10/9/58. *Not repaired.*

BOILERS:
1808.
1817 *(ex8817)* 26/8/15.
1853 *(ex8824)* 18/10/18.
1800 *(ex8790)* 7/10/21.
1799 *(ex8845)* 12/7/29.
3625 *(ex8854)* 8/5/31.
3622 *(ex8810)* 2/6/33.
3647 *(ex8840)* 13/4/35.
4255 *(new)* 2/6/37.
4286 *(new)* 29/4/39.
4313 *(new)* 18/2/42.
4258 *(ex8797)* 11/12/43.
4253 *(ex8802)* 12/12/45.
4234 *(ex8797)* 17/6/47.
4235 *(ex8783)* 19/11/49.
4235 reno. 23326 20/1/51.
23454 *(ex8845)* 30/1/54.
23387 *(ex8858)* 12/5/56.

SHEDS:
Cambridge.
Norwich 3/10/25.
Cambridge 12/12/25.
March ?/?.
Cambridge 26/5/29.
Lincoln 26/7/29.
Norwich 17/10/31.
Yarmouth 30/9/45.
Norwich 6/1/46.
Trafford Park 23/4/50.
Norwich 8/6/52.
Cambridge 22/6/52.
Pbo. Spital Bridge 12/10/52.
Lincoln 24/3/57.

RENUMBERED:
8808 18/12/24.
2599 9/8/46.
62599 19/11/49.

CONDEMNED: 15/9/58.
Cut up at Stratford.

8809

To traffic 11/1910.

REPAIRS:
Str. 25/3—11/7/16.**G**.
Bd. 8/12/19—15/6/20.**G**.
Str. 24/8—14/12/23.**G**.
Str. 4/5—23/7/25.**G**.
Str. ?/?—5/7/29.**G**.
Superheated boiler fitted.
Vacuum brake added.
Coal guard on tender.
Str. 23/4—5/6/31.**G**.
Str. 30/3—22/6/33.**G**.
Rebuilt to D16/3.
Str. 3/12/34—17/1/35.**G**.

Str. ?/?—?/12/36.**G**.
Str. ?/?—31/3/39.**G**.
Str. ?/?—15/7/39.**L**.
Str. ?/?—2/10/41.**G**.
Str. ?/?—23/6/43.**L**.
Str. ?/?—15/4/44.**G**.
Str. ?/?—8/12/44.**L**.
Str. ?/?—31/8/45.**G**.
Str. ?/?—9/3/46.**L**.
Str. ?/?—2/8/47.**L**.

BOILERS:
1809.
1831 *(ex8831)* 11/7/16.
1837 *(ex8837)* 15/6/20.
1808 *(ex8834)* 23/7/25.
3627 *(ex8815)* 5/7/29.
3594 *(ex8848)* 5/6/31.
4208 *(new)* 22/6/33.
4205 *(ex8802)* 17/1/35.
4203 *(exJ19 8146)* ?/12/36.
4262 *(ex8797)* 31/3/39.
4272 *(ex8788)* 2/10/41.
4252 *(exJ19 8264)* 15/4/44.
4232 *(ex8861)* 31/8/45.

SHEDS:
Norwich.
Ipswich 22/6/37.
Stratford 29/9/45.
Norwich 9/8/47.
Lowestoft 12/10/47.
Norwich 16/11/47.

RENUMBERED:
1809E ?/?/24.
8809 ?/?/??.
2600 20/9/46.

CONDEMNED: 12/6/48.
Cut up at Stratford.

Concurrently with rebuilding with new boilers but retaining the original front end, ten further engines were also fitted with new cylinders having 8" piston valves and long travel valve gear. Between 3rd February 1933 (8900) and 6th July 1934 (8817), the ten converted were: 8798, 8804, 8809, 8816, 8817, 8837, 8849, 8855, 8866, 8900.

The reason as to why no.8900 is carrying a somewhat different name in the above photgraph is fully explained by the following extract from a letter, written in 1965, by the legendary Arthur English, Technical Assistant at Stratford Works, to Eric Fry, Editor of the RCTS *Locomotives of the LNER* series. Arthur English was responsible for drawing up the long travel valve gear designs for the B12's, Clauds and N7.

    '...When it was decided to rebuild no.8900, questions arose as to whether or not to perpetuate the name "Claud Hamilton" on the engine and if so, the best means of so doing.

    As you are no doubt aware, the first and only S.46 Class engine (March 1900), was mainly Frederick V.Russell's child and ever since it was built the engine had carried the name "Claud Hamilton" in black letters, inset on the brass beadings round the driving splashers.

    As a mark of respect for and in honour of the former GER Chairman and also in order to maintain the full identity of a former famous GER locomotive, it was eventually considered proper to continue to name the engine, but by means of the currently modern style of a gunmetal name plate - external to the splasher top.

    Another question also arose - "how would it look"? - and here a subtle idea was born since it was then realised that the general appearance and physical construction of the engine would be altered and thus a F.V.R. 'magnum opus' would virtually be destroyed. Hence the idea developed of making a "modern" wooden name plate "Frederick the Great" (The notable king - scholarly potentate and creator of masterly Government), fixing it to No.8900 and photographing, not only to decide appearance but to perpetuate F.V.R.'s great connection with No.1900. Apart from the relatively small (although important) aspect of appearance, the whole exercise was carried out as a very fine leg-pulling tribute (and in honour) to a really great locomotive man who not only helped considerably to place the G.E.R. on the map in 1900 but who later became a masterly governor of Railway Operation. A photograph was sent him suitably mounted and endorsed. A similar photograph was also taken after rebuilding to show and commemorate F.V.R. before and after the event...'

As the piston valve engines showed a marked advantage over those with slide valves, ten more (8791, 8803, 8808, 8810, 8812, 8825, 8832, 8861, 8864, 8865) were fitted with piston valves of 9½" diameter between April 1936 and June 1937. No further Clauds were fitted with piston valves. These engines had screw operated reversing rod instead of by air and a noticeably shorter arm. Yarmouth South Town, 24th October 1936.

8790

To traffic 3/1911.

REPAIRS:
Str. 22/12/14—6/4/15.**G.**
Str. 12/4—2/9/21.**G.**
Str. 9/11/23—29/3/24.**G.**
Vacuum brake added.
Str. 13/3—11/6/25.**G.**
Str. 2/5—20/8/27.**G.**
Altered to D15/2.
Superheated boiler fitted.
Str. 17/1—26/4/29.**G.**
Rebuilt to D16/2.
Coal guard on tender.
Str. 10/4—13/6/31.**G.**
Str. 12/2—27/3/33.**G.**
Str. 6/2—28/3/34.**G.**
Ash ejector fitted.
Str. 24/5—13/6/35.**H.**
Str. 23/3—8/5/36.**G.**
Str. 27/3—10/5/38.**G.**
Str. 13/5—18/7/40.**G.**
Str. 6/5—9/6/42.**G.**
Str. 16/7—2/9/44.**G.**
Rebuilt to D16/3.
Str. 3/3—19/4/46.**G.**
Str. 30/11/47—24/1/48.**G.**
Str. 28/2—20/3/48.**L.**
Str. 1/3—28/4/50.**G.**
Str. 1/6—26/7/52.**G.**
Str. 13/9—16/10/54.**G.**

BOILERS:
1790.
1800 *(ex8800)* 6/4/15.
1853 *(ex8808)* 2/9/21.
1792 *(ex8795)* 29/3/24.
1859 *(ex8835)* 11/6/25.
3603 *(ex8850)* 20/8/27.
3908 *(ex8851)* 26/4/29.
3934 *(new)* 13/6/31.
3922 *(ex8841)* 28/3/34.
3904 *(ex8846)* 8/5/36.
3905 *(ex8852)* 10/5/38.
3922 *(ex8792)* 18/7/40.
3924 *(ex8829)* 9/6/42.
4329 *(new)* 2/9/44.
4230 *(exJ19 8247)* 19/4/46.
4259 *(ex8882)* 24/1/48.
4343 *(new)* 28/4/50.
23355 *(exJ19 8269)* 26/7/52.
23350 *(ex8875)* 16/10/54.

SHEDS:
Cambridge.
Norwich 7/10/24.
Cambridge 22/12/24.
Norwich 3/10/25.
Cambridge 10/12/25.
Norwich 9/10/26.
Cambridge 31/12/26.
March 26/5/29.

Cambridge 16/11/40.
King's Lynn 13/6/48.

RENUMBERED:
8790 29/3/24.
2601 6/10/46.
62601 28/4/50.

CONDEMNED: 1/1/57.
Cut up at Stratford.

8791

To traffic 3/1911.

REPAIRS:
Str. 13/9/22—5/4/23.**G.**
Superheated boiler fitted.
Str. ?/?—?/6/24.**G.**
Weir feedwater heater removed.
Str. 18/12/25—22/4/26.**G.**
Str. 15—22/6/27.**N/C.**
Vacuum brake added.
Str. 17/2—12/5/28.**G.**
Altered to D15/2.
Str. 30/11/31—21/1/32.**G.**
Str. ?/?—?/10/33.**G.**
Str. 24/4—7/6/35.**G.**
Str. ?/?—19/2/37.**G.**
Rebuilt to D16/3.
Str. ?/?—6/10/38.**G.**
Str. ?/?—6/8/40.**G.**
Str. ?/?—?/9/44.**G.**
Str. ?/?—16/1/46.**L.**
Str. ?/?--20/7/46.**G.**
Str. ?/?—17/1/47.**L.**
Str. ?/?—21/5/47.**L.**
Str. ?/?—20/11/47.**L.**
Str. ?/?—20/2/48.**L.**

BOILERS:
1791.
3639 *(new)* 5/4/23.
3612 *(ex8810)* 12/5/28.
3603 *(ex8803)* 21/1/32.
3685 *(ex8807)* ?/10/33.
3456 *(exJ17 8231)* 7/6/35.
4258 *(new)* 19/2/37.
4264 *(ex8793)* 6/10/38.
4248 *(ex8864)* 6/8/40.
4239 *(ex8816)* ?/9/44.
4287 *(ex8899)* 20/7/46.

SHEDS:
Stratford.
Southend ?/??
Stratford 14/12/29.
Southend 11/1/30.
Stratford 18/1/30
Southend 9/4/30.
Stratford 16/5/30.
Southend 17/5/30.
Stratford 25/10/30.
Cambridge 20/3/39.

Stratford 13/6/39.
Colchester 25/9/39.
Stratford 3/12/39.
Cambridge 4/6/40.
March 14/11/40.
Stratford 21/11/42.
Colchester 2/1/43.
Stratford 11/11/44.

RENUMBERED:
8791 ?/6/24.
2602 20/10/46.

CONDEMNED: 23/9/48.
Cut up at Stratford.

8792

To traffic 4/1911.

REPAIRS:
Str. 11/3—28/7/14.**G.**
Superheated boiler fitted.
Str. 16/8/22—6/2/23.**G.**
Str. 1/2—16/4/24.**G.**
Str. 7—26/7/24.**L.**
Str. 23/12/25—1/5/26.**G.**
Str. 1/11/27—1/3/28.**G.**
Rebuilt to D16/2.
Coal guard on tender.
Str. 13—21/9/28.**N/C.**
Vacuum brake added.
Str. 2/10—14/12/29.**G.**
Str. 16/9—20/11/31.**G.**
Str. 4/9—25/10/33.**G.**
Str. 29/4—4/7/35.**G.**
Str. 1/11—11/12/36.**G.**
Str. 2/3—29/4/38.**G.**
Str. 7/1—2/3/40.**G.**
Str. 1/3—6/5/42.**G.**
Str. 9/12/43—1/1/44.**L.**
Str. 9/7—19/8/44.**G.**
Str. 24/4—5/6/46.**G.**
Str. 26/1—22/3/48.**L.**
Str. 7/4—4/5/48.**L.**
Str. 22/11/48—1/2/49.**G.**
Str. 22/8/51. *Not repaired.*

BOILERS:
1792.
3561 *(new)* 28/7/14.
3562 *(ex8797)* 6/2/23.
3913 *(new)* 1/3/28.
1780 *(ex8780)* 20/11/31.
3915 *(ex8805)* 25/10/33.
3910 *(ex8795)* 4/7/35.
3929 *(ex8831)* 11/12/36.
3922 *(ex8826)* 29/4/38.
3920 *(ex8829)* 2/3/40.
3919 *(ex8801)* 6/5/42.
3935 *(ex8841)* 19/8/44.
3929 *(ex8847)* 5/6/46.

SHEDS:
Cambridge.
Peterborough East 1/3/29.
Cambridge 9/6/29.
Peterborough East 21/4/30.
Cambridge 17/5/30.
King's Lynn 11/10/30.
Cambridge 5/7/31.
King's Lynn 6/12/31.
March 21/11/42.
Cambridge 3/12/50.

RENUMBERED:
8792 16/4/24.
2603 3/11/46.
62603 1/5/48.

CONDEMNED: 3/9/51.
Cut up at Stratford.

8793

To traffic 5/1911.

REPAIRS:
Str. 12/7/18—20/3/19.**G.**
Str. 18/4—14/7/23.**G.**
Str. 19/11/24—24/3/25.**G.**
Str. 31/3—23/7/26.**G.**
Str. 14/1—3/5/27.**G.**
Vacuum brake added.
Coal guard on tender.
Str. 22/1—27/5/29.**G.**
Altered to D15/2.
Str. 2/3—9/5/31.**G.**
Str. 13/3—30/4/32.**H.**
Str. 30/3—18/5/33.**G.**
Str. 22/3--30/5/35.**G.**
Str. 25—28/5/36.**L.**
Str. 4/5—28/7/37.**G.**
Rebuilt to D16/3.
Str. 9/8—20/9/38.**G.**
Str. 17/3—13/5/40.**G.**
Str. 19/2—10/4/43.**G.**
Str. 19/2—23/3/45.**G.**
Str. 12/9—2/11/46.**G.**
Str. 2/5—23/6/48.**G.**
Str. 16—31/1/49.**L.**
Str. 3/12/50—13/1/51.**G.**
Str. 5/10—8/11/52.**G.**
Str. 5/9—21/10/55.**G.**
Str. 16/10—2/11/56.**C/L.**
Str. 16/9—4/10/57.**C/L.**

BOILERS:
1793.
1799 *(ex8799)* 20/3/19.
3595 *(ex8825)* 24/3/25.
3563 *(ex8826)* 27/5/29.
3643 *(ex8806)* 9/5/31.
3649 *(ex8798)* 30/4/32.
3598 *(ex8849)* 18/5/33.
3653 *(exJ17 8152)* 30/5/35.
4264 *(new)* 28/7/37.

4278 (new) 20/9/38.
4301 (ex8806) 10/4/43.
4250 (exJ19 8145) 23/3/45.
4284 (ex8780) 2/11/46.
4319 (ex8872) 23/6/48.
23322 (ex ?) 13/1/51.
23420 (ex ?) 8/11/52.
23422 (ex8786) 21/10/55.

SHEDS:
Stratford.
Cambridge 24/6/27.
March ?/??
Cambridge 26/5/29.
Peterborough East 9/6/29.
Norwich 30/6/36.
Yarmouth 12/10/41.
Lowestoft 17/10/45.
Yarmouth 10/11/45.
Lowestoft 25/10/59.

RENUMBERED:
8793 24/3/25.
2604 24/11/46.
62604 19/6/48.

CONDEMNED: 5/2/60.
Cut up at Stratford.

8794

To traffic 6/1911.

REPAIRS:
Str. 23/4—29/7/14.**G.**
Str. 1/7—12/11/21.**G.**
Ca. 5/3—11/4/23.**H.**
Str. 4/10/24—6/2/25.**G.**
Vacuum brake added.
Str. 14—26/8/25.**L.**
Str. 25/2—28/5/27.**G.**
Str. 1/11/28—15/2/29.**G.**
Rebuilt to D16/2.
Coal guard on tender.
Str. 10/1—19/3/31.**G.**
Str. 20/2—27/4/34.**G.**
Str. 28/12/36—12/2/37.**G.**
Str. 1/1—21/3/40.**G.**
Rebuilt to D16/3.
Str. 7—24/5/40.**L.**
Str. 21/4—5/6/42.**G.**
Str. 2/2—6/3/43.**L.**
Str. 10/9—13/10/44.**G.**
Str. 18—25/10/44.**L.**
Str. 10—14/8/45.**L.**
Str. 9/9—26/10/46.**G.**
Str. 9—21/4/47.**L.**
Str. 21/7—1/10/48.**H.**
Str. 16/5—25/6/49.**G.**
Str. 30/11—17/12/49.**C/L.**
Str. 7/1—16/2/52.**G.**
W.P.U. gear removed.
Str. 17/5—2/8/52.**C/H.**
Str. 4/6—24/7/54.**C/L.**

Str. 13/12/54—22/1/55.**G.**
Str. 5—25/5/55.**C/L.**

BOILERS:
1794.
1797 (ex8797) 29/7/14.
3564 (ex8855) 12/11/21.
3643 (ex8798) 28/5/27.
3923 (new) 15/2/29.
3905 (ex8847) 19/3/31.
3934 (ex8790) 27/4/34.
3936 (ex8800) 12/2/37.
4308 (new) 21/3/40.
4307 (ex8830) 5/6/42.
4257 (ex8873) 13/10/44.
4302 (ex8830) 26/10/46.
4228 (ex8844) 1/10/48.
4257 (ex8873) 25/6/49.
23329 (ex8821) 16/2/52.
23414 (ex ?) 2/8/52.
23408 (ex8813) 22/1/55.

SHEDS:
King's Lynn.
Cambridge 14/5/28.
March 26/5/29.
Cambridge 31/7/30.
March *by* 5/32.
Cambridge 11/12/55.
March 30/9/56.

RENUMBERED:
8794 ?/?/??.
2605 24/10/46.
62605 1/10/48.

CONDEMNED: 7/6/57.
Cut up at Stratford.

8795

To traffic 7/1911.

REPAIRS:
Str. 24/6—5/12/18.**G.**
Bd. 24/12/19—24/7/20.**G.**
Str. 17/10/23—22/1/24.**G.**
Str. 14/1—26/4/26.**G.**
Str. 16/12/26—25/1/27.**L.**
Str. 26/4—31/5/27.**G.**
Coal guard on tender.
Str. 28/2—23/5/29.**G.**
Vacuum brake added.
Str. 12/2—22/4/31.**G.**
Rebuilt to D16/2.
Superheated boiler fitted.
Str. 1/5—23/6/33.**G.**
Str. 29/1—8/3/34.**L.**
Str. 20/2—12/4/35.**G.**
Str. 4/10—12/11/36.**G.**
Str. 8/9—20/10/38.**G.**
Str. 24/7—1/10/40.**G.**
Str. 15/10—2/12/42.**G.**
Str. 3/5—17/6/44.**G.**

Str. 28/1—2/3/46.**G.**
Rebuilt to D16/3.
Str. 1/6—22/7/46.**L.**
Str. 30/1—18/2/47.**L.**
Str. 21/12/47—6/3/48.**G.**
Str. 26/5—24/6/50.**G.**
Str. 18/6—9/8/52.**G.**
Str. 19/12/54—29/1/55.**G.**
Str. 30/3—17/5/57.**G.**
Str. 15/9/59. *Not repaired.*

BOILERS:
1795.
1792 (ex8796) 5/12/18.
3557 (ex8829) 22/1/24.
3556 (ex8820) 31/5/27.
3931 (new) 22/4/31.
3910 (ex8800) 23/6/33.
1787 (ex8796) 12/4/35.
3912 (ex8801) 12/11/36.
3917 (ex8851) 20/10/38.
3932 (ex8819) 1/10/40.
3927 (ex8818) 2/12/42.
3931 (ex8833) 17/6/44.
4258 (ex8808) 2/3/46.
4312 (exJ19 8260) 6/3/48.
4274 (ex8816) 24/6/50.
23412 (ex ?) 9/8/52.
23467 (new) 29/1/55.
23300 (exJ19 8254) 17/5/57.

SHEDS:
Stratford.
Cambridge 2/7/26.
Peterborough East 24/3/32.
Cambridge 5/9/32.
Stratford 5/6/38.
Bishops Stortford 11/6/38.
Cambridge 9/1/39.
South Lynn 23/10/46.
Cambridge 5/11/46.
King's Lynn 4/7/47.
Cambridge 3/8/47.
King's Lynn 11/11/48.
Norwich 22/12/48.
Lowestoft 27/2/49.
Norwich 30/7/50.
King's Lynn 7/6/53.

RENUMBERED:
1795ᴇ 22/1/24.
8795 26/4/26.
7665 2/12/42.
8795 14/7/44.
2606 10/11/46.
ᴇ**2606** 6/3/48.
62606 24/6/50.

CONDEMNED: 28/9/59.
Cut up at Stratford.

8796

To traffic 7/1911.

REPAIRS:
Str. 21/8—19/11/14.**G.**
Str. 1/3—22/7/18.**G.**
Str. 28/4—12/7/23.**G.**
Str. 13/11/24—24/4/25.**G.**
Superheated boiler fitted.
Str. 11/11/26—18/2/27.**G.**
Str. 28/6/27.**N/C.**
Vacuum brake added.
Str. 22/9—19/12/28.**G.**
Rebuilt to D16/2.
Coal guard on tender.
Str. 19/9—9/12/30.**G.**
Str. 25/2—14/4/32.**G.**
Str. 18/9—2/11/33.**G.**
Str. 5/2—14/3/35.**G.**
Str. 23/11/36—8/1/37.**G.**
Str. 31/10/38—6/1/39.**G.**
Str. 2/3—16/4/41.**G.**
Str. 29/5—4/8/43.**G.**
Str. 21/1—12/2/44.**L.**
Str. 22/4—1/6/45.**G.**
Str. 2/11—13/12/46.**G.**
Rebuilt to D16/3.
Str. 16/4—19/5/47.**L.**
Str. 12/12/48—22/1/49.**G.**
Str. 25—30/12/49.**C/L.**
Str. 23/2—30/3/51.**G.**
Str. 9/12/51—2/1/52.**C/L.**
Str. 27/7—29/8/53.**G.**
Str. 2—20/8/55.**C/L.**

BOILERS:
1796.
1792 (ex8792) 19/11/14.
1813 (ex8804) 22/7/18.
3551 (ex8840) 12/7/23.
1798 (ex8857) 24/4/25.
1797 (ex8812) 18/2/27.
3919 (new) 19/12/28.
3935 (new) 14/4/32.
1787 (ex8782) 2/11/33.
3923 (ex8831) 14/3/35.
3910 (ex8792) 8/1/37.
3930 (ex8788) 6/1/39.
3903 (ex8789) 16/4/41.
3916 (ex8784) 4/8/43.
3936 (ex8842) 1/6/45.
4220 (ex8863) 13/12/46.
4213 (ex8879) 22/1/49.
23338 (ex ?) 30/3/51.
23405 (exJ19 8244) 29/8/53.

SHEDS:
Stratford.
Southend ?/??.
Stratford 15/2/30.
Southend 15/3/30.
Stratford 22/3/30.
Southend 10/5/30.

85

Stratford 17/5/30.
Norwich 24/1/39.
Cambridge 1/2/39.
Stratford 22/10/44.
Cambridge 10/8/45.
South Lynn 16/5/48.
Cambridge 26/5/48.
Bury St Edmunds 19/6/49.
Cambridge 7/11/54.

RENUMBERED:
  1796E 12/7/23?
  8796 24/4/25.
  2607 6/12/46.
  62607 22/1/49.

CONDEMNED: 28/11/55.
Cut up at Stratford.

8797

To traffic 8/1911.

REPAIRS:
Str. 3/4—31/7/14.**G.**
Superheated boiler fitted.
Str. 11/4—2/8/22.**G.**
Str. 4/1—14/3/24.**G.**
Str. 14/12/25—18/3/26.**G.**
Str. 24/11/27—14/4/28.**G.**
Altered to D15/2.
Coal guard on tender.
Str. 21/8—4/9/28.**N/C.**
Vacuum brake added.
Str. 28/9—8/11/28.**L.**
Str. 21/12/29—22/2/30.**G.**
Str. 19/9—5/12/31.**G.**
Str. 18—29/1/32.**H.**
Str. 7/10—1/12/33.**G.**
Str. 30/4—27/6/35.**G.**
Str. 4—7/5/36.**L.**
Str. 13/4—13/7/37.**G.**
Rebuilt to D16/3.
Str. 22/12/38—17/2/39.**G.**
Str. 12/12/40—8/2/41.**G.**
Str. 15/4—12/6/43.**G.**
Str. 14/10—13/11/43.**L.**
Str. 15/4—16/5/45.**G.**
Str. 10/2—2/4/47.**G.**
Str. 7/7—20/8/49.**G.**
Str. 6/4—10/5/52.**G.**
W.P.U. gear removed.
Str. 20—27/5/52.**N/C.**
Str. 29/11/54—8/1/55.**G.**

BOILERS:
  1797.
  3562 (new) 31/7/14.
  3570 (ex8848) 2/8/22.
  3562 (ex8792) 14/4/28.
  3570 (ex8816) 22/2/30.
  3573 (ex8857) 5/12/31.
  3567 (ex8857) 1/12/33.
  3603 (ex8803) 27/6/35.

  4262 (new) 13/7/37.
  4260 (ex8798) 17/2/39.
  4258 (ex8804) 8/2/41.
  4321 (new) 12/6/43.
  4234 (exJ19 8248) 16/5/45.
  4286 (exJ19 8142) 2/4/47.
  4236 (ex8807) 20/8/49.
  23401 (ex ?) 10/5/52.
  23384 (ex8855) 8/1/55.

SHEDS:
Cambridge.
Stratford 25/7/30.
Cambridge 31/7/30.
King's Lynn 1/3/31.
Cambridge 16/10/32.
Stratford 10/8/45.
Colchester 17/8/46.
Norwich 20/5/51.
Melton Constable 24/6/51.
Norwich 16/12/51.
Cambridge 2/10/55.

RENUMBERED:
  8797 14/3/24.
  2608 17/10/46.
  62608 20/8/49.

CONDEMNED: 1/1/57.
Cut up at Stratford.

8798

To traffic 9/1911.

REPAIRS:
Str. 24/5—18/10/18.**G.**
Bd. 14/2—17/7/20.**G.**
Str. 20/4—30/6/23.**G.**
Str. 13/10—18/12/24.**G.**
Str. 21/1—30/4/27.**G.**
Vacuum brake added.
Str. 7/12/28—3/4/29.**G.**
Coal guard on tender.
Str. 12/9—20/11/30.**G.**
Str. 29/2—15/4/32.**G.**
Altered to D15/2.
G.N. chimney and cowl.
Str. 16/1—6/4/34.**G.**
Rebuilt to D16/3.
Str. 13/8—14/10/35.**G.**
Str. 4/5—1/7/37.**G.**
Str. 26/9—9/11/38.**G.**
Str. 29/12/40—6/5/41.**G.**
Str. 4/4—29/5/43.**G.**
Str. 23/4—31/5/45.**G.**
Str. 29/12/45—2/2/46.**L.**
Str. 28/2—26/4/48.**G.**
Str. 2/8—2/9/50.**G.**
Str. 16—29/11/52.**N/C.**
Str. 25/10—11/12/54.**G.**
Str. 22/1/57. *Not repaired.*

BOILERS:
  1798.
  3572 (new) 18/10/18.
  3643 (new) 30/6/23.
  1798 (ex8796) 30/4/27.
  3656 (ex8835) 3/4/29.
  3649 (ex8836) 20/11/30.
  3595 (ex8823) 15/4/32.
  4212 (new) 6/4/34.
  4260 (new) 1/7/37.
  4280 (new) 9/11/38.
  4287 (ex8820) 29/5/43.
  4306 (ex8825) 31/5/45.
  4303 (exJ19 8262) 26/4/48.
  4304 (ex8865) 2/9/50.
  23395 (ex8799) 11/12/54.

SHEDS:
Stratford.
Norwich 16/4/29.
Yarmouth 7/6/42.
Norwich 9/8/42.
Stratford 21/11/42.
Colchester 2/1/43.
Stratford 18/11/44.
Colchester 3/3/47.
Trafford Park 11/6/50.
Cambridge 8/6/52.
South Lynn 29/6/52.
Cambridge 22/9/52.
Pbo. Spital Bridge 12/10/52.
Cambridge 13/9/53.
Pbo. Spital Bridge 29/11/53.

RENUMBERED:
  8798 by 8/24.
  2609 22/9/46.
  62609 17/4/48.

CONDEMNED: 4/2/57.
Cut up at Stratford.

8799

To traffic 9/1911.

REPAIRS:
Str. 27/3—17/9/18.**G.**
Str. 20/1—24/3/23.**G.**
Str. 3/4—3/7/24.**G.**
Str. 14—30/4/26. *Not repaired.*
Gr. 1/5—26/11/26.**G.**
Str. 2/11/28—5/2/29.**G.**
Vacuum brake added.
Coal guard on tender.
Str. 21/12/30—10/3/31.**G.**
Str. 2/2—16/4/32.**G.**
Str. 5/1—23/2/34.**G.**
Altered to D15/2.
Str. 23/4—28/5/35.**H.**
Str. 10/1—12/2/36.**G.**
Str. 27—30/4/36.**L.**
Str. 9/2—18/3/38.**G.**
Cab side screen fitted.

Str. 18/10/39—13/2/40.**G.**
Rebuilt to D16/3.
Str. 16/3—5/4/41.**L.**
Str. 25/7—7/9/42.**G.**
Str. 12—30/1/43.**L.**
Str. 5/11—8/12/44.**G.**
Str. 20/3—13/5/46.**G.**
Str. 29/11/47—30/1/48.**G.**
Str. 15/10—16/12/49.**G.**
Str. 16/2—28/3/52.**G.**
W.P.U. gear removed.
Str. 9—17/10/53.**C/L.**
Str. 8—19/12/53.**C/L.**
Str. 28/9—30/10/54.**G.**
Str. 15/2—28/3/57.**G.**

BOILERS:
  1799.
  3571 (new) 17/9/18.
  3561 (ex8792) 24/3/23.
  1793 (ex8844) 5/2/29.
  3656 (ex8798) 10/3/31.
  3624 (ex8850) 16/4/32.
  3627 (ex8836) 23/2/34.
  3595 (ex8830) 12/2/36.
  3437 (ex8830) 18/3/38.
  4304 (new) 13/2/40.
  4256 (exJ19 8149) 7/9/42.
  4307 (ex8794) 8/12/44.
  4276 (exJ19 8243) 13/5/46.
  4230 (ex8790) 30/1/48.
  23395 (ex ?) 28/3/52.
  23466 (new) 30/10/54.
  23381 (ex8838) 28/3/57.

SHEDS:
Stratford.
Ipswich 3/7/24.
Colchester 16/7/34.
Stratford 25/9/39.
Colchester 12/12/42.
Stratford 18/11/44.
Colchester 28/7/45.
Stratford 20/10/45.
Norwich 13/5/46.
Melton Constable 13/6/46.
Norwich 18/12/46.
Melton Constable 5/1/47.
Norwich 16/7/47.
Melton Constable 19/8/51.
Norwich 25/11/51.
Cambridge 13/11/55.
King's Lynn 13/10/57.

RENUMBERED:
  8799 3/7/24.
  2610 10/11/46.
  E**2610** 30/1/48.
  62610 16/12/49.

CONDEMNED: 1/1/59.
Cut up at Stratford.

(top) The rebuilds which had piston valves could be distinguished because the frames at the front end were strengthened by extra pieces welded on to give a convex instead of concave profile. The first ten rebuilds got boilers with twin anti-vacuum valves, but the next batch all got boilers with single Gresley type anti-vacuum valve and had hand holes instead of plugs for washout purposes, still two on each side. All Part 3 engines were fitted with two Ross 'pop' safety valves throughout. Note also the exhaust steam injector beneath the cab, behind the steps and the supply pipe projecting from the bowels of the smokebox. Instructions in 1945 decreed that exhaust steam injectors were to be taken or blanked off - live steam only to be used - and by the end of the LNER they had gone.

(right) The first thirty boilers built to Diagram 28A were put to work January 1933 to June 1935. All had the twin GER type anti-vacuum valves, and had two washout plugs on each side of the firebox. Four of them were first used to rebuild J19 Class engines. These first boilers were particularly durable. 62585 at Bletchley in February 1954 with the 12.10 p.m. for Oxford.

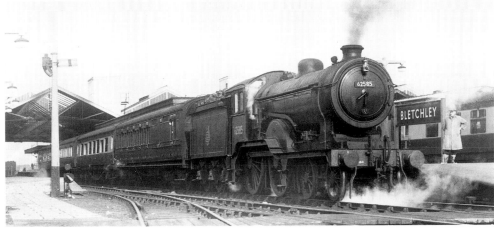

(right) Rebuilding from Part 2 began when no.8851 was ex works 28th June 1938, and all except four of the forty D16/2 changed to round top firebox, no.62570 being the last on 29th September 1949, bringing the number of rebuilds to D16/3 to 104. Change from Part 2 to 3 required no modification to footplating or splashers so the valance was retained. Apart from boiler, dome and chimney only a new front plate to the cab was needed. The boiler put on 8851 was new.

Only one Part 2 engine lost its valances, when no.8783 had a level crossing accident at Hilgay on 1st June 1939. The repairs included rebuilding to Part 3 and the damaged valances were not restored. 8783 remained that way until withdrawal as 62614. *F.W.Day.*

The round top firebox boilers were pitched 1" higher than the Belpaires and all had LNER pattern chimney in place of GER type, which cut height from rail to 12' 11", although over the dome it was now 13' 1". In May 1939 instructions were issued for all D16/3 to have their height reduced by 1" and the class then conformed to the 13' 0" composite loading gauge. Stratford 13th October 1945.

During the war many had the forward cab side window replaced by a steel sheet as fitted to no.62592. It is not known if all were so treated or whether restitution was made on some engines as was the case with no.62610. Certainly some restoration took place but some kept the steel plate to withdrawal, as late as November 1959 in the case of no.62618.

Five of those rebuilt in 1934 (nos.8804, 8816, 8828, 8859, 8869) were fitted with ash ejector in the smokebox. The steam supply pipe for working it ran along the right hand side from cab to smokebox. By the end of 1935 another eleven engines (8798, 8802, 8809, 8814, 8817, 8821, 8837, 8840, 8848, 8849, 8855) had also been so fitted. On some, provision of the ash ejector was short lived, 8840 losing it in March 1937 for instance. All those still fitted lost the equipment during WW2.

At rebuilding it was usual for Group Standard buffers to be fitted but there were some exceptions. Among the 1933 rebuilds, nos.8802, 8848 and 8854 retained their GER parallel shank buffers with circular flange and packing piece. The hybrid type introduced in 1939 with the longer parallel shanks but large head and square flange was used on some D16/3 as on 62577. Wells-next-the-Sea, 15th June 1952. *L.R.Peters.*

When rebuilt to Part 3, a new cab roof was put on. This was steel and had curved rain strips, also a sliding ventilator on the centre line. From 1937 hinged glass sight screens began to be fitted between the cab side windows. The nine rebuilds that year all got them, and some of the earlier rebuilds acquired them but nos.8802 and 8855 never did so. Screen fitting was suspended during the war and was not resumed except for 62613.

The ten engines built in 1923, nos.8780 to 8789, which became 62611 to 62620 were originally equipped with sight feed lubricator in the cab. At least no.62615 retained this type whilst nos.62613, 62614, 62618 were changed to Wakefield which was standard for all other engines in the class.

All Part 3 engines were dual braked, and 22 of them had the larger Westinghouse pump supplied whilst they were mainly Part 2. The other engines kept the smaller version to withdrawal. Note Wakefield mechanical lubricator mounted on frame behind smokebox. Where the coupling rod valances were removed, the front footsteps were separate and were fixed to the rear of the running plate angle. On engines which had been D16/2 and where the valance was not disturbed at rebuilding, the footsteps remained integral with the decorative framing. *Photomatic.*

The GER standard tender of 5 tons coal and 3450 gallons water capacity was coupled to all Part 3 engines. Many of these tenders eventually had Group Standard buffers. Stratford, October 1945.

Only the one Part 3 engine was ever named and when no.8900 was rebuilt in February 1933 new plates of LNER style were fitted. These remained on 8900, 7770 and 2500 until its withdrawal on 27th May 1947. The nameplates from 2500 were transferred to 2546 in mid-August 1947 and remained on that engine until withdrawal in June 1957. During 1945 instructions were issued for the exhaust steam injectors to be taken off, or blanked off so as to work on live steam only. Before the end of the LNER they had all gone, although no.2500 was still so fitted to its withdrawal. Stratford, 4th June 1947.

The nameplates from no.2500 remained with no.62546 until that engine was withdrawn on 18th June 1957. Yarmouth South Town 26th May 1956.

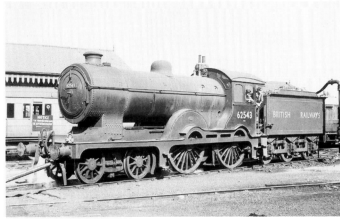

During the war some Part 3 engines began working from M&GN sheds. These engines had tablet exchange apparatus fitted on their tender. When no.62543 left the M&GN section in November 1950 the tablet exchange apparatus was removed for further use on another engine.

When the 1946 re-numbering to 2500-2620 took place, no.8815 became 2586 on Saturday 21st September 1946 at Norwich shed. The cab side numbers are unusual in being only 9" high. 2586 is at Yarmouth Vauxhall shed , 22nd June 1947. *L.W.Perkins.*

8780

To traffic 21/6/1923.

REPAIRS:
Str. 1/11/24—11/2/25.**G.**
Str. 20—21/5/26. *Not repaired.*
Gr. 22/5—19/11/26.**G.**
Str. 30/7—6/11/28.**G.**
Altered to D16/2.
Vacuum brake added.
Coal guard on tender.
Str. 22/11—24/12/29.**G.**
Str. 11/4—15/6/31.**G.**
Str. 9/11/33—2/1/34.**G.**
Str. 24/5—18/7/35.**G.**
Str. 3/4—26/5/37.**G.**
Str. 3/7—1/9/39.**G.**
Str. 4/6—24/7/42.**G.**
Str. 16/7—2/9/44.**G.**
Rebuilt to D16/3.
Str. 16/11—9/12/44.**L.**
Str. 5/5—28/6/46.**G.**
Str. 24/10—10/12/48.**G.**
Str. 10/3—14/4/51.**G.**
Str. 8/9—3/10/53.**G.**

BOILERS:
1780.
3904 *(ex8853)* 15/6/31.
1786 *(ex8833)* 2/1/34.
3915 *(ex8792)* 18/7/35.
3900 *(ex8784)* 26/5/37.
3934 *(ex8841)* 1/9/39.
3923 *(ex8813)* 24/7/42.
4284 *(ex8837)* 2/9/44.
4318 *(ex8876)* 28/6/46.
4330 *(ex8855)* 10/12/48.
23344 *(ex8847)* 14/4/51.
23451 *(ex8843)* 3/10/53.

SHEDS:
Colchester.
Ipswich 7/3/28.
Norwich 18/7/35.
Yarmouth 4/10/36.
Norwich 13/12/36.
Yarmouth 22/1/38.
Norwich 20/3/38.
Yarmouth 20/10/39.
Norwich 14/4/40.
Yarmouth 30/9/45.
Norwich 28/10/45.
Ipswich 11/11/45.
Melton Constable 3/1/46.
Ipswich 30/1/46.
Norwich 17/10/48.
Yarmouth 11/6/50.

RENUMBERED:
1780ᴇ ?/?/??.
8780 11/2/25.
2611 1/12/46.
62611 4/12/48.

CONDEMNED: 1/1/57.
Cut up at Stratford.

8781

To traffic 26/6/1923.

REPAIRS:
Str. 10/10—5/12/24.**G.**
Str. 16—30/4/26. *Not repaired.*
Gr. 1/5—26/11/26.**G.**
Str. 8/6—29/8/28.**G.**
Altered to D16/2.
Vacuum brake added.
Coal guard on tender.
Str. 5—20/12/29.**L.**
Str. 2/5—16/8/30.**G.**
Str. 16/1—23/5/31.**H.**
After Thorpe collision.
Str. 4/7—1/9/32.**G.**
Str. 27/1—21/3/35.**G.**
Str. 6/11—22/12/36.**G.**
Str. 23/2—11/3/38.**L.**
Str. 12/3—29/4/39.**G.**
Str. 11/12/41—7/2/42.**G.**
Str. 18/4—8/5/43.**L.**
Str. 23/5—5/6/43.**L.**
Str. 16—24/6/43.**N/C.**
Str. 13/8—16/9/44.**G.**
Str. 3/5—25/6/46.**G.**
Str. 20/2—15/4/49.**G.**
Rebuilt to D16/3.
Str. 20/3—21/4/51.**G.**
Str. 27/11—20/12/52.**C/L.**
Str. 23/8—18/9/53.**G.**
Str. 15—31/10/53.**C/L.**
Str. 19/3—28/4/56.**G.**
Str. 29/10—23/11/56.**C/L.**

BOILERS:
1781.
3921 *(new)* 29/8/28.
1781 *(ex8842)* 1/9/32.
1784 *(ex8833)* 21/3/35.
3907 *(ex8839)* 22/12/36.
1783 *(ex8782)* 29/4/39.
3913 *(ex8846)* 7/2/42.
3919 *(ex8792)* 16/9/44.
3935 *(ex8792)* 25/6/46.
4206 *(ex8871)* 15/4/49.
23345 *(ex8796)* 21/4/51.
23303 *(exJ19 8252)* 18/9/53.
23357 *(ex8864)* 28/4/56.

SHEDS:
Colchester.
Ipswich 29/7/33.
Norwich 18/11/45.
Yarmouth 17/3/46.
Norwich 3/5/46.
Ipswich 7/7/46.
Norwich 17/10/48.
Lowestoft 2/1/49.
Norwich 20/2/49.

Ipswich 24/7/49.
Norwich 28/8/49.
Ipswich 13/6/54.
Pbo. Spital Bridge 12/4/59.

RENUMBERED:
1781ᴇ ?/?/23.
8781 5/12/24.
2612 1/11/46.
62612 14/4/49.

CONDEMNED: 24/11/59.
Cut up at Stratford.

8782

To traffic 30/6/1923.

REPAIRS:
Str. 15/10/24—6/1/25.**G.**
Str. 24—30/4/26. *Not repaired.*
Gr. 1/5—10/11/26.**G.**
Str. 8/6/27.**N/C.**
Vacuum brake added.
Str. 4/8—2/9/27.**L.**
Str. 9/3—23/6/28.**G.**
Coal guard on tender.
Str. 16/11/29—27/1/30.**G.**
Str. 8/4—29/5/31.**G.**
Altered to D16/2.
Str. 23/3—11/5/33.**G.**
Str. 20/11—31/12/34.**G.**
Str. 7—24/1/36.**H.**
Str. 1/10—6/11/36.**G.**
Str. 22/9—8/12/38.**G.**
Str. 8/7—29/8/41.**G.**
Str. 25/3—29/4/44.**G.**
Str. 24—26/10/44.**L.**
Str. 15/9—18/11/46.**G.**
Str. 31/10—27/12/48.**G.**
Rebuilt to D16/3.
Str. 13/8—16/9/50.**C/L.**
Str. 16/10—28/11/51.**G.**
W.P.U. gear removed.
Str. 11/2—20/3/54.**G.**
Str. 18/10—8/11/56.**C/L.**
Str. 13/4—31/5/57.**G.**

BOILERS:
1782.
3918 *(new)* 23/6/28.
1787 *(ex8856)* 29/5/31.
3906 *(ex8831)* 11/5/33.
3932 *(ex8800)* 31/12/34.
1786 *(ex8780)* 24/1/36.
1783 *(ex8843)* 6/11/36.
3909 *(ex8787)* 8/12/38.
3906 *(ex8784)* 29/8/41.
1783 *(ex8800)* 29/4/44.
3932 *(ex8853)* 18/11/46.
4285 *(exJ19 8243)* 27/12/48.
4285 reno. 23304 16/9/50.
23374 *(ex8870)* 28/11/51.
23369 *(ex8851)* 20/3/54.

23417 *(ex8861)* 31/5/57.

SHEDS:
Stratford.
Southend 22/2/30.
Stratford 15/3/30.
Southend 29/3/30.
Stratford 19/4/30.
Southend 17/5/30.
Stratford 14/6/30.
Southend 21/6/30.
Stratford 8/11/30.
Colchester 18/11/44.
Norwich 14/8/46.
Yarmouth Beach 19/1/47.
Norwich 10/10/48.
Yarmouth 11/1/49.
Pbo. Spital Bridge 12/4/59.
March 31/1/60.

RENUMBERED:
1782ᴇ ?/?/23.
8782 6/1/25.
2613 9/11/46.
62613 24/12/48.

CONDEMNED: 25/10/60.
Cut up at Stratford.

8783

To traffic 10/7/1923.

REPAIRS:
Str. 7/11/24—16/1/25.**G.**
Str. 25/3—4/8/26.**G.**
Str. 26/3/27.**N/C.**
Vacuum brake added.
Str. 24/2—1/6/28.**G.**
Altered to D16/2.
Coal guard on tender.
Str. 28/3—18/6/30.**G.**
Str. 24/5—23/8/32.**G.**
Str. 2/5—27/7/34.**G.**
Str. 3—11/10/36.**L.**
Str. 2/5—17/7/37.**G.**
Str. 12/3—21/4/39.**H.**
Str. 2/6—2/12/39.**G.**
Rebuilt to D16/3.
Str. 6/12/41—17/1/42.**G.**
Str. 19/12/43—12/2/44.**G.**
Str. 18/11/45—31/1/46.**G.**
Painted green.
Str. 25/8—29/10/47.**G.**
Str. 11/9—19/11/49.**G.**
Str. 5—21/4/51.**C/H.**
Str. 10/3—24/4/52.**G.**
W.P.U. gear removed.
Str. 7—16/12/52.**C/L.**
Str. 28/3—15/5/54.**G.**
Str. 26/2—21/4/56.**G.**
Str. 23/2—1/3/57.**C/L.**

BOILERS:
1783.
3916 *(new)* 1/6/28.
3936 *(new)* 23/8/32.
1788 *(ex8813)* 27/7/34.
3924 *(ex8829)* 17/7/37.
4299 *(new)* 2/12/39.
4300 *(ex8811)* 17/1/42.
4285 *(exJ19 8266)* 12/2/44.
4325 *(ex8837)* 31/1/46.
4235 *(exJ19 8254)* 29/10/47.
4272 *(exJ19 8266)* 19/11/49.
4272 reno. 23350 21/4/51.
23399 *(ex ?)* 24/4/52.
23365 *(ex8818)* 15/5/54.
23463 *(ex8854)* 21/4/56.

SHEDS:
Stratford.
Cambridge 7/10/30.
King's Lynn 6/2/46.

RENUMBERED:
1783E ?/?/23.
8783 16/1/25.
2614 3/11/46.
62614 19/11/49.

CONDEMNED: 18/8/58.
Cut up at Stratford.

8784

To traffic 14/7/1923.

REPAIRS:
Str. 24/10/24—7/1/25.**G**.
Str. 24—30/4/26. *Not repaired.*
Gr. 1/5—11/11/26.**G**.
Str. 1—30/4/27.**G**.
Str. 14/6/27.**N/C**.
Vacuum brake added.
Str. 23/2—10/6/29.**G**.
Altered to D16/2
Coal guard on tender.
Str. 21/2—17/4/31.**G**.
Str. 31/12/32—9/2/33.**G**.
Str. 29/11/34—16/1/35.**G**.
Str. 12/10—23/11/36.**G**.
Str. 12/2—31/3/39.**G**.
Str. 19/12/40—7/2/41.**G**.
Str. 27/5—12/6/41.**L**.
Str. 11/4—1/7/43.**G**.
Str. 14/11—16/12/44.**G**.
Str. 16/2—28/3/46.**L**.
Str. 26/1—9/4/47.**G**.
Rebuilt to D16/3.
Str. 28/1—28/3/49.**G**.
Str. 9—25/6/49.**C/L**.
Str. 28/4—16/6/51.**G**.
Str. 29/5—27/6/53.**G**.
Str. 16/6—13/8/55.**G**.
Str. 24/10—14/11/55.**C/L**.
Str. 7—29/8/56.**C/L**.

BOILERS:
1784.
3906 *(ex8856)* 10/6/29.
3923 *(ex8794)* 17/4/31.
3928 *(ex8813)* 9/2/33.
3900 *(ex8843)* 16/1/35.
3911 *(ex8785)* 23/11/36.
3906 *(ex8843)* 31/3/39.
3916 *(ex8831)* 7/2/41.
3915 *(ex8826)* 1/7/43.
1788 *(ex8852)* 16/12/44.
4231 *(exJ19 8252)* 9/4/47.
4290 *(ex8825)* 28/3/49.
23453 *(new)* 16/6/51.
23427 *(ex ?)* 27/6/53.
23391 *(ex8853)* 13/8/55.

SHEDS:
Stratford.
Southend ?/??.
Stratford 21/12/29.
Southend 15/2/30.
Stratford 22/2/30.
Southend 25/10/30.
Stratford 1/11/30.
Cambridge 18/5/39.
Bury St Edmunds 3/1/43.
Cambridge 15/4/51.
Bury St Edmunds 10/8/52.
March 16/6/57.

RENUMBERED:
1784E ?/?/23.
8784 7/1/25.
2615 10/11/46.
62615 26/3/49.

CONDEMNED: 13/10/58.
Cut up at Stratford.

8785

To traffic 31/7/1923.

REPAIRS:
Str. 8/12/24—12/2/25.**G**.
Str. 22/5/26.*Not repaired.*
Gr. 22/5—30/10/26.**G**.
Str. 31/3—30/6/28.**G**.
Altered to D16/2.
Coal guard on tender.
Str. 16/11/29—27/1/30..**G**.
Str. 10/10—12/12/31.**G**.
Str. 18/4—25/5/33.**G**.
Str. 13/12/34—1/2/35.**G**.
Str. 26/8—1/10/36.**G**.
Str. 27/9—1/12/38.**G**.
Str. 8/5—27/6/41.**G**.
Str. 16/1—6/5/44.**G**.
Rebuilt to D16/3.
Str. 31/3—29/5/46.**G**.
Str. 5/12/47—1/1/48.**L**.
Str. 16/10—26/11/48.**G**.
Str. 14/2—17/3/51.**G**.

Str. 7—18/10/51.**C/L**.
Str. 11/2/53. *Not repaired.*

BOILERS:
1785.
3920 *(new)* 30/6/28.
1785 *(ex8787)* 12/12/31.
3911 *(ex8819)* 25/5/33.
3935 *(ex8787)* 1/10/36.
3929 *(ex8853)* 27/6/41.
4290 *(ex8840)* 6/5/44.
4243 *(exJ19 8141)* 29/5/46.
4267 *(ex8851)* 26/11/48.
23336 *(ex ?)* 17/3/51.

SHEDS:
Ipswich.
Stratford 12/10/27.
Southend 15/3/30.
Stratford 29/8/30.
Southend 20/9/30.
Stratford 25/10/30.
Colchester 18/11/44.
Stratford 17/8/46.
Norwich 8/3/47.
Melton Constable 10/4/47.
Norwich 13/7/47.
Yarmouth 22/2/48.
Norwich 14/4/48.
Cambridge 9/3/52.

RENUMBERED:
1785E ?/?/23.
8785 12/2/25.
2616 9/11/46.
62616 20/11/48.

CONDEMNED: 23/2/53.
Cut up at Stratford.

8786

To traffic 24/8/1923.

REPAIRS:
Str. 21/3—7/7/25.**G**.
Str. 27/1—18/5/27.**G**.
Str. 2/3—7/6/29.**G**.
Altered to D16/2.
Coal guard on tender.
Str. 13/12/30—27/2/31.**G**.
Str. 13/9—28/10/32.**G**.
Str. 8/4—13/6/34.**G**.
Str. 19/1—28/2/36.**G**.
Str. 8/11—3/12/37.**G**.
Str. 26/10/39—9/1/40.**G**.
Str. 27/6—5/11/42.**G**.
Str. 16/8/44.**N/C**.
Str. 2/12/44—6/1/45.**G**.
Rebuilt to D16/3.
Str. 30/6—20/9/46.**G**.
Str. 7—10/1/48.**N/C**.
Tablet exchange gear fitted.
Str. 10/8—22/9/48.**G**.

Str. 21/10—30/11/50.**G**.
Str. 22/12/52—23/1/53.**G**.
Str. 9/3—6/4/55.**C/L**.
Str. 24/7—20/8/55.**G**.
Str. 10/5—25/7/56.**C/L**.

BOILERS:
1786.
3907 *(ex8843)* 7/6/29.
1782 *(ex8788)* 27/2/31.
3921 *(ex8781)* 28/10/32.
3908 *(ex8789)* 13/6/34.
1785 *(ex8818)* 28/2/36.
3927 *(ex8818)* 3/12/37.
1788 *(ex8846)* 9/1/40.
3926 *(ex8827)* 5/11/42.
4308 *(ex8806)* 6/1/45.
4229 *(ex8854)* 20/9/46.
4218 *(ex8845)* 22/9/48.
23315 *(ex ?)* 30/11/50.
23422 *(ex ?)* 23/1/53.
23336 *(ex8831)* 20/8/55.

SHEDS:
Stratford.
Cambridge 24/8/26.
Stratford 20/5/27.
Southend 19/4/30.
Stratford 17/5/30.
Colchester 18/11/44.
Norwich 13/1/48.
Melton Constable 22/2/48.
Norwich 26/1/49.
Melton Constable 17/6/51.

RENUMBERED:
1786E ?/?/23.
8786 7/7/25.
7656 7/11/42.
8786 16/8/44.
2617 24/11/46.
62617 18/9/48.

CONDEMNED: 20/5/57.
Cut up at Stratford.

8787

To traffic 31/8/1923.

REPAIRS:
Str. 8/12/24—19/3/25.**G**.
Str. 21/5—12/11/26.**G**.
Str. 22/9/28—3/1/29.**G**.
Altered to D16/2.
Coal guard on tender.
Str. 23/7—3/10/31.**G**.
Str. 31/10—30/12/31.**L**.
Re-painting for Royal engine.
Str. 25/1—13/4/34.**G**.
Str. 28/6—21/8/36.**G**.
Str. 26/9—21/12/38.**G**.
Str. 25/8—9/10/40.**G**.
Str. 21/1—13/3/42.**G**.

Str. 21/6—12/8/44.**G.**
Rebuilt to D16/3.
Str. 28/2—16/4/46.**G.**
Str. 31/12/47—11/3/48.**G.**
Str. 19/9—29/10/49.**G.**
Str. 4/11—7/12/49.**N/C.**
Str. 26/8—6/10/51.**G.**
Str. 26/4—10/5/52.**C/L.**
Str. 10/8—19/9/53.**G.**
Str. 10—22/10/54.**C/L.**
Str. 28/10—13/11/54.**C/L.**
Str. 8/5—11/6/55.**G.**
Str. 15/3—3/5/57.**G.**

BOILERS:
1787.
1785 *(ex8785)* 3/1/29.
3918 *(ex8782)* 3/10/31.
3935 *(ex8796)* 13/4/34.
3909 *(ex8829)* 21/8/36.
3933 *(ex8834)* 21/12/38.
3911 *(ex8800)* 13/3/42.
4311 *(exJ19 8252)* 12/8/44.
4277 *(ex8850)* 16/4/46.
4301 *(ex8801)* 11/3/48.
4244 *(ex8882)* 29/10/49.
23363 *(ex ?)* 6/10/51.
23459 *(new)* 19/9/53.
23406 *(ex8828)* 11/6/55.
23366 *(ex8836)* 3/5/57.

SHEDS:
Stratford.
Cambridge 22/10/30.
King's Lynn 9/3/58.
March 30/11/58.

RENUMBERED:
1787E 31/8/23 *as built.*
8787 19/3/25.
2618 24/11/46.
E2618 11/3/48.
62618 29/10/49.

CONDEMNED: 23/11/59.
Cut up at Stratford.

8788

To traffic 15/9/1923.

REPAIRS:
Str. 19/3—2/7/25.**G.**
Str. 5/2—11/6/27.**G.**
Str. 28/9—14/12/28.**G.**
Altered to D16/2.
Coal guard on tender.
Str. 28/12/29—29/1/30.**L.**
Str. 21/8—14/11/30.**G.**
Str. 8/2—1/4/32.**G.**
Str. 13/10—24/11/33.**G.**
Str. 17/3—22/5/35.**G.**
Str. 25/1—18/3/37.**G.**
Str. 10/12/37—13/1/38.**L.**

Str. 19/10—29/12/38.**G.**
Rebuilt to D16/3.
Str. 24/9—29/10/40.**H.**
Str. 21/7—30/8/41.**G.**
Str. 23/8—20/10/43.**G.**
Str. 22/11—8/12/44.**L.**
Str. 1—28/6/45.**G.**
Str. 28/4—3/6/46.**G.**
Str. 4/1—6/3/48.**G.**
Str. 21/9—28/10/50.**G.**
Str. 7—16/2/52.**C/L.**
Str. 17/10—22/11/52.**G.**
Str. 6/2—5/3/55.**G.**

BOILERS:
1788.
1782 *(ex8782)* 14/12/28.
1783 *(ex8805)* 14/11/30.
3903 *(ex8789)* 1/4/32.
3930 *(ex8847)* 24/11/33.
3920 *(ex8826)* 22/5/35.
3930 *(ex8813)* 18/3/37.
4281 *(new)* 29/12/38.
4272 *(exJ19 8246)* 29/10/40.
4295 *(exJ19 8243)* 30/8/41.
4296 *(ex8850)* 20/10/43.
4294 *(ex8865)* 3/6/46.
23311 *(ex ?)* 28/10/50.
23322 *(ex8793)* 22/11/52.
23367 *(exJ19 8146)* 5/3/55.

SHEDS:
Stratford.
Cambridge 24/8/26.
Stratford 11/6/27.
Colchester 26/3/39.
Stratford 12/11/39.
Colchester 1/12/39.
Stratford 10/3/40.
Colchester 17/3/40.
Stratford 21/9/41.
Colchester 2/1/43.
Norwich 3/6/46.
Yarmouth 24/8/47.
Norwich 21/9/47.
Yarmouth 16/11/47.
Norwich 14/12/47.

RENUMBERED:
1788E 15/9/23 *as built.*
8788 28/1/25.
2619 12/11/46.
E2619 6/3/48.
62619 28/10/50.

CONDEMNED: 7/10/57.
Cut up at Stratford.

8789

To traffic 29/9/1923.

REPAIRS:
Str. 20/3—7/7/25.**G.**

Str. 3/3—16/6/27.**G.**
Str. 14/9—25/12/28.**G.**
Altered to D16/2.
Coal guard on tender.
Str. 14/3—22/5/30.**G.**
Str. 7/11/31—8/1/32.**G.**
Str. 24/2—10/5/34.**G.**
Ash ejector fitted.
Str. 27/1—26/3/36.**G.**
Str. 28/10—1/12/37.**G.**
Str. 18/11—16/12/39.**L.**
Str. 15/6—19/7/40.**G.**
Str. 26/11/41—19/1/42.**H.**
Str. 8/10—7/11/42.**H.**
Str. 3/11—2/12/44.**G.**
Str. 5—13/1/45.**L.**
Str. 19/9—20/10/45.**G.**
Str. 28/11/47—27/3/48.**G.**
Rebuilt to D16/3.
Str. 1/9—30/11/49.**C/L.**
Str. 28/1—3/3/51.**G.**
Str. 16/6—7/8/53.**G.**
Str. 29/12/54—27/1/55.**C/L.**
Str. 29/9/55. *Not repaired.*

BOILERS:
1789.
1781 *(ex8781)* 25/12/28.
3903 *(ex8813)* 22/5/30.
3908 *(ex8790)* 8/1/32.
3902 *(ex8845)* 10/5/34.
3903 *(ex8845)* 1/12/37.
3925 *(ex8826)* 19/7/40.
3909 *(ex8782)* 19/1/42.
3913 *(ex8781)* 2/12/44.
3928 *(ex8856)* 20/10/45.
4324 *(ex8873)* 27/3/48.
23333 *(ex ?)* 3/3/51.
23453 *(ex8784)* 7/8/53.

SHEDS:
Stratford.
Southend 8/11/30.
Stratford *by* 1931.
Colchester 2/1/43.
Norwich 29/8/45.
Yarmouth 2/12/45.
Norwich 16/1/46.
Yarmouth 3/5/46.
Norwich 24/5/46.
Yarmouth Beach 30/10/46.
Yarmouth 12/10/47.
Norwich 26/10/47.
Melton Constable 1/9/48.

RENUMBERED:
1780E 29/9/23 *as built.*
8789 7/7/25.
2620 27/10/46.
E2620 27/3/48
62620 30/11/49.

CONDEMNED: 10/10/55.
Cut up at Stratford.

(opposite, top) **No.2554 was ex works 10th June 1947 from a 'general' and had numbers and letters put on in shaded transfers, although stock of these was being run down never to be replenished. By September, Stratford was already applying painted unshaded numbers and letters in Gill Sans style - two early recipients of these changes were 2513 (19th September) and 2521 (5th October).**

(opposite, centre) **Although demoted to the reserve Royal engine, no.8783 was restored to green and fully lined when ex works 31st January 1946. King's Lynn shed changed its number to 2614 on Sunday 3rd November 1946 and were supplied with shaded transfers to do the renumbering properly. However, no.2614 had a 'general' in late 1947 from which it was out in green paint but now had yellow painted and unshaded numbers and letters in Gill Sans style but with modified 6.** *A.R.Goult.*

(opposite, bottom) **Except for the two nominated Royal engines, unlined black was the standard livery at the end of the LNER and this was carried on by British Railways at least until mid-1951, as far as the D16/3's were concerned, when lining was brought back in. Lettering and numbering however was quickly standardised from the 6" high examples of January and February of 1948. By the beginning of March 7½" high letters and 10" high numbers, in Gill Sans style, became the norm though with modified 6 and 9. A Regional prefix 'E' had been introduced almost at once after Nationalisation but this application was to last only until the end of March when E2620 was ex works. E2524 got its prefix just ten days before. Stratford in the meantime continued to apply all sorts of combinations of different sized letters and numbers - 12" numbers, 7½" letters; 12" numbers, 6" letters; 12" numbers, 10" letters; 10" numbers, 12" letters; 10" numbers, 10" letters, etc.**

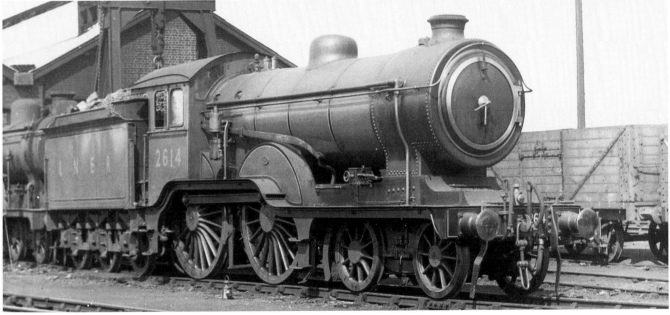

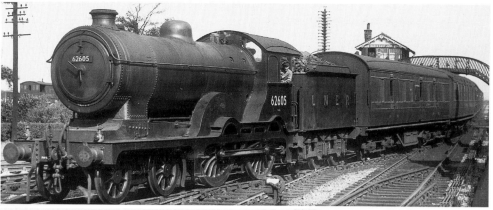

(left) **By the time no.62605 was out on 1st October 1948, correct 6 and 9 were being used and smokebox number plates were being fitted. Standard 10" numbers were used on the cab. Still carrying LNER on the tender, 62605 negotiates March East junction.**

(left) **Effective from 20th August 1949 on no.62521, there was a change to the BR emblem on the tender but still no lining even though D16/3 had been chosen in July 1948 to be amongst those to receive the red, cream and grey lining. It was not until May 1951 that the first D16/3 received full lining and that was no.62575. Many engines such as 62511, 62513, 62521, 62522, 62524, never received lining.**

(second from bottom) **The two which had been the pre-war 'Royal' engines continued to be treated by BR as special cases. From a 'general' on 19th November 1949, no.62614 came out still in LNER green with black and white lining although with smokebox number plate and BR emblem on tender. It kept this livery until it went into works 10th March 1952 but came out on 24th April in lined black livery. The other 'Royal', 8787, remained in the wartime unlined black until ex works from a 'general' 29th October 1949 when, rather surprisingly, it came out in LNER green with black and white lining. It kept that style until it next went to works on 26th August 1951 and came out from that repair in lined black. King's Lynn, 26th August 1950.** *H.C.Casserley.*

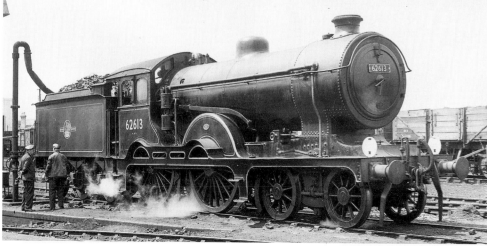

(left) **The last general repairs were in April/May 1957 and no.62613, ex works 31st May in red, cream and grey lining, concluded them. Besides this last one, three other engines managed to receive the new BR crest during that two month period: 62543 (24th April), 62618 (3rd May), 62606 (17th May). Like many other engines at that period, the four D16/3's had the right hand crest facing forward with the lion facing right - a serious heraldic mistake - but as they had no subsequent painting attention they were never corrected. Cambridge, 1960.** *L.R.Peters.*